Logistics Management and Strategy

We work with leading authors to develop the strongest educational materials in logistics, bringing cutting-edge thinking and best learning practice to a global market.

Under a range of well-known imprints, including Financial Times Prentice Hall, we craft high quality print and electronic publications which help readers to understand and apply their content, whether studying or at work.

To find out more about the complete range of our publishing, please visit us on the World Wide Web at: **www.pearsoneduc.com**

Logistics Management and Strategy

Alan Harrison

Remko van Hoek

FINANCIAL TIMES

Prentice Hall

An imprint of **Pearson Education**

Harlow, England · London · New York · Reading, Massachusetts · San Francisco
Toronto · Don Mills, Ontario · Sydney · Tokyo · Singapore · Hong Kong · Seoul
Taipei · Cape Town · Madrid · Mexico City · Amsterdam · Munich · Paris · Milan

Pearson Education Limited

Edinburgh Gate
Harlow
Essex CM20 2JE

and Associated Companies throughout the world.

Visit us on the World Wide Web at:
www.pearsoneduc.com

First published 2002

© Pearson Education Limited 2002

The rights of Alan Harrison and Remko van Hoek to be identified as authors
of this work have been asserted by them in accordance with the Copyright,
Designs and Patents Act 1988.

ISBN 0273 64674 5

British Library Cataloguing-in-Publication Data
A catalogue record for this book is available from the British Library

Library of Congress Cataloging-in-Publication Data

Harrison, Alan, 1926–
    Logistics management and strategy / Alan Harrison & Remko van Hoek.
        p. cm.
    Includes bibliographical references and index.
    ISBN 0–273–64674–5
    1. Business logistics. 2. Industrial management. I. Hoek, Remko I. van. II. Title.

    HD38.5 .H367 2001
    658.5–dc21

                                                    2001046012

10 9 8 7 6 5 4 3 2 1
06 05 04· 03 02

Typeset in Great Britain by 3
Printed and bound in Great Britain by Ashford Colour Press

Contents

Part One INTRODUCTION

Foreword

Logistics and supply chain management have emerged over the last decade or so to become critical agenda items in the boardrooms of the world. The reasons for this are self-evident. Firstly the increased competitiveness of markets has forced organisations to review both their cost structures and their value delivery processes. Secondly, there has been a realisation that companies no longer compete as stand-alone entities but rather as part of an increasingly inter-dependent network.

The implications of these changes to the competitive landscape are profound. New ways of managing are needed along with new skills and new organisational formats. Logistics management provides a set of tools to enable a market-facing orientation to be achieved whilst supply chain management takes these ideas a step further by seeking to manage the upstream and downstream interfaces in a way that facilitates a more cost-effective response to customer demand.

Today's turbulent markets also require a focus on agility. In the past the emphasis in organisations tended to be on achieving process efficiency at the expense of responsiveness. Now, the priority has switched to responsiveness, i.e. the ability to meet the ever-changing needs of customers.

My colleagues, Alan Harrison and Remko van Hoek, have built on these ideas to produce a valuable guide to managing logistics and supply chains in these uncertain times. It will be welcomed by students and practitioners alike.

Professor Martin Christopher
Chairman, Cranfield Centre for Logistics and Transportation
Cranfield School of Management
October 2001

Preface

Logistics has been emerging from Peter Drucker's shadowy description as 'the economy's dark continent' for some years. Its emergence has been facilitated by such pioneers as Doug Lambert and John Gattorna, and by our Cranfield colleague Martin Christopher. From its largely military beginnings, logistics has accelerated into becoming one of the key business issues of the day, presenting formidable challenges for managers and occupying some of the best minds. Its relatively slow route to this exalted position can be attributed to two causes. First, logistics is a cross-functional subject. In the past, it has rightly drawn on contributions from marketing, finance, operations and corporate strategy. The late Jim Cooper referred to it as a 'pariah subject' for this reason. Within the organisation, a more appropriate description would be a *business process*, cutting across functional boundaries yet with a contribution from each. Second, logistics extends beyond the boundaries of the organisation into the supply chain. Here, it engages with the complexities of synchronising the movement of materials and information between business processes. The *systems nature* of logistics has proved a particularly difficult lesson to learn, and individual organisations still often think that they can optimise profit conditions for themselves by exploiting others in the supply chain. Often they can – in the short term. But winners in one area are matched by losers in another, and the losers are unable to invest or to develop the capabilities needed to keep the chain healthy in the long term. The emergence of logistics has therefore been dependent on the development of a cross-functional model of the organisation, and on an understanding of the need to integrate business processes across the supply chain.

While its maturity as a discipline in its own right is still far from complete, we believe that the time has come to take a fresh look at logistics management and strategy. Tools and concepts to enable integration of the supply chain are starting to work well, and developments such as e-marketplaces offer far more in the future. Tomorrow's competitive advantage will not come from implementing ERP in itself. It will come from responding to customers at the end of the supply chain better than competition. Logistics plays a key role in this response, and it is this role that we seek to describe in this book.

Accordingly, we start in Part One with the strategic role of logistics in the supply chain. We continue by a focus on responding to customer needs and then on the concept of value and logistics costs. In Part Two, we review leveraging logistics operations in terms of their global dimensions, and of the lead time frontier. Part Two continues by examining the impact on logistics of lean thinking and the agile supply chain. Part Three reviews managing supplier interfaces, first in terms of supply chain management and second in terms of partnerships. Our book ends with Part Four, in which we outline the logistics future challenge.

This text is intended for MSc students on logistics courses, and as an accompanying text for open learning courses such as the global MSc degrees and virtual universities. It will also be attractive as a management textbook and as recommended reading on MBA options in logistics and supply chain management.

We hope that our book will offer support to further professional development in logistics, which is much needed. In particular, we hope that it encourages the reader to challenge existing thinking, and to break old mindsets by creating a new and more innovative future.

Acknowledgements

We should like to acknowledge our many friends and colleagues who have contributed to our thinking and to our book. Professor Martin Christopher has provided much stimulating thought. For example, the three of us developed the logistics thinking around the agile supply chain discussed in Chapter 7. Other Cranfield colleagues deserve a special mention: Dr Paul Chapman, Mark Barrett and Dr Richard Wilding have been particularly helpful. Sri Srikanthan helped us a lot with the financial concepts used in Chapter 3. Our colleagues in the Performance Measurement Research Unit, Professor Andy Nealey and Dr Mike Kennerley, helped us with the balanced measurement portfolio in the same chapter. Members of the Agile Supply Chain Research Club at Cranfield also deserve special mention, especially David Aldridge of Cussons and Chris Poole of Procter & Gamble. Many of our MSc students, such as Steve Walker and Simon Templar, have also made important contributions, including checking parts of the text for us. Dr Yemisi Bolumole gave us a lot of help in redrafting earlier versions, and we are very grateful to her. Dr Jim Aitken contributed the Global case study in Chapter 2, and we have used his work on supplier associations in Chapter 9. Ulrich Franke has contributed much to our thinking on virtual organisations, and we quote his case study on Bearing Partners in Chapter 10. We also acknowledge the support given by Pearson Education in the preparation of this text and the encouragement to write it faster! Also, we thank the reviewers who made many valuable comments on earlier versions of the book. We are very grateful to all of these, and to the many others who made smaller contributions to making this book possible. Finally, we thank Tricia Pritchard for helping to sort out the rather convoluted MS in addition to being instrumental in setting up our Global MSc in Logistics!

How to use this book

This book is divided into four parts, centred around a model for logistics. The model for logistics is introduced in the first chapter of Part One, which offers an introduction to logistics and its basic contribution to competitiveness, customer service and the creation of value. Part Two of the book focuses on leveraging logistics operations within the overall context of service and cost performance objectives. Part Three focuses on supplier interfaces, and Part Four pulls together elements of leading-edge thinking in logistics, homing in on future challenges for the subject.

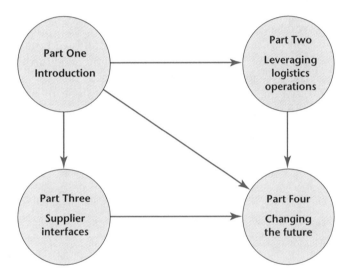

The book has been arranged to take the reader through the subject in logical stages. The limitation of a text presentation is that the subjects are then arranged in sequence, and links between stages have to be made by the reader. We have set out to facilitate cross-linkage task by including:

- *activities* at the end of many of the sections, which are aimed at helping you to think about the issues raised and how they could be applied;
- *discussion questions* at the end of each chapter to help you to assess your understanding of the issues raised, and to give you practice in using them;
- *case studies*, which draw together a number of issues and help you to think about how those issues are linked together in a practical setting. Use the study questions at the end of each case to guide your thinking.

We have sought continually to break up the text with figures, tables, activities and case studies, so you will rarely find two successive pages of continuous text. You should therefore regard the activities and case studies as an integral part of the method used in this book to help you to learn.

Where possible, discuss the activities and case study questions in groups after you have prepared them individually. Discussion helps to broaden the agenda and create confidence in handling the issues! While you are studying this book, think about the logistics issues it raises – in your own organisation or ones that you know well, and in articles in newspapers such as the *Financial Times* and magazines such as *Business Week*. Follow up the web site addresses we have included in the text and again link them with the issues raised in the book.

A few words on terminology are appropriate here. We have taken the view that logistics and supply chain management are sufficiently different for separate definitions to be needed. We have included these definitions in Chapter 1: logistics is a subset of SCM. 'Supply chain' and 'supply network' are used interchangeably, although we favour 'chain' for a few organisations linked in series and 'network' to describe the more complex interlinkages found in most situations. Again, our position is explained in Chapter 1.

A summary is provided at the end of each chapter to help you to check that you have understood and absorbed the main points in that chapter. If you do not follow the summary points, go back and read the relevant section again. If need be, follow up on references or recommended further reading. Summaries are also there to help you with revision.

We have designed this book to help you to start out on the logistics journey and to feel confident with its issues. We hope that you enjoy it.

Plan of the book

Part One INTRODUCTION	
Chapter 1 Logistics and the supply chain	**Chapter 2** Serving the customer

Chapter 3 Value and logistics costs

Part Two LEVERAGING LOGISTICS OPERATIONS	
Chapter 4 Managing logistics internationally	**Chapter 5** Managing the lead-time frontier
Chapter 6 Just-in-time and lean thinking	**Chapter 7** The agile supply chain

Part Three SUPPLIER INTERFACES	
Chapter 8 Managing the supply chain	**Chapter 9** Partnerships in the supply chain

Part Four CHANGING THE FUTURE

Chapter 10 Logistics future challenge

Publisher's acknowledgements

We are grateful to the following for permission to reproduce copyright material:

Figure 1.1 and Case Study 1.1 from *Operations Management,* 2e, Financial Times Prentice Hall (Slack *et al*, 1998); Figure 1.11 from What is the right supply chain for your product? from *Harvard Business Review* March/April (Fisher, M. 1997); Figure 2.1 and Table 2.1 from *Logistics and Supply Chain Management,* 2e, Financial Times Prentice Hall (Christopher, M. 1998); Figure 3.10 from Supply Chain Council and Supply Chain Operations Reference (SCOR) model overview at www.supply-chain.org; Case Study 5.2 based on a study by Dr Paul Chapman and Dr Richard Wilding, Cranfield Centre for Logistics and Transportation; Case Study 6.1 from ENIMM module 7 unit 6, reproduced by courtesy of Dr Paul Chapman, Cranfield School of Management; Figure 7.1 and Table 7.2 from Agile, or leagile: matching your supply chain to the marketplace in *Proceedings 15th International Conference on Production Research*, Limerick (Mason-Jones, R., Naylor, B. and Towill, D.R. 1991); Figure 9.1 from *International Journal of Physical Distribution and Logistics Management* **23** (6), 14–26 (Cooper and Gardner, 1993); Figure 9.2 from *Improving Purchase Performance*, Pitman (Syson, 1992); Figure 9.4 from The Impact of Modular Production on the Dynamics of Supply Chains in *The International Journal of Logistics Management*, Vol. 9 No. 2, p. 38. (Van Hoeken, R. and Weken A.M, 1998) http:www.ijlm.org; Case Study 9.2 and Figure 9.7 from *Integration of the Supply Chain: The Effect of Inter-Organisational Interactions between Purchasing-Sales-Logistics.* PhD thesis, Cranfield School of Management, (Aitken, J. 1998); Figure 10.3 from *Marketchansen durch dynamische Netzerke.* Carl Hansen Verlag, (Schuh, G., Millarg, K. and Göransson, A, 1998); Case Study 10.1, Figures 10.4 and 10.5 from *Virtual logistics: an explanatory case study.* Cranfield University working paper. (Franke, U. and Jockel, O. 2000).

Whilst every effort has been made to trace the owners of copyright material, in a few cases this has proved impossible and we take this opportunity to offer our apologies to any copyright holders whose rights we may have unwittingly infringed.

Part One

INTRODUCTION

Our model of logistics structures the supply network around three main factors: the flow of materials, the flow of information, and the time taken to respond to demand from source of supply. The scope of the network extends from 'our organisation' in the centre across supplier and customer interfaces, and therefore typically stretches across functions, organisations and borders. The network is best seen as a system of interdependent processes, where actions in one part affect those of all others. The key 'initiator' of the network is end customer demand on the right: only the end-customer is free to make up their mind when to place an order. After that, the system takes over.

- *Chapter 1* explains how networks are structured, the different ways in which they may choose to compete, and how their capabilities should be aligned to end-customer needs.

- *Chapter 2* addresses customer service and the setting of customer service priorities.

- *Chapter 3* considers how value is created in a supply network, how logistics costs can be managed, and how a balanced measurement portfolio can be designed.

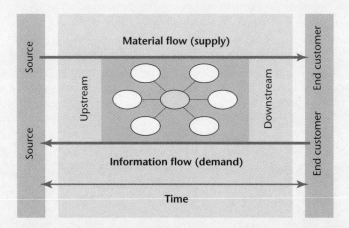

Logistics and the supply chain

The objectives of this chapter are to:

- identify and explain logistics definitions and concepts that are relevant to managing the supply chain;
- identify how supply chains compete in terms of time, cost and quality;
- show how different supply chains may adopt different and distinctive strategies for competing in the marketplace.

By the end of this chapter you should be able to:

- understand how supply chains are structured;
- understand different ways in which supply chains may choose to compete in the marketplace;
- understand the need to align supply chain capabilities with the needs of the end customer.

Introduction

A car takes only 20 hours or so to assemble, and a couple more days to ship it to the customer via the dealers. So why does it take a month for a manufacturer to make and deliver the car I want? And why are the products I want to buy never available on the shelf at the local supermarket? These are questions that go to the heart of logistics management and strategy. Supply chains today are slow, costly, and don't deliver particularly good value to the end consumer. But let us start at the beginning, by thinking about logistics and the supply chain in terms of what they are trying to do. It is easy to get bogged down in the complexities of how a supply chain actually works (and very few people actually know how a whole supply chain works!). We shall address many of those details later in this textbook. First, let us focus on how a supply chain competes, and on what the implications are for logistics management and strategy.

The overall aim of this chapter is to provide an introduction to logistics, and to set the scene for the book as a whole. The need is to look outside the individual organisation and to consider how it aligns with all other organisations in a given supply chain. This is both a strategic and a managerial task: strategic, because it brings in long-term decisions about how logistics will be structured and the systems it will use; managerial, because it encompasses decisions about sourcing, making and delivering products and services within an overall 'game plan'.

Key issues   *This chapter addresses four key issues:*

1 **Logistics and the supply chain:** definitions, structure, tiering.

2 **Material and information flow:** the supply chain and the demand chain.

3 **Competing through logistics:** competitive criteria in the marketplace.

4 **Supply chain strategies:** aligning capabilities across the supply chain.

1.1 Logistics and the supply chain

Key issues: What is the supply chain, and how is it structured? What is the purpose of a supply chain?

Logistics is a big word for a big challenge. Let us begin by giving an example of that challenge in practice, because that is where logistics starts and ends.

**CASE STUDY
1.1**

Tesco

Tesco is the UK's largest food retailer, with a sales turnover of Euro 30bn. While it has over 800 stores in Europe and the Far East, most are in the UK, where it has 646. The product range held by the stores has grown rapidly in recent years, and currently stands at 40 000 stock-keeping units (sku's). This massive range is supported by 2000 suppliers, who are expected to provide service levels (correct time and quantities) of at least 98.5% by delivering to Tesco within half-hour time 'windows'. Volumes are equally impressive. In a year, some 1 billion cases of product are shipped from suppliers to the stores.

Tesco states that its core purpose is 'to create value for customers to earn their lifetime loyalty'. Wide product range and high on-shelf availability across that range are key enablers of that core purpose. So how do you maintain high availability of so many sku's in so many stores? This question goes to the heart of logistics management for such a vast organisation. Logistics is about material flow, and about information flow. Let's look at how Tesco deals with each of these in turn.

An early reform for supermarket operation was to have suppliers deliver to a distribution centre rather than to every store. During the 1980s, distribution to retail stores was handled by 26 depots. These operated on a single-temperature basis, and were small and relatively inefficient. Delivery volumes to each store were also relatively low, and it was not economic to deliver to all stores each day. Goods that required temperature-controlled environments had to be carried on separate vehicles. Each product group had different ordering systems. The network of depots simply couldn't handle the growth in volumes and the increasingly high standards of temperature control. A new distribution strategy was needed.

Under the 'composite' distribution system, many small depots with limited temperature control facilities were replaced by composite distribution centres (called *Regional Distribution Centres*, RDCs), which can handle many products at several temperature ranges. The opportunity is to provide a cost-effective daily delivery service to all stores. Typically, a composite distribution centre can handle over 30 million cases per year on a 15-acre site. The warehouse building comprises 250 000 square feet divided into three temperature zones: frozen ($-25°C$), $+1°C$ (chilled) and $+12°C$ (semi-ambient). Each distribution centre serves a region of about 50 retail stores. Delivery vehicles for composite depots use insulated trailers which can be divided into chambers by means of movable bulkheads so they can operate at different temperatures. Deliveries are made at agreed, scheduled times. Ambient goods like cans and clothing are delivered through separate systems.

So much for the method of transporting goods from supplier through to the stores, but how much should be sent to each store? With such a huge product range today, it's impossible for the individual store to reorder across the whole range (store-based ordering). Instead, sales of each product line are tracked continuously through the till by means of electronic point of sale (EPOS) systems. As a customer's purchases are scanned through the bar code reader at the till, the sale is automatically recorded for each sku. Cumulative sales are updated every four hours on *Tesco Information Exchange* (TIE). This is a system based on Internet technology that allows Tesco and its suppliers to communicate trading information. The aim of improved communication is to reduce response times from manufacturer to stores and to ensure product availability on the shelf. Among other things, TIE aims to improve processes for introducing new products and promotions, and to monitor service levels.

Based on the cumulative sales, Tesco places orders on its suppliers by means of electronic data interchange (EDI). As volumes and product ranges increased during the 1990s, food retailers such as Tesco aimed to destock their distribution centres by ordering only what was needed to meet tomorrow's forecast sales. For fast-moving products such as types of cheese and washing powders, the aim is *day 1 for day 2*: that is, to order today what is needed for tomorrow. For fast-moving products, the aim is to *pick to zero* in the distribution centre: no stock is left after store orders have been fulfilled. And deliveries to stores are made in *waves*: specific products are delivered in different cycles through the day. This means that the same space in the distribution centre can be used several times.

Questions

1 Describe the key logistics processes at Tesco.

2 What do you think are the likely problems in running the Tesco operation?

So why is Tesco growing in an intensely competitive market? It describes its core purpose as being 'to create value for customers to earn their lifetime loyalty'. In order to achieve this, Tesco needs to understand customer needs and how they can be served. Its products must be recognised by its customers as representing outstanding value for money. In order to support such goals, it must ensure that the products that its customers want are available on the shelf at each of its stores at all times, day and night. The task of planning and controlling the purchase and distribution of Tesco's massive product range from suppliers to stores is one of logistics. Logistics is the task of providing:

- *material flow* of the physical goods from suppliers through the distribution centres to stores;
- *information flow* of demand data from the consumer back to purchasing and to suppliers so that material flow can be accurately planned and controlled.

The logistics task of managing material flow and information flow is a key part of the overall task of *supply chain management*. Supply chain management is concerned with managing the entire process of raw material supply, manufacture, packaging and distribution to the end customer. The Tesco UK supply chain structure comprises three main functions:

- *distribution*: the operations and support task of managing Tesco's distribution centres (DCs), and the distribution of products from the DCs to the associated stores;
- *network and capacity planning*: the task of planning and implementing sufficient capacity in the supply chain to ensure that the right products can be procured in the right quantities now and in the future;
- *supply chain development*: the task of improving Tesco's supply chain so that its processes are stable and in control, that it is efficient, and that it is correctly structured to meet the logistics needs of material flow and information flow.

Thus logistics can be seen as part of the overall supply chain challenge. While the terms 'logistics' and 'supply chain management' are often used interchangeably, logistics is actually a subset of supply chain management. It is time for some definitions.

1.1.1 Definitions and concepts

A supply chain as a whole ranges from basic commodities (what's in the ground, sea or air) to selling the final product to the end customer. Material flows from a basic commodity (e.g. a bauxite mine as a source of aluminium ore) to the final product (e.g. a can of Cola). The analogy to the flow of water in a river is often used to describe organisations near the source as *upstream*, and those near the end customer as *downstream*. The definition of supply chain management used in this book is as follows:

> **The alignment of upstream and downstream capabilities of supply chain partners to deliver superior value to the end customer at less cost to the supply chain as a whole.**

Thus the focus of management strategy for the supply chain as a whole is on *alignment* between supply chain members, of which the end customer is the key one. As Gattorna (1998) puts it:

> **Materials and finished products only flow through the supply chain because of consumer behaviour at the end of the [chain].**

The degree to which the consumer is satisfied with the finished product depends crucially on the management of material flow and information flow along the supply chain. If delivery is late, or the product has bits missing, the whole supply chain is at risk from competitors who can perform the logistics task better. Logistics is a key enabler for supply chain management. Christopher (1998) defines logistics as:

> **Strategically managing the procurement, movement and storage of materials, parts and finished product inventory and the related information flows, through the organisation and its marketing channels in such a way that the current and future profitability are maximised through the cost-effective fulfilment of orders.**

Tesco is in no doubt about the opportunities here. A breakdown of costs in Tesco's part of the UK supply chain is as follows:

- Supplier delivery to Tesco distribution centre (DC)   18%
- Tesco DC operations and deliver to store   28%
- Store replenishment   46%
- Supplier replenishment systems   8%

Nearly half of supply chain costs are incurred in-store. In order to reduce these in-store costs, Tesco realises that the solution is 'to spend more upstream and downstream to secure viable trade-offs in store replenishment'. If a product is not available on the shelf, the sale is lost. By aligning external manufacturing and distribution processes with its own, Tesco seeks to deliver superior value to the consumer at less cost to the supply chain as a whole.

1.1.2 Supply chain: structure and tiering

The concept of a supply chain suggests a series of processes linked together to form a chain. A typical Tesco supply chain is formed from five such links:

To some extent, the term 'supply chain' is misleading in that it models a simple series of links between a basic commodity such as milk and a final product such as packaged cheese. Thus the supplier will need packaging materials such as film, labels and cases. Cheese requires materials additional to milk in the manufacturing process. Once made, the cheese is dispatched for maturation to the supplier's national distribution centre (NDC), and it is dispatched to many customers in addition to Tesco. Once at one of Tesco's Regional Distribution Centres (RDCs), the 'chain' again spreads because several stores are served by a given RDC. A more realistic representation of the supply chain is shown in Figure 1.1, where each link can connect with several others. Our own company ('our organisation') is shown at the centre of many possible connections with other supplier and customer companies.

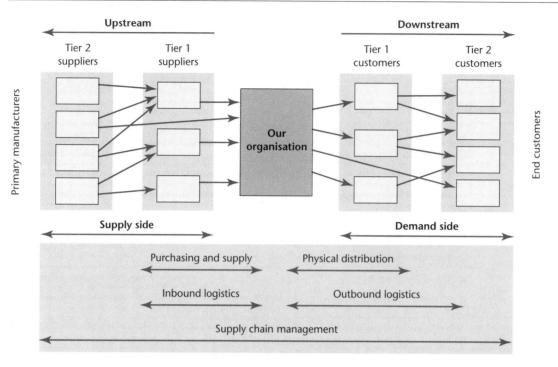

Figure 1.1 Relationships in the supply chain
(Source: After Slack *et al.*, 1998)

The supply chain can be seen in this diagram as a number of processes that extend across organisational boundaries. 'Our organisation' is embedded within the chain, and our operational processes must coordinate with others that are part of the same chain. Materials flow from left (upstream) to right (downstream). End customer demand information, on the other hand, flows from right to left. If everything is as orderly as it seems, then only the end customer (to the extreme right of the chain) is free to place orders when he or she likes: after that, the supply chain takes over.

The supply chain is *tiered* in that supply side and demand side can be organised into groups of organisations with which we deal. Thus if we place an assembler such as the Ford plant at Valencia as the 'operation', tier 1 comprises suppliers of major parts and subassemblies who deliver directly to Ford, while tier 2 suppliers deliver to the tier 1s, etc. On the demand side, Ford supplies to the national sales companies as tier 1 customers, who in turn supply to dealers as tier 2, and so on.

In the box at the bottom of the diagram we have placed supply chain management and various part-manifestations of supply chain management. Thus:

- *Purchasing and supply* deals with the 'organisation's' immediate suppliers.
- *Physical distribution* deals with the tier 1 customer processes.
- *Logistics* refers to management of materials and information. Inbound logistics deals with links between our organisation and tier 1 suppliers, while out-

bound logistics refers to the links between our organisation and tier 1 customers.

- *Materials management* refers to flow of materials and information through the immediate supply chain – that is, tier 1 customers and suppliers and our organisation.

Supply chain management thus appears as the 'end to end' (or 'cow to customer' as a cheese manufacturer might say) management of the network as a whole, and of the relationships between the various links. The essential points have been summarised by Oliver and Webber (1982):

- Supply chain management views the supply chain as a *single entity*.
- It demands strategic decision-making.
- It views *balancing inventories* as a last resort.
- It demands *system integration*.

A natural extension of this thinking is that the supply chain should be viewed as a *network*. Figure 1.2 shows how 'our organisation' can be seen at the centre of a network of upstream and downstream organisations.

The supply network can be defined (Zheng *et al.*, 1998) as:

a number of organisations that are linked together for the purpose of supply of goods or services that are required by end customers.

The terms 'supply chain' and 'supply network' both attempt to describe the way in which buyers and suppliers are linked together to serve the end customer. 'Network' describes a more complex structure, where organisations can be cross-linked; 'chain' describes a simpler, sequential set of links. We have used the terms interchangeably in this book, preferring 'chain' to describe simpler sequences of a few organisations and 'network' where there many organisations linked in a more complex way.

Figure 1.2 takes a basic view of the network, with 'our organisation' linked to three upstream suppliers and three downstream customers. If we then add material flow and information flow to this basic model, and place a boundary around the network, Figure 1.3 shows the network in context. Here we have added arrows showing the logistics contribution of material and information flows, together with the time dimension. Material flows from primary

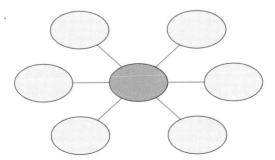

Figure 1.2 **A network of organisations**

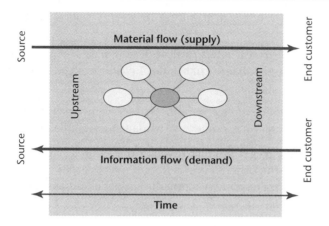

Figure 1.3 The network in context

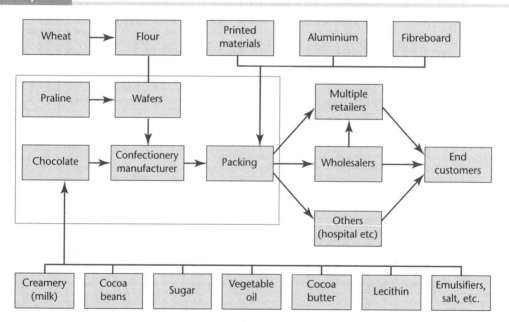

Figure 1.4 Example of a confectionery network map
(Source: After Zheng et al., 1998)

Figure 1.4 shows an example network map of a chocolate bar. Draw a network map showing how your organisation, or one that you know well, links with other organisations. Explain the upstream and downstream processes as far as you can. We expect you to address at least the first tiers of demand and supply. You will derive further benefit from researching additional tiers, and by developing the linkage of relationships that is involved. Explain how these work in practice, and how materials flow between the different tiers.

manufacture (for example farming, mining or forestry) through various stages of the network to the end customer. Material flow represents the *supply* of product through the network in response to demand from the next (succeeding) organisation. Information flow broadcasts *demand* from the end customer to preceding organisations in the network. The time dimension addresses the question 'How long does it take to get from primary source to the end customer?' That is, how long does it take to get product through the various stages from one end of the supply chain to the other? Time is important because it measures how quickly a given network can respond to demand from the end customer. In fact, the concept of flow is based on time:

> **Flow measures the quantity of material (measured in input terms such as numbers of components, tonnes and litres) that passes through a given network per unit of time.**

An important point here is that the supply network should be viewed as a *system*. All processes within the network need to be understood in terms of how they interact with other processes. No organisation is an island: its inputs and outputs are affected by the behaviour of other players in the network. One powerful, disruptive player can make life very difficult for everyone else. For example, several auto assemblers optimise their own processes, but disrupt those of upstream suppliers and downstream distributors. The effect is to increase total system costs *and* reduce responsiveness to end-customer demand.

1.2 Material and information flow

Key issue: What is the relationship between material flow and information flow?

As we've already seen, logistics is about material flow and information flow. In this section, we examine each flow in more detail.

1.2.1 Material flow

The aim within a supply chain must be to keep materials flowing from source to end customer. The time dimension in Figure 1.3 suggests that parts are moved through the supply chain as quickly as possible. And in order to prevent local build-ups of inventory, flow must be orchestrated so that parts move in a coordinated fashion. The term often used is *synchronous*. Caterpillar Inc. make complex earth-moving equipment, and have literally thousands of component parts and subassemblies that must come together in final assembly processes. Their view is that these parts and subassemblies must flow continuously through the supply chain, like water along a river bed (Knill, 1992):

The goal is continuous, synchronous flow. Continuous means no interruptions, no dropping the ball, no unnecessary accumulations of inventory. And synchronous means that it all runs like a ballet. Parts and components are delivered on time, in the proper sequence, exactly to the point they're needed.

Often it is difficult to see the 'end to end' nature of flow in a given supply chain. The negative effects of such difficulty include build-ups of inventory and sluggish response to end customer demand. And sheer greed by the major players in a supply chain often means that it is weaker partners (notably SMEs) who end up holding the inventories. So management strategies for the supply chain require a more holistic look at the links, and an understanding that organisational boundaries create barriers to flow.

Case study 1.2 describes how one company – Xerox in this case – re-engineered material flow in their distribution system.

<table>
<tr><td>CASE STUDY
1.2</td><td></td></tr>
</table>

Xerox

Once the problems of introducing 'just-in-time' production systems had been solved at the Xerox plant making photocopiers at Venray in Holland, attention shifted towards the finished product inventory. Historically, stocks of finished products had been 'managed' by trying to turn the tap of sales on or off as stocks developed. This was characterised by the familiar 'feast or famine' situations. The objective of the next move for Xerox became clear: making only what you need when you need it, then shipping direct to the customer. But the key question had to be answered: just-in-time for what? The answer is – the customer! And customer surveys showed that three types of delivery were needed:

● Commodity products should be delivered 'off the shelf'.
● Middle-range products were required in 5 days.
● Larger products that had to be integrated into existing customer processes and systems had to be planned months ahead: but the quoted delivery date had to be met 100%.

It was envisaged that this would lead to a radically different inventory 'profile' in the supply chain. Figure 1.5 shows a traditional inventory profile on the left. Most of the stock was held in local depots waiting for customer orders. If the mix had been incorrectly forecast, too many of the wrong products were in plentiful supply, while needed products were unavailable! Further, a batch of replacement products would take a long time to fight their way through the pipeline. A new 'just in time' strategy was conceived to make the supply chain much more responsive. This strategy had a profound effect on the inventory profile, pushing much of the inventory away from the end customer (where it has maximum added value and is already committed to a given finished product specification). Instead, inventory was mostly held further upstream, where it could be finally assembled to known orders, and where it had lower value. Of course, it has since been possible to remove several of the stages of the distribution process, thereby eliminating some of the sources of inventory altogether!

For commodity products, Xerox coined the term *deliver JIT*: that is, the product had to be delivered out of stock. Where sales forecasts are traditionally poor, the challenge

Note: WIP = work in progress, i.e. products being worked on, but not yet ready for sale.
Shaded areas indicate days of stock. The wider the area, the more days of stock in that position

Figure 1.5 Xerox: the impact on inventories

was one of flexibility, simplicity and speed of manufacture. For mid-range products, it was unrealistic to hold 'just in case' inventories of products that are too complex to be assembled quickly. Instead, *finish JIT* was the term coined to describe the new policy of building semi-finished products with the minimum of added value, consistent with being able to complete and deliver the product in the five-day target. Finally, *build JIT* was the term used to describe the new philosophy of building larger products quickly within a defined lead time.

The impact of the new build philosophies on the downstream supply chain processes can be judged from Figure 1.5. While the traditional inventory profile shows a maximum number of days of stock (shown in the shaded area) at finished product level, this is risky. It always seems that demand is greatest for the very items that are not available! *Postponing* the decision on exact specification until as late as possible in the process helps to create the much flattened inventory profile to the right of the diagram. These are issues to which we return in Chapters 6 and 7 of this textbook.

(Source: After Eggleton, 1990)

Question

How did inventory reduction in the supply chain lead to improved competitiveness at Xerox?

1.2.2 Information flow

As asked in the Xerox case study, just-in-time *for what*? It's all well and good to get materials flowing and movements synchronised, but the 'supply orchestra' needs to respond in unison to a specific 'conductor'. The 'conductor' in this analogy is actually the end customer, and it is the end customer's demand signals that trigger the supply chain to respond. By sharing the end-customer demand

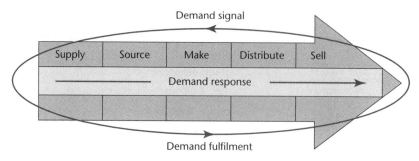

Figure 1.6 Integrating demand and supply chains
(Source: After Jeff Beech, Andersen Consulting)

information across the supply chain, we create a *demand chain*, directed at providing enhanced customer value. Information technology enables the rapid sharing of demand and supply data at increasing levels of detail and sophistication. The aim is to *integrate* such demand and supply data so that an increasingly accurate picture is obtained about the nature of business processes, markets and consumers. Such integration provides increasing competitive advantage.

The greatest opportunities for meeting demand in the marketplace with a maximum of dependability and a minimum of inventory come from implementing such integration across the supply chain. You cannot become 'world class' by yourself!

Figure 1.6 gives a conceptual model of how supply chain processes (supply, source, make, distribute and sell) are integrated together in order to meet end customer demand (Beech, 1998). Demand signals are shared across the chain rather than being interpreted and massaged by the 'sell' process next to the market. Demand fulfilment is also envisaged as an integrated process, as materials are moved from one process to the next in a seamless flow. Information is the 'glue' that binds the supply chain processes together.

Activity 1.2

Write a brief (200 words) appraisal of material and information flow in the supply network affecting *one* of the major products in the response you gave in Activity 1.1. Perhaps the current situation is very different from the above ideals?

1.3 Competing through logistics

Key issues: **How do products win orders in the marketplace? How does logistics contribute to competitive advantage?**

There are many potentially conflicting demands on an organisation today. All those unreasonable customers seem to want it yesterday, at no cost, and to be compensated if it goes wrong! Within a given supply chain, it is important that each organisation understands how each group of products competes in the marketplace, and that it aligns its capabilities with those of its partners. It is impossible to be outstanding at everything, and supply chain partners need to give priority to capabilities that give each product group its competitive edge. These are the advantages where supply chain partners 'dig in deep' by giving priority to investment, by training, and by focusing product development and marketing efforts. They need only match the industry average on other criteria. Let us look at the competitive priorities that can be delivered by logistics in the supply chain.

1.3.1 Competitive advantage

There are various ways in which products compete in the marketplace. Perhaps a given product is something that no one else can match in terms of price. Or maybe you offer a product that is technically superior, such as Gillette razor blades. While new product development has logistics implications, the key advantage provided by logistics – as suggested in the Tesco example in section 1.1 – is *product availability in the marketplace at low cost.* Logistics supports competitiveness of the supply chain as a whole by

> **meeting end customer demand through supplying what is needed in the form it is needed, when it is needed, at a competitive cost.**

Extending Slack's (1991) performance objectives to the supply chain, there are five ways of competing through logistics. These are quality, speed, dependability, flexibility and cost. Let us look at each of these performance objectives in turn.

Doing things right: the quality advantage

The most fundamental objective – in that it is a foundation for all the others – is to carry out all processes across the supply chain so that the end product does what it is supposed to do. Quality is the most visible aspect of the supply chain. Unavailability of the product, defects and late deliveries are all symptoms of quality problems in supply chain processes. Such problems are visible to the end customer, and negatively influence that customer's loyalty. Robust processes are at the heart of supply chain performance. Internally, robust processes help to reduce costs by eliminating errors, and help to increase dependability by making processes more certain. Commenting on the Japanese attitude to 'quality – above all' at Nissan, former personnel director Peter Wickens (1987) states:

> **Commitment to a zero defects product is absolute – not only at top management levels but throughout the company – particularly at the 'sharp end' where the products are actually made.**

Part of Nissan UK's continuing concerns is to extend such thinking to all tiers of the inbound supply chain. A basic goal is to reduce defects to 50 parts per million (ppm) for all inbound components. Externally, superior performance of supply chain processes shows up as unavailability of the product, defects and late deliveries, as stated above. For example, a 'league table' of defects per hundred vehicles is published by J.D. Power Associates (www.jdpower.com). The *Initial*

Quality Study is based on responses from more than 47 000 purchasers and lessees of new model-year vehicles, and monitors the number of reported problems that consumers experience in the first 90 days of ownership. The study has been the industry standard benchmark of initial vehicle quality since 1987, and is based on problems-per-100 vehicles covering 135 specific problem areas. Consistent top performers are Japanese producers such as Toyota and Nissan, who have established a tough pace for Western competitors to match.

Doing it fast: the speed advantage

Time measures how long a customer has to wait in order to receive a given product or service. VW call this time the *customer to customer* lead time: that is, the time it takes from the moment a customer places an order to the moment that customer receives the car he or she specified. Such lead times can vary from zero (the product is immediately available, such as goods on a supermarket shelf) to months or years (such as the construction of a new building). Time can be used to win orders by companies who have learned that some customers don't want to wait – and are prepared to pay a premium to get what they want quickly. An example is Vision Express, who offer prescription spectacles 'in about one hour'. Technicians machine lenses from blanks on the premises. Staff are given incentives to maintain a 95% service level against the one-hour target. Vision Express has been successful in the marketplace by re-engineering the supply chain so that parts and information can flow rapidly from one process to the next. Compare this with other opticians in the high street, who must send customer orders to a central factory. Under the 'remote factory' system, orders typically take about 10 days to process. An individual customer's order must be dispatched to the factory, and then compete in a queue with orders from all the other high street branches around the country. Once it has been processed, it must return to the branch that raised the order. While this may be cheaper to do (a single, remote factory replaces many small 'factories' in the branches), it takes much longer.

Doing things on time: the dependability advantage

Time is not just about speed. It is also about meeting promises. Firms who do not offer instantaneous availability need to tell the customer *when* the product or service will be delivered. Delivery dependability measures how successful the firm has been in meeting those promises. For example, the UK-based Royal Mail offers a 'first class' service for letters whereby there is a 92% chance that a letter posted today will reach its destination tomorrow. It is important to measure dependability in the same 'end to end' way that speed is measured. Although Vision Express offers a one-hour service for prescription glasses, the 95% service level target is a measure of the dependability of that service. Dependability measures are widely used in industries such as train and air services to monitor how well published timetables are met. And in manufacturing firms, dependability is used to monitor a supplier's performance in such terms as:

- *on time* (% orders delivered on time);
- *in full* (% orders delivered complete).

The implication of dependability for supply chain processes is that they need to be robust and predictable. Toyota UK manages inbound deliveries of parts from suppliers in southern Europe by a process called *chain logistics*. Trailers of parts are moved in four-hour cycles, after which they are exchanged for the returning empty trailer on its way back from the UK. One hitch in this highly orchestrated process means that incoming parts don't arrive just in time at the assembly plant. Toyota demands that its suppliers and logistics partner ALUK plan *counter-measures*. This means that alternative routes have been planned in advance to deal, for example, with a French Channel ferry strike at Calais.

Ability to change what is done: the flexibility advantage

While doing things the same way at the same time may be great from a point of view of keeping costs down, few markets are in tune with such an idealised way of doing business. A supply chain needs to be responsive to new products and markets, and to changing customer demand. This means in turn that it must be capable of changing what is done. Flexibility takes four forms. First, *product* flexibility measures how quickly a new product can be introduced. Second, *mix* flexibility measures the time it takes to change between different products in a given range. Third, *volume* flexibility measures the time it takes to respond to increases or decreases in overall demand. And fourth, *delivery* flexibility measures the ability to change deliveries (intentionally) by bringing them forward or pushing them back.

The Britvic case study (1.3) shows some of the pressures for flexibility at a soft drinks manufacturer.

CASE STUDY 1.3

Britvic Soft Drinks

The Britvic Soft Drinks canning operation at Rugby, central UK, is one of the largest in Europe. Apart from its own brands, such as Tango, it also cans and distributes Pepsi-Cola. There are four state-of-the-art canning lines, each producing 1500 cans per minute. Thus the maximum capacity over a 24-hour period with no changeovers would be 8.5 million cans. There are strict delivery windows for major customers (the super-markets), and all products have a limited shelf-life. Thus production must be moderated according to demand. Only a limited amount of anticipation stocks can be set up in April prior to the summer peak.

To make the task even more challenging, demand is very sensitive to the unpredictable British weather. A few hot days, and demand can double. While the chart in Figure 1.7 shows the average monthly demand, which is very uneven but at least predictable, the day-to-day demand is not only uneven, but also highly unpredictable. While Britvic has invested in the most sophisticated forecasting packages, it has found that they are at best 50% accurate under such circumstances.

In order to provide flexible production capacity, canning lines are run for up to 24 hours a day in pairs 'back to back'. Only one line of the pair is run when demand is low; the other line is brought in immediately demand increases. In periods of very high demand weekends are worked, and a flexible 'annual hours' contract is worked by employees. Labour productivity is a distant second to material productivity: whether a

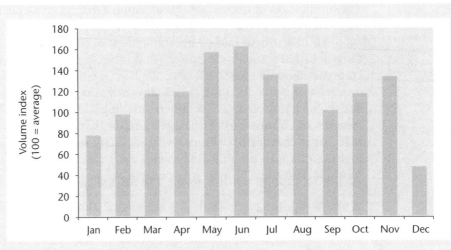

Figure 1.7 Britvic Soft Drinks: monthly sales

crew works one line or two is less important than matching demand with output so that customer service levels are maintained with minimum inventories.

(Source: After Slack *et al.*, 1998)

Question

What types of flexibility are most evident in the Britvic example?

Cost: *the productivity advantage*

Cost is important for all supply chain processes – that goes without saying! Low costs translate into advantages in the marketplace in terms of low prices or high margins, or a bit of each. Many products compete specifically on the basis of low price. This is supported from a supply chain point of view by low-cost manufacture, distribution, servicing and the like. Examples of products that compete on low price are 'own brand' supermarket goods that reduce the high margins and heavy advertising spend of major brands. They also perhaps cut some of the corners in terms of product specification in the hope that the customer will consider low price as being more important than minor differences in product quality.

The pressure to reduce prices at automotive component suppliers is intense. The assemblers have been setting annual price reduction targets for their inbound supply chains for some years. Unless a supplier can match reduced prices for which products are being sold by means of reduced costs, that supplier will gradually go out of business. As a result, many suppliers are cynical about the 'price down' policies of the assemblers. Reduced prices are the reward of cost cutting, and that is most often a collaborative effort on the part of several partners in the supply chain. As indicated in section 1.1, Tesco can make only limited inroads into its in-store costs without collaboration from its supply chain partners. Many small UK dairy farmers are being forced out of business because the price of milk paid by supermarkets is 'less than the price of water'. For them, there are few opportunities to cut costs.

Logistics is not the only way in which product competitiveness in the market-place can be enhanced. The five performance objectives listed above can be added to (and in some cases eclipsed by) other ways in which products may win orders, such as design and marketing features. Thus superior product or service design – often supported by brand image – may create advantage in the market-place, as it does for BMW cars and the Dorchester Hotel, for example. Here, the logistics task is to support the superior design. BMW's supply chain is one of the most efficient there is, mainly because its products are sold (at least in Europe) as soon as they have been made. Finished cars do not accumulate in storage on air-fields like those of the mass producers. Finished product storage adds cost, with no value to the end consumer.

1.3.2 Order winners and order qualifiers

The relative importance of the five performance objectives is usually different for a given product or service. A helpful distinction is that between order winners and order qualifiers (Hill, 1993):

Order winners are factors that directly and significantly help products to win orders in the marketplace. Customers regard such factors as key reasons for buying that product or service. If a firm raises its performance on those factors, it will increase its chances of getting more business. Thus a product that competes mainly on price would benefit in the marketplace if productivity improvements enabled further cost reductions.

Order qualifiers are factors that are regarded by the market as an 'entry ticket'. Unless the product or service meets basic performance standards, it will not be taken seriously. An example is quality accreditation: a possible supplier to major utilities such as PowerGen in the UK and EDF in France would not be considered seriously without ISO 9000 certification. And delivery reliability is a must for newspapers: yesterday's news is worthless! Note that, in both examples, order qualifiers are *order-losing sensitive*: loss of ISO 9000 accreditation would make it impossible to supply to major utilities, and late delivery of newspapers would miss the market.

The different impacts of the two sets of criteria are illustrated in Figure 1.8. Increased performance in an order winner, shown by the solid line, increases competitive benefit for the product in proportion. Order qualifiers, shown by the dotted line, have different characteristics. Attainment of a required performance standard, such as ISO 9000 accreditation, gains entry to the market but no more than that.

Note that order winners and qualifiers are *specific to individual product lines* and the market segments they serve. Table 1.1 provides an example of how two different products made by the same manufacturer and passing through the same distribution channel have different performance objectives. The first product group comprises standard shirts that are sold in a limited range of 'standard'

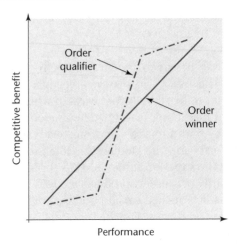

Figure 1.8 Order winners and order qualifiers

colours and sizes. The second product group comprises fashion blouses that are designed specially for each season in many colours and a choice of styles with associated designer labels.

Analysis of the order winners and qualifiers shows that the two product ranges have very different performance criteria in the marketplace. Of the two, the range of fashion blouses presents more logistics challenges because individual sku's are much more difficult to forecast. It is not until the season is under way that a picture begins to emerge about which colours are selling most in which region of the market. The logistics challenge is therefore concerned with speed of response

Table 1.1 Different product groups have different logistics performance objectives

	Standard shirts	**Fashion blouses**
Product range	Narrow: few colours, standard sizes	Wide: many colours, choice of styles, designer labels
Design changes	Occasional	Frequent (at least every season)
Price	Everyday low price	Premium prices
Quality	Consistency, conformance to (basic) specification	High grades of material, high standards of workmanship
Sales volumes	Consistent sales over time	Sales peak for given fashion season
Order winners	Price	Product range Brand/label Quality
Order qualifiers	Quality Availability	Price Availability
Logistics priorities	Cost Dependability Quality	Speed Flexibility Quality

and flexibility to changing demand. The logistics challenges between the two ranges are quite distinctive.

Not only can order winners and qualifiers be different for different products and services. They can also *change over time*. Thus, in the early phase of a new product life cycle, such as the launch of a new integrated circuit, the order winners are availability and design performance. Price would often be a qualifier: provided the price is not so exorbitant that no one can afford it, there is a market for innovators who want the best-performing chip that is available. But by the maturity phase of the life cycle, competitors have emerged, the next generation is already on the stocks, and the order winners have changed to price and product reliability. The former order winners (availability and design performance) have changed to become order qualifiers. The logistics challenge is to understand the market dynamics and to adjust capabilities accordingly.

The *actions of competitors* are therefore a further influence on logistics performance objectives. For example, low-price competitors are a feature of most markets, and attempt to differentiate themselves from the perhaps higher-grade but pricier incumbents. Thus competitors like Matalan have sparked fundamental changes in logistics strategy at the long-established UK clothing retailer Marks and Spencer (www.marks&spencer.co.uk). In response to massive loss of sales to cheaper new entrants, Marks and Spencer have ditched 30-year-old agreements with local UK suppliers in favour of sourcing garments from suppliers in the Far East.

In section 7.1 of Chapter 7 we introduce the terms *market qualifiers* and *market winners* as supply chain extensions of these basic concepts.

Activity 1.3

Select the top two product lines (in terms of sales) for your firm or one that you know well. Using the headings in Table 1.1, fill in the details for characteristics of both product lines. Aim to use precise details, so identify the actual sales figures instead of putting 'high' or 'low'. Use additional or alternative headings if they describe the situation better. Go on to identify the principal order winners and qualifiers for each product.

1.4 Supply chain strategies

Key issues: What is 'strategy'? How can competitive criteria be aligned within a supply chain? How can supply chain strategies be timed to different product needs?

1.4.1 Defining 'strategy'

Strategy is about planning as distinct from doing. It is about formulating a long-term plan for the supply chain, as distinct from solving the day-to-day issues and problems that inevitably occur. Extending the concept of 'strategy' from Hayes and Wheelwright (1984), the aim for the supply chain as a whole should be

> the set of guiding principles, driving forces and ingrained attitudes that help to communicate goals, plans and policies to all employees that are reinforced through conscious and subconscious behaviour at all levels of the supply chain.

Five important characteristics of 'strategy' are as follows:

- *Time horizon*: this is long-term rather than short-term.
- *Pattern of decisions*: decisions are consistent with each other over time.
- *Impact*: changes are significant rather than small-scale.
- *Concentration of effort*: the focus is on selected, defined capabilities rather than 'broad brush'.
- *Comprehensiveness*: all processes in the supply chain are coordinated.

All too often, supply chain 'strategy' is set using few such characteristics: decisions are made piecemeal by accident, muddle or inertia. We need, however, to recognise that strategic decisions may indeed be made by such means.

Whittington (1993) proposes four approaches to setting strategy. He starts by proposing different motivations for setting strategy:

- *How deliberate are the processes of strategy setting?* These can range from clearly and carefully planned to a series of ad hoc decisions taken on a day-to-day basis.
- *What are the goals of strategy setting?* These can range from a focus on maximising profit to allowing other business priorities such as sales growth to be included.

If we make these two considerations the axes of a matrix, Figure 1.9 suggests four options for crafting strategy.

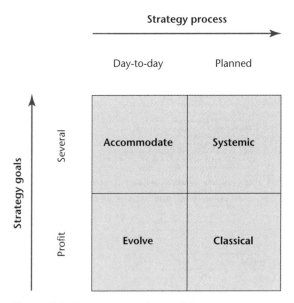

Figure 1.9 Four options for crafting strategy

What are the implications for the way in which supply chain strategy is approached in different organisations? Here is a brief description of the four options:

- *Evolve.* 'Strategy' is not something that is formally undertaken at all. 'Our strategy is not to have a strategy' is a typical viewpoint. Operating decisions are taken in relation to the needs of the moment, with financial goals the main guiding principle.

- *Classical.* While financial goals are again the main guiding principle, these are achieved through a formal planning process. This is called 'classical' because it is the oldest and most influential option.

- *Accommodate.* Here, decisions are back to the day-to-day mode, but financial objectives are no longer the primary concern. Strategy is accommodated instead to the realities of the firm and the markets in which it operates.

- *Systemic.* This option for strategy-setting sees no conflict between the ends and means of realising business goals. While goal-setting takes place across all major aspects of the business (including human resources, marketing and manufacturing policies), these are linked to the means by which they will be achieved in practice.

1.4.2 Aligning strategies

In section 1.1 we showed the supply chain as a network of operating processes. In section 1.2 we emphasised the need to 'integrate' these processes to maximise flow and focus on the end customer. And in section 1.3 we saw how supply chains can choose to compete on a range of different competitive priorities. Now is the time to put these ideas together and show how strategies need to be *aligned* across the supply chain.

If different links in the supply chain are directed towards different competitive priorities, then the chain will not be able to serve the end customer as well as a supply chain in which the links are directed towards the same priorities. That is the basic argument for alignment in the supply chain. Where the links are directed by a common and consistent set of competitive criteria, then that supply chain will compete better in the marketplace than one in which the links have different, conflicting priorities.

And the concept on *focus* says that a given operation should not be subject to too many conflicting priorities. It is difficult to handle high-volume, low-cost products in the same supply chain channel as low-volume high-variety products, for which flexibility is the name of the game. While the assembly line is the method of choice for assembling cars in volume, development of new models is kept well away from the factory in special facilities until close to launch. This is because the development process demands quite different technical skills and equipment that are better physically separated from the more routine, repetitive assembly line. In the example of the standard shirts and fashion blouses in section 1.3, the associated operations processes would be kept separate ('focused') for similar reasons.

What happens when the processes are not aligned within a supply chain? Let us address that question with case study 1.4 to show the problems that can arise.

Talleres Auto

Talleres Auto (TA) is an SME based in Barcelona. TA attends to broken-down vehicles, providing a roadside repair and recovery service. Two of the parts that TA frequently uses are starters and alternators, which were obtained from a local distributor. In turn, the local distributor ordered parts from a prime distributor. Starters and alternators were obtained from a remanufacturer, who replaced the windings and tested the products using parts bought from a component supplier. A diagram of this part of the supply chain is shown in Figure 1.10.

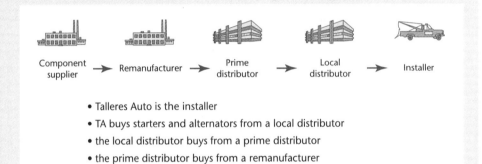

- Talleres Auto is the installer
- TA buys starters and alternators from a local distributor
- the local distributor buys from a prime distributor
- the prime distributor buys from a remanufacturer
- the remanufacturer buys components from a component supplier

Figure 1.10 **The Talleres Auto supply chain**

Most of TA's customers made 'distress purchases': their car had broken down and they wanted it to be fixed quickly! So TA needed a fast replacement service from the local distributor. While the distributors both recognised the need for fast replacements, the performance of the purchasing department at the remanufacturer was measured on cost savings. Thus the component supplier thought that the name of the game was low cost.

(Source: Harland, 1997)

Questions

1 What were the order winners and order qualifiers at TA?

2 What were the order winners and order qualifiers at the component supplier?

3 What impact on customer service was this mismatch likely to cause?

1.4.3 Differentiating strategies

A supply chain, then, may choose to compete on different criteria. Such criteria need in turn to be recognised and form a part for the business strategies of all of the members of a given network. The choices so made have major implications for the operation of each member. Failure to recognise competitive criteria and their implications for a given product or service *by any member* means that the supply chain will compete less effectively. It is like playing football when the goalkeeper makes an error and lets in a goal that should not have happened: he lets the whole side down.

We complete Chapter 1 with a look at two commonly used supply chain strategies that have very different operational implications. Consider two products with different order winners:

- *Product 1*: a high-volume dishwashing product for which demand is relatively stable throughout the year. While subject to occasional enhancements, these are usually small scale: the life cycle is comparatively long.
- *Product 2*: a fashion ski jacket, which is produced for a given season and which is completely redesigned for the next season. Demand is very difficult to forecast, and the life cycle is short.

Product 1 sells because it is a well-known brand that performs reliably and well, and because it represents good value for money. Order winners are price and brand; qualifiers are quality and delivery reliability. Product 1 demands a supply chain that is focused on low-cost, reliable supply. Efficient operations processes are the name of the game.

Product 2 also sells because it is a well-known brand, but it is also recognised as this season's fashion offering. Price is now a qualifier, while order winners are style and brand. The operations task for the supply chain is flexibility and responsiveness to support the new offering in the marketplace. If it sells well, then the supply chain must be in a position to respond quickly to cash in on the short window of opportunity.

These two different sets of characteristics can be positioned on a matrix to aid the comparison, as shown in Figure 1.11. Product 1 emerges from this analysis as

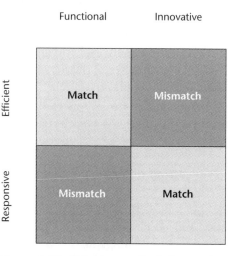

Figure 1.11 Fisher's supply chain matrix

characteristic of a *functional-efficient* supply chain. The product performs a well-known, reliable but scarcely innovative task. Product 2, on the other hand, is a fashion product that is indeed innovative, and which must be supported by a responsive supply chain. Hence its supply chain is described as *innovative-responsive*.

1 Using the concepts from this section, analyse the supply chain support for both of the products you analysed in Activity 3.3. What should the supply chain be (*functional-efficient* or *innovative-responsive*)? What is the reality, and why are the two different?

2 To what extent is there alignment of strategy in the supply chains for these two products?

Summary

How does logistics work within the supply chain?

● Supply chain management is defined as 'the alignment of upstream and downstream capabilities of supply chain partners to deliver superior value to the end customer at less cost to the supply chain as a whole'.

● Logistics is defined as 'strategically managing the procurement, movement and storage of materials, parts and finished product inventory and the related information flows, through the organisation and its marketing channels in such a way that the current and future profitability are maximised through the cost-effective fulfilment of orders'. Logistics is thus concerned with material flow and information flow in the supply chain.

● In a supply chain, materials flow from upstream to downstream. Demand information from the end customer flows in the opposite direction. A given organisation is positioned within a supply 'network', with tier 1 suppliers and tier 1 customers its immediate neighbours. Material flow measures the quantity of material that passes through a given network per unit of time.

● A supply network is a system, wherein each organisation is linked to the others. Therefore the overall performance of the network results from the combined performance of the individual players.

● Logistics supports competitiveness of the supply chain as a whole by meeting end customer demand through supplying what's needed when it's needed at low cost.

What are the performance objectives of the supply chain, and how does logistics support those objectives?

● There are five ways of competing through logistics. These are quality, speed, dependability, flexibility and cost objectives. Briefly, quality is about doing things right, speed is about doing things fast, dependability is about doing things on time, flexibility is about being able to change what is done, and cost is about doing things cheaply.

- Such performance objectives can, and often are, augmented by other objectives that are outside logistics. These include product superiority and brand. Here the logistics task is to support other such performance objectives.

- The relative importance of the five performance objectives varies from one situation to another. It can also vary over time. The concept of order winners and qualifiers helps to prioritise the logistics task. Key influences on relative importance are individual product needs in the marketplace, position in the product life cycle, and competitor activity.

- Logistics strategy is the set of guiding principles, driving forces and ingrained attitudes that help to communicate goals, plans and policies to all employees and which are reinforced through conscious and subconscious behaviour at all levels of the supply chain.

Discussion questions

1 Bill Gates of Microsoft describes the 2000s as 'business @ the speed of thought'. Discuss the importance of speed in the supply chain. How can speed be increased within the supply chain?

2 Suggest logistics performance objectives for the following, explaining why you have come to your conclusions:
   a a low-fare airline such as Ryanair
   b a fast food chain such as McDonald's
   c an overnight parcels service such as TNT

3 What is meant by the term *alignment* in relation to supply chain processes? Why is alignment important in setting a strategy for a given supply chain?

4 What does *flow* mean in a supply chain context? Explain how material flow relates to information flow in a supply network.

References

Beech, J. (1998) The supply–demand nexus. In Gattorna, J. (ed.), *Strategic Supply Chain Alignment*, pp 92–103. Aldershot: Gower.

Christopher, M. (1998) *Logistics and Supply Chain Management: Strategies for reducing cost and improving service*, 2nd edn. London: Financial Times Pitman.

Eggleton, D.J. (1990) JIT in a distribution environment. *International Journal of Logistics and Distribution Management*, 9(1), 32–4.

Fisher, M. (1997) What is the right supply chain for your product? *Harvard Business Review*, March/April, 105–16.

Gattorna, J. (ed.) (1998) *Strategic Supply Chain Alignment: Best practice in supply chain management*. Aldershot: Gower.

Harland, C. (1997). Talleres Auto. In Johnston, R., Chambers, S., Harland, C., Harrison, A. and Chambers, S. (eds), *Cases in Operations Management*, 2nd edn, pp 420–8. London: Pitman.

Hayes, R.H. and Wheelwright, S.C. (1984) *Restoring our Competitive Edge*. John Wiley.

Hill, T. (1993) *Manufacturing Strategy*. London: Macmillan.

Knill, B. (1992) Continuous flow manufacturing, Material Handling Engineering, May, pp 54–7.

Oliver, R.K. and Webber, M.D. (1982) *Supply Chain Management: Logistics catches up with strategy*, Outlook.

Slack, N. (1991) *The Manufacturing Advantage*. London: Mercury.

Slack, N., Chambers, S., Harland, C., Harrison, A. and Johnston, R. (1998) *Operations Management*, 2nd edn. London: Pitman.

Whittington, R. (1993) *What is Strategy and Does it Matter?* London: Routledge (repr. 1996 by International Thompson Business Press).

Wickens, P. (1987) *The Road to Nissan*. Basingstoke: Macmillan.

Zheng, J., Harland, C., Johnsen, T. and Lamming, R. (1998). Initial conceptual framework for creation and operation of supply networks. *Proceedings of 14th AMP Conference, Turku, 3–5 September*, Vol. 3, pp 591–613.

Suggested further reading

Christopher, M. (1998) *Logistics and Supply Chain Management: Strategies for reducing cost and improving service*, 2nd edn. London: Financial Times Prentice Hall.

Stock, J.R. and Lambert, M. (2001) *Strategic Logistics Management*, 4th edn. Boston, MA: McGraw-Hill/Irwin.

CHAPTER 2

Serving the customer

Objectives

The objectives of this chapter are to:

- introduce customer service concepts;
- show how customer service bridges marketing and logistics;
- explain the need for customer retention;
- provide an approach for setting customer service priorities.

By the end of this chapter you should be able to:

- understand how companies compete through managing customer service;
- understand how to apply an approach for setting customer service priorities.

Introduction

In Chapter 1 we looked at the logistics task from the perspective of material flow and information flow. We also saw how logistics contributes to competitive strategy and the performance objectives by which we can measure this contribution. But what is it that drives the need for flow in the first place? The essential point to recognise here is that it is the behaviour of the end customer that should dictate what happens. As quoted in Chapter 1, 'materials and finished products only move through the supply chain because of consumer behaviour at the end of the [chain] . . .' (Gattorna, 1998). Only end customers should be free to make up their minds about when they want to place an order on the network; after that, the system takes over.

Customer service addresses the process of handing over our products or services into the hands of our customers. Only after this process has been completed does the product or service reach its full value. And the process offers many opportunities for adding value. Instead of picking up a product from a distributor who is remote from our business, there are opportunities during the sales transaction (for example, help and advice in using our products), as well after the sales transaction (for example, after sales service and warranty).

The overall aim of this chapter is to introduce customer service by examining the link between marketing and logistics. Examining this link helps to show how it is possible to identify the differing logistics needs of various groups of customers.

Key issues   *This chapter addresses four key issues as follows:*

1 **Introduction to customer service:** the impact of increasing customer expectations and technological know-how.

2 **Customer service as a link between logistics and marketing:** pre-transaction, transaction and post-transaction categories.

3 **Customer service and customer retention:** measuring loyalty and retention.

4 **Setting customer service priorities:** a three-stage model.

2.1 Introduction to customer service

Key issue: **Why is customer service vital to logistics strategy?**

Customer service is an increasingly important aspect of competitiveness. This has been caused by two widespread changes that have affected industry. These are an increase in customer expectations, and the dispersion of technological know-how. As Hutter (1998) explains:

> The battleground is the customer's wallet. The protagonists are the world's largest corporations. Their weapons are technologies which increase understanding of individual customers and offer better access to those customers. The victors will be those that can order their entire organisation around the challenges of getting cheaper [access to] more profitable and more loyal customers. The backdrop to this scene is the growing sophistication of consumers themselves. We live in an age of expert buyers. Customers are becoming ever more critical and demanding. They know that they can play the market and are placing higher and higher demands on [suppliers] to give them what they want – and immediately.

In Chapter 1 we referred to 'tier 1 customers' with whom our organisation deals directly, and to 'end customers' who are the consumers at the end of the supply network. It is therefore usual to refer to two types of customer:

- *business customers*, who represent our organisation's immediate trading environment (see Figure 1.1);
- *end customers*, who represent the ultimate customer for the network as a whole (see Figure 1.3).

It is becoming common practice to refer to the relationships as *business to business* (B2B) and *business to customer* (B2C) accordingly. In section 1.2.2 of Chapter 1 we referred to the need to integrate supply chain processes so that they are aligned towards end customer needs. In this sense, B2B integration should be aligned towards the ultimate B2C process.

2.1.1 Increasing customer expectations

Expectations have risen amongst consumers in line with a general increase in wealth amongst developed countries over the latter half of the twentieth century. This increase in expectations has many causes, including:

- better levels of general education;
- better ability to discern between alternative products;
- exposure to more lifestyle issues in the media.

These expectations have not only led to consumers aspiring to more desirable products; they are also demanding much better levels of service to be associated with those products.

Businesses are also expecting more from their vendors. Suppliers need to pay increasing attention to the service aspects of their dealings with industrial customers. This is especially true when the customer has implemented more customer-centric management systems such as just-in-time.

2.1.2 Technological know-how

Technological know-how disperses across and between industries and between competitors through a number of routes, including:

- benchmarking projects;
- product tear-down;
- employee turnover;
- educational programmes (such as this textbook).

When technologies mature, the rate at which new developments occur can be overtaken by the rate of dispersal. This leads to competing products having broadly the same characteristics and capabilities, with only marginal differences between them. This leads to customers becoming increasingly unable to perceive differences between them. While this process is a gradual one, it leads to products being eventually viewed as commodities.

Faced with rising customer expectations and lowering product differentiation, companies are increasingly turning to customer service as their way to gain competitive advantage.

2.2 Customer service as a link between logistics and marketing

Key issues: What are the elements of customer service? How do these relate to the marketing mix?

'Marketing' is a philosophy that can be applied to the network as a whole. Adapting Doyle's (1994) definition:

> Marketing is the philosophy that integrates the disparate activities and functions that take place within the network. Satisfied customers are seen as the only source of profit, growth and security.

Marketing in practice is a series of plans and decisions that address how the philosophy will be actioned. The starting point is *segmentation*, which describes how a given market might be broken up into groups of customers with different needs. For example, segmentation of the market for suntan creams and lotions would begin with an understanding of:

- the benefits wanted (e.g. water resistance, oil/non-oil, sun factor);
- the price consumers are prepared to pay;
- the media to which they are exposed (TV programmes, magazines, etc.);
- the amount and timing of their purchases.

We can then develop profiles of the segments and evaluate their relative attractiveness to our organisation. The next step is to select target segments and to identify how our organisation is going to win orders in each – in other words, to define our organisation's *differential advantage* that distinguishes our offerings from those of our competitors. In logistics terms, the important issues here are the order winning criteria (OWC) and qualifying criteria (QC) for the target segments. These help in turn to define the *marketing mix*.

The marketing mix is the set of marketing decisions that is made to implement positioning strategy (target market segments and differential advantage) and to achieve the associated marketing and financial goals. The marketing mix has been popularly termed the *4 Ps*:

- *product*: range, sizes, presentation and packaging, design and performance;
- *price*: list price, discounts, geographical pricing, payment terms;
- *promotion*: sales force, advertising, consumer promotion, trade promotion, direct marketing;
- *place*: channel selection, market coverage, distribution systems, dealer support.

Logistics contributes fundamentally to the place decisions, as well as supporting product and promotion decisions. All too often the distribution activities are viewed as the bit bolted to the back of production that gets inventory away from the factory and into stockholding points such as warehouses.

In order to achieve the goal of the right product in the right place at the right time', logistics systems and processes must designed to support products in the marketplace. An effective interface between marketing and logistics requires the development and implementation of practices that deliver *customer service*.

Customer service is embodied in the marketing mix referred to above. The elements that make up customer service are many and varied, so for the purpose of simplicity they are often categorised under three headings:

- pre-transaction (before the sale);
- transaction (during the sale);
- post-transaction (after the sale).

These three categories are detailed in Table 2.1, and explained below.

Table 2.1. **The components of customer service**

Category	Explanation	Examples
Pre-transaction	Elements set up in advance of a transaction relating to customer service policy	● Written customer service policy ● Accessibility
Transaction	Elements directly involved when performing distribution	● Inventory availability ● Order fill rate
Post-transaction	Elements that support the product when it is in use	● Spares availability ● Call-out time

(Source: Christopher, 1998)

2.2.1 Pre-transaction elements of customer service

The pre-transaction elements of customer service are those set up in advance of a transaction. They result from planning undertaken to ensure that subsequent transactions occur smoothly, in line with customer needs. Examples of these elements are as follows.

Written customer service policy

- Does one exist?
- Is it communicated to internal staff?
- Do customers know about it and how it to use it?
- Does it contain specific measures on how you aim to perform?

Accessibility

- How easy is it for customers to deal with you?
- Are you easy to find physically and on the Web?
- Is it easy to find your phone, fax and e-mail?
- Is there a specified first point of contact for customers?

Organisational structure

- Is someone designated as responsible for customer service?
- Do they have the authority to make changes in order to help customers?

System flexibility

- How flexible is your logistics system in accommodating special needs of customers?

2.2.2 Transaction elements of customer service

Transaction elements are the customer service components of physical distribution. These are all the aspects necessary for and directly involved in getting the right product to the right place at the right time. Examples of these elements are as follows.

Order cycle time

- How long does it take from receiving an order to delivering it?
- How reliable is delivery? That is, do you achieve the target delivery dates/times?
- What is the variation between shortest, average and longest order cycle times?

Inventory availability

- Where orders are picked from stock, what is the availability for each item?

Order fill rate

- What percentage of orders are met in full within the order lead time? This measure considers an order to be fulfilled only when the full amount of *all* items on an order is delivered.

2.2.3 Post-transaction elements of customer service

Following a transaction, customers will usually need further services from a supplier. These are necessary to overcome problems they encounter and as ongoing support during product use. Some of these services are opportunities to increase revenue from the customer and provide an essential part of a business's income. Examples of these elements are as follows.

Spares availability

When a low-cost item can disable a high-value product, spares availability will be very important.

- What are the stock levels and delivery times?

Call-out time

Specialist skills and equipment may be needed to service or repair a product.

- What is the time taken to arrive?
- How long does a repair take?
- On what percentage of occasions is a repair completed at the first call-out?

Customer complaints

Complaints are an opportunity to learn from customers where the logistics system is failing. Skilful resolution of complaints can leave customers feeling better about a supplier than if there had been nothing wrong in the first place.

- What is the speed with which complaints are resolved?
- How many people does a customer have to speak with to resolve their complaint?
- What percentage of complaints can be solved by the first person the customer speaks to?

CASE STUDY 2.1

Powerdrive Motors

Tom Cross took over as Managing Director at Powerdrive three years ago. At the time, the company was an established manufacturer of small electric motors with a strong reputation for product reliability and technical leadership. On the downside, it was also regarded in the trade as having high prices and variable delivery. Tom's first actions were to tackle the huge product variety on offer. He saw this as the major problem in addressing the negative views in the marketplace, and also saw opportunities in streamlining design and production. The product range was replaced with a new generation of designs based on a few hundred 'modules', which could be assembled in many different combinations to give variety at low cost. This meant the loss of some customers who had gone to Powerdrive because they could rely on the company's technical leadership to produce designs that suited their particular needs. This was not considered important because the combined sales volume of such customers was under 5%.

Using the new designs, Tom was now able to reorganise the factory into cells that produced major subassemblies such as rotors and stators. The work flow was transformed, and manufacturing throughput time was reduced from 6 weeks to just 4 days. Cost improvements mean that average price reductions of between 10 and 15% could be offered.

Powerdrive's customer service policy was redrafted to offer quotations within a maximum of one hour of any enquiry, and for deliveries of finished product to be made within one week 'anywhere in Northern Europe'. This new policy was explained to internal sales staff, and to sales representatives and agents employed by the organisation. If 'old' customers wanted special designs that were no longer in the range, the sales staff were instructed to explain Powerdrive's new policy and to politely decline the order.

At first, business soared. Impressed by the lower prices and short delivery times, customers flocked to Powerdrive and sales jumped by 50%. But then things began to go sour. First, the factory could no longer cope with the demands being placed on it. The addition of a large order for lawnmower motors blocked out a lot of production capacity from January to June. Order lead times during this period in particular slid back to former levels. Second, a Brazilian supplier spotted the opportunity to enter the market with prices that undercut Powerdrive by 20%. While only half of the product range was covered by this new entrant, it was the high-volume products that were especially threatened. Further, the new competitor offered 3-day lead times from stock

▶

that had been established in Europe. Third, some of the former customers who could no longer obtain their bespoke designs from Powerdrive were complaining within the industry that Powerdrive's technical leadership had been sacrificed. Although small in number, such customers were influential at trade fairs and conferences.

Questions

1 Evaluate the changes that took place in the transaction elements of Powerdrive's customer service policy.

2 Use Fisher's supply chain matrix (Figure 1.11) to suggest what impact the changes to Powerdrive's strategy have had on customer service.

2.3 Customer service and customer retention

Key issue: **What is customer loyalty, and how can it be measured?**

Getting a customer to try your product for the first time, or winning a new customer account, often takes a long time and substantial effort. After all this, a company will see a return on this effort only if it can retain this customer. Despite this fact, it is all too common for current customers to be overlooked in the enthusiasm to win new ones. An obvious example is building societies who offer special low rates of interest in order to attract new borrowers, while existing customers are allowed to stay in old-style accounts that are no longer competitive. As consumer knowledge increases, these anomalies are becoming only too apparent, leading to a rush of rate cuts for existing borrowers. The realisation is dawning that retaining existing customers is often cheaper than finding new ones. This is hardly a new discovery: for example, a study by the US Department of Consumer Affairs (Peters, 1987) showed that the cost of winning new customers is five times greater than that of keeping existing customers.

The change in mindset is to value the loyal customer in terms of his or her lifetime spending. Thus a customer of VW Audi Group could be viewed as worth €300k rather than the €30k of today's sales transaction. As Johnston and Clark (2001) put it, loyal customers:

* generate long-term revenue streams (high lifetime values);
* tend to buy more than new customers;
* tend to increase spending over time;
* may be willing to pay premium prices;
* provide cost savings in relation to attracting new customers.

The logistics challenge is to reinforce customer loyalty by contributing to the marketing mix as indicated in section 2.2. Supporting product availability through such means as channel selection, market coverage, distribution systems and dealer support all helps to nourish customer loyalty. So does logistics support of product characteristics (such as variety or product range) and promotions.

2.3.1 Measuring customer retention

For many B2B situations, the measurement of customer retention is relatively straightforward. The question 'How many customers that we had 12 months ago do we still have today?' (Christopher, 1998) can readily be answered. Figure 2.1 shows the split between the new customers that have been picked up in the last 12 months and the ones retained from last year. If 20% of last year's customers are no longer doing business, the recognition of this is a powerful wake-up call that should be used to analyse what must be done to reverse such a decline.

The other important measure is a comparison of the value of purchases 12 months ago with the value of purchases by retained customers.

Measuring retention in B2C environments is often more problematic because of the difficulty of tracking individual retail customers. The proliferation of 'loyalty' cards in recent years is an attempt by retailers to get to grips with this issue by recording spending patterns by individual account. The 'lifetime' value of an average customer can then be calculated as follows:

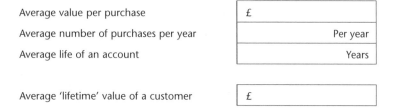

Average value per purchase	£
Average number of purchases per year	Per year
Average life of an account	Years
Average 'lifetime' value of a customer	£

A natural extension of such thinking is to divide customers into such categories as 'gold, silver and bronze' and to resource them accordingly. From a logistics perspective, this could imply additional quality checks and a willingness to organise 'panic' deliveries for gold customers.

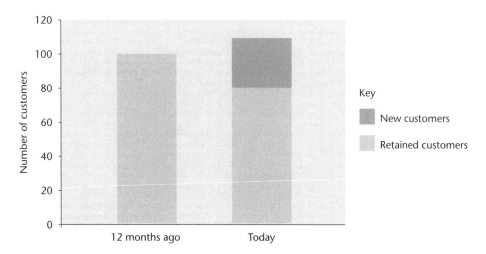

Figure 2.1 Retained customers as a proportion of the total
(Source: After Christopher, 1998)

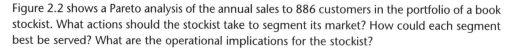

Activity 2.1

Figure 2.2 shows a Pareto analysis of the annual sales to 886 customers in the portfolio of a book stockist. What actions should the stockist take to segment its market? How could each segment best be served? What are the operational implications for the stockist?

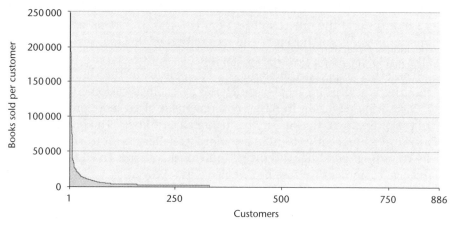

Figure 2.2 **Annual sales per customer for a book distributor, shown as a Pareto diagram**

2.3.2 Customer relationship management

The principle behind relationship marketing is that marketing strategies are continuously extended in order to strengthen customer loyalty. Eventually, customer and supplier are so closely intertwined that it would be difficult to sever the relationship. Figure 2.3 shows the two extremes. Such thinking works particularly well for industrial marketing or B2B situations. Case study 2.2, Batman, illustrates the evolution of diamond-type relationships.

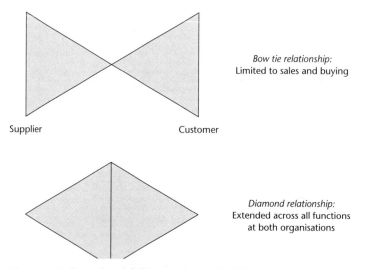

Figure 2.3 **Bow tie and diamond relationships**

(Source: after Payne *et al.*, 1995)

CASE STUDY
2.2

Batman: Adding value through customer service

Everglo Battery SA viewed the development of its marketing strategy in four stages, each signalled by extended concepts of what is meant by 'customer service'. Stage 1 had been the basic product: a sealed lead–acid battery for use in mining applications. Batteries were regarded by customers as a mature product and as a 'grudge buy'. Each year, the basic product was under heavy downward price pressure. Stage 2 had been the industry reaction to customer service: the addition of warranty replacement of defective product, of quality assurance (QA) audits of a supplier's design and manufacturing processes, and of parts and service provision.

Stage 3 had recognised the need to go much further in terms of customer service. A whole raft of additional services had been conceived with a view to adding value. Breakdowns were fixed at short notice by means of field service engineers. Everglo products could now be delivered and installed at customer premises. Price lists were simplified by including peripheral equipment, such as contactors, that had to be added

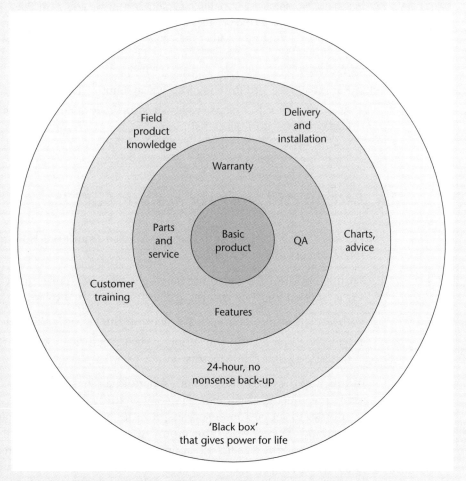

Figure 2.4 **Adding value by customer service**

to a battery rack in order to make it work. Advice and tips were added to help customers warm to Everglo products. In a proactive move, Everglo introduced charts and advice about the application of battery products in general, and the resulting tables became an industry standard. Parts and service in the field were upgraded to a '24 hour, no-nonsense back-up service'. And customer training built on Everglo's position as an industry leader. Rather than sales seminars, Everglo's were customer training seminars, where the company spoke on behalf of the industry rather than as a supplier.

In spite of having reached a pre-eminent position in mining power supply, Everglo recognised that the centre of Figure 2.4 was in effect a 'black hole'. Each year, competitors added more services to their basic products too. In effect, the second and to some extent the third circles were being absorbed into the 'commodity' category, and customer expectations increased all the time. A new stage 4 strategy was conceived to take Everglo into a position that competitors would find it even more difficult to follow. The new strategy was coined 'Batman': battery management for life. The aim was nothing less than a total, customer-oriented product management service that provides 'power for life'. The supplier takes over the task of managing the customer's assets, including problem identification, training and managing cash flow. The objective of 'Batman' is to look at the product the way the customer does, performing best at what the customer values most rather than at what the supplier values most.

Questions

1 Has Everglo reached the end of the line in terms of its customer service strategy?

2 As a competitor to Everglo, what would be your options in response to Everglo's latest moves?

2.4 Setting customer service priorities

Key issues: **How can we set customer service priorities? How do such priorities relate to customer segments?**

Setting priorities for customer service establishes performance measures for a service-driven logistics system. These should be used to ensure that:

● the organisation maintains its focus on the factors valued by customers;

● everyone involved in the supply network can see how well the system is performing against these factors.

In this way they can judge whether performance is improving or declining, and assess the effect on customer service of changes to the system.

In order to set customer service priorities, the needs of the customer, must be understood. These needs differ from customer to customer so it is usually a mistake to take a 'one size fits all' approach to servicing them. Instead it is necessary to find groups of customers that have similar needs that should be serviced in focused, targeted ways. These particular needs define groups and give them a special identity. Identifying them is what marketing people refer to as *segmenta-*

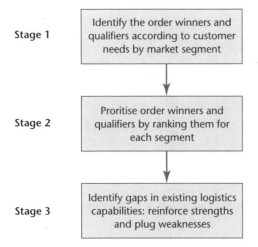

Figure 2.5 **Three-stage process for creating logistics advantage**

tion, referred to in section 2.2. The approach to finding groups in the market follows the three-stage process shown in Figure 2.5. Each of these stages is examined in more detail below.

2.4.1   Stage 1: Identify order winners and qualifiers by segment

In Table 1.11, we referred to order winners and qualifiers in terms of *product lines and the markets they serve.* In Figure 2.5, we have used the marketing term of *segments.* These are intended to be equivalent terms, and they must be clearly understood by different parts of the business. Each segment has different needs, and each need must be translated into its logistics equivalent. Thus a bottle of Coke that is 'always within reach' translates into product availability objectives. 'Marketing speak' needs to be translated into what are the logistics implications, the marketing vision into the logistics reality. Order winners and qualifiers are thus the bridge between marketing and logistics, enabling general statements to be given form the substance. This demands that logistics and marketing explicitly align their roles in delivering value to the customer. Since order winners and qualifiers change over time, this alignment must be regularly updated *and* anticipated future trends included.

2.4.2   Stage 2: Prioritise order winners for each segment

The next stage is to prioritise the order winners for each segment. This is essentially a marketing-led task, and involves allocating points for each order winning criterion for each segment. A convenient way to do this is to allocate 100 percentage points across the order winners that have been identified. In this way,

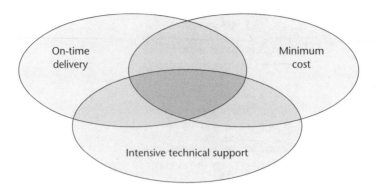

Figure 2.6 Customer segmentation using order winners

not only can the order of importance be found but also the scale of the difference in importance between criteria can be quantified. A further refinement is to involve sample customers from key market segments in this process, thereby gaining a 'reality check' in this somewhat subjective task.

The relative importance of these measures varies according to the relative priorities of the order winners for each segment. Segment A for example, may place a high priority on delivery speed. Here, response-related measures are the key measures of performance. Segment B on the other hand may place high priority on delivery consistency: speed is less important than dependable order cycle times. Having researched customer needs, the next step is to design a logistics system that delivers competitive service levels and to monitor performance of the system by means of suitably designed controls. We outline performance monitoring principles in sections 4 and 5 of the next chapter.

Discussing the data with a cross-functional group in a workshop setting helps to spawn ideas on patterns. It is often easier to make sense of the data if it is used to plot graphs and charts. Venn diagrams such as the one shown in Figure 2.6 are helpful to illustrate patterns that may appear among the analysed data.

2.4.3 Stage 3: Identify gaps, reinforce strengths and plug weaknesses

Having prioritised order winners by segment, the third stage is to compare these priorities with current logistics performance. For example if on-time delivery has been given top priority for a given segment and current logistics performance is rated as poor relative to competitors, the direction of future logistics strategy will be clear. Note that there will be a need for *several different logistics strategies*, because each segment will reveal its own strengths and weaknesses relative to competitors. This point was initiated in section 1.4.3, where we showed how two different products could have quite distinctive strategic needs. A common failure of strategy making is to assume a 'one size fits all' approach to logistics capabilities. Products that need more investment – not less – are left to compete internally for resources with products with low-cost needs. Logistics strategy making must address the differences inherent in different segments. Due attention must also be given to qualifiers that are identified for a given segment. Here, the issue is that logistics capabilities must support performance in the marketplace, so that they do not become *order losing* (see page 19).

2.4.4 Using market segments to set logistics priorities

Undertaking the above three-stage process helps to create an action plan for creating logistics advantage. In order to ensure that progress is being made in the right directions, performance must be monitored over time against key measures for each segment. Table 2.2 lists examples of service level measures used in retail supply chains (Stern *et al.*, 1989).

Table 2.2 **Selected service level measurements**

Major category	Subcategory
Product availability	Line item availability Product group availability Invoice fill Cases/units
Order cycle time	Order entry Order processing Total cycle time
Consistency	In order cycle time In shipment dispatch In transit time In arrival time In warehouse handling
Response time	Order status Order tracing Back order status Order confirmation Product substitution Order shortages Product information requests
Error rates	Shipment delays Order errors Picking and packing errors Shipping and labelling errors
Product/shipment-related malfunction	Damaged merchandise Merchandise refusals Claims Returned goods Customer complaints
Special handling	Trans-shipment Expedited orders Panic deliveries Special packaging Customer backhauls

(Source: Stern *et al.*, 1989)

The relative importance of these measures varies from one customer to another. Customer A, for example, may be interested primarily in speed. Here, response-related measures are top priority. Customer B may be primarily interested in consistency: speed is less important than dependable order cycle times. Having researched customer needs, the next step is to design a logistics system that delivers competitive service levels, and to monitor performance of the system by means of suitably designed controls. We outline performance monitoring principles in sections 3.4 and 3.5 of the next chapter.

Summary

What is customer service in the context of logistics?

- Business to business (B2B) refers to upstream relationships between members of a network. Business to customer (B2C) refers to handover to the end customer. B2B relationships therefore need to be aligned towards B2C.

- Marketing is a philosophy that integrates the disparate activities and functions that take place within the network. Satisfied customers are seen as the only source of profit, growth and security. Marketing in practice starts with analysing segments, evaluating those segments and targeting them. It continues by market positioning, which requires differential advantage to be defined, and the marketing mix to be formulated.

- The key logistics contribution to marketing mix is in the 'fourth P', place. This includes decisions about factors such as channel selection, market coverage, distribution systems and dealer support. Logistics also supports product decisions (for example, product range), and promotion activity.

- The components of customer service were defined as pre-transaction, transaction and post-transaction. The key logistics issue here is that logistics objectives (for example, inventory availability, order fill rate, spares availability and call-out time) are formalised as part of this process.

How do we retain customers through logistics?

- The principle here is that loyal customers have many advantages over new ones. The logistics challenge is to reinforce loyalty by exceeding customer expectations via superior performance.

- Customer relationship management is based on the principle that marketing strategies should be continuously extended to strengthen customer loyalty. Phases of logistics development are needed, each phase placing increasing demands on the development of logistics capabilities.

- Customer retention should be measured between time periods (e.g. annually) to track the percentage of customers who have been retained, and their relative value.

Discussion questions

1 Suggest ways in which logistics can play a part in the marketing mix for:

   a an airline
   b a supermarket
   c an automotive manufacturer
   d a hospital

   In each case, specify the organisation you have in mind and explain the reasons for your suggestions.

2 Referring to the Batman case study 2.2 in section 2.3, explain the likely logistics challenges at each stage of development, and suggest how these might be addressed.

3 Read case study 2.3, Global Lighting, and answer the study questions at the end.

CASE STUDY 2.3

Global Lighting

This case study contains information on how Global's expectations of customer service from their suppliers evolved over a number of years. Further changes are affecting these suppliers as Global's own customers continue to demand higher levels of service. If you are unfamiliar with the terms *kanban* and MRP, they are explained in Chapter 6.

Global is one of the UK's largest manufacturers of lighting products. The market for architectural lighting, one of its major product lines, has become increasingly volatile and competitive in recent years. Pressure to supply products more cheaply and more quickly to a higher standard on an international basis has meant that Global has had to work hard on shortening product life cycles and reducing delivery lead times.

During 1996, the new managing director raised the profile of logistics by making an appointment at Board level. Following this change in organisational structure, a 'lean' approach to supply chain management and manufacturing was implemented over the next 3 years. But recently the lean approach to managing the supply chain has been found to have serious shortcomings in terms of meeting increased demand for customised products such as architectural lighting. Consequently, Global's supply chain management strategy has evolved to accommodate the rapid growth in the market for these products. This change resulted in a multifaceted supply chain strategy, which increases Global's ability to meet the mass customisation needs of its customer base. This multiple strategy approach has created many challenges for suppliers.

Prior to 1996

Before 1996 Global's organisation and management of its internal and external supply chains was based on a single, familiar approach. Global managed internal manufacturing operations and material flow on a push principle driven by MRP.

The supply base was managed through an essentially adversarial approach. The supply base was broad, as the strategy of the buying function of the company operated on the principle of *lowest price is best*. Buyers routinely moved the sourcing of components to a new supplier if the price was lower. New suppliers would be assessed on

▶

the basis of price and component quality only, and no obligation of repeat purchase was expected if the supplier did not retain the lowest price. Price, not cost, was the major objective of the buying group.

After 1996

During 1996, the managing director and his changed board of directors developed a new strategy to manage internal and external operations. Manufacturing was restructured to improve customer service and to increase profitability. Following an extensive programme of data collection and analysis, the production facility was segmented into two distinct sections. One section became a low-volume, irregular-demand factory employing operators with broad product knowledge. The other area became the high-volume, regular-demand factory, with focused and repetitive build tasks. These two areas also operated their internal supply chains in distinctly different formats. The low-volume area continued with a push (MRP) strategy, while the high-volume section operated a pull strategy using *kanban*, as shown in Table 2.3.

Table 2.3 Focused factory structure

	Low volume	High volume
Material control	MRP	*Kanban*
Product codes	>5000	<800
Material flow	Push	Pull
Demand predictability	Low	High
Minimum order quantity	1	pallet
Service offer	MTO	MTS

In addition to restructuring the internal supply chain, the historical approach to managing the external chain of suppliers was altered. Because materials constituted more than 80% of the cost of sales, the decision was made to acknowledge vendors as an intrinsic part of the organisation. Improving the performance of the suppliers and the efficiency of the exchange between the firms was recognised as key to Global's success. In order to achieve the necessary improvements a four-phase plan was conceived. Figure 2.7 gives an overview of the four phases.

Phase 1: Supply base reduction
Before Global committed any substantial resource to develop its suppliers, it was necessary to reduce the number of companies that it dealt with. Reducing the number of direct suppliers was essential to maximise the limited time and resources available. In order to reduce the number of suppliers who dealt directly with Global, resourcing and tiering activities were put in place. Suppliers were selected for the ongoing supply base on the following criteria:

- ppm defects (quality performance);
- ability to operate with *kanban* system (delivery performance);
- CAD/CAM facilities (new product development);

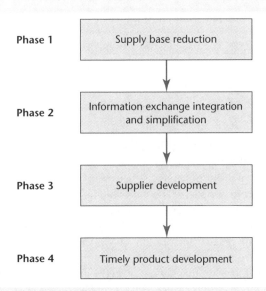

Figure 2.7 The four-phase plan for supplier improvement

● geographical location (new product development and delivery performance);
● price.

If a supplier could not or planned not to operate in accordance with Global's quality, logistical or product development criteria, they were either delisted (and the components switched to another current supplier) or became a tier 2 supplier.

For example, the principal supplier of injection moulding components coordinated purchase and delivery of plastic parts from the other smaller suppliers, which had formerly all been tier 1. The 'before' and 'after' scenarios are shown in Figure 2.8.

The result of these activities was a reduction in direct supplier numbers from 267 to less than 100. This is shown in Table 2.4.

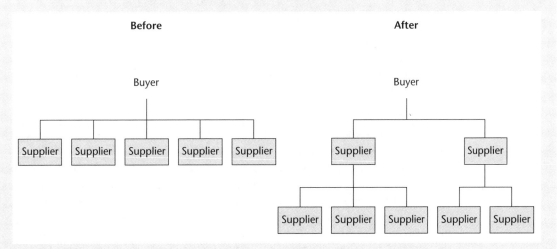

Figure 2.8 Restructuring the supplier base

Table 2.4 **Supplier reduction figures**

Year	No. of suppliers
1995	267
1996	198
1997	132
1998	106
1999	<100

Phase 2: Information exchange integration and simplification

Following the segmentation of the factory into low- and high-volume sections, and reduction of the supply base, it became possible to simplify communications between Global and its suppliers. The high-volume factory introduced, with the assistance and agreement of the suppliers, a two-bin, *kanban* material-ordering system. The support of the suppliers in introducing the simple material-ordering system was an early example of greater integration of working practices within the supply base. Only through the agreement of a new way of trading was it possible to stop posting weekly MRP schedules, which were out of step with 'real time' customer demand. Introduction of the *kanban* system reduced waste created by the delay in transmitting demand data. Similarly, waste related to inappropriate processing, unnecessary inventory, unnecessary motion, waiting and transporting was reduced.

Phase 3: Supplier development

Introducing *kanban* proved to be an early and rewarding example of supplier development for Global and its suppliers. However, development was not limited to one-off, functional improvements. Before improvements were attempted in the more complicated arena of new product development, it was planned to introduce cross-functional teams between Global and its supply base through team-building weekends. For example, the managing director of the main die-casting supplier attended a team-building weekend with Global engineers, sales people, manufacturing managers and finance personnel. This weekend experience prompted the die-caster to introduce team building within their own operation, thus helping to reduce new product development times between the two companies.

Phase 4: Timely product development

Lead times for new product development in the lighting industry in 1996 were typically 18–24 months. For an industry that was becoming more and more fashion conscious the time from concept to product delivery was proving costly in terms of competitiveness in the market.

One of the prime driving forces for Global's new management approach towards suppliers was the desire drastically to reduce time and cost to market. Suppliers within this new ethos became involved at the concept stage for new products. Product development activities became concurrent rather than sequential. Designers and engineers of suppliers with CAD and CAM technologies began to interact directly with Global's designers and engineers at each stage of the development process. At the same time, shopfloor operators became involved with designers to bring cohesion between design and build activities. The result of these changes in approach, internally and externally, was a reduction in development lead times for standard production items from 18 months to 14 weeks by early 1999.

Outcomes

Restructuring Global's approach to managing suppliers would have provided limited benefits if it had not occurred in conjunction with changes to Global's internal operations. For example, improvements in the efficiency of the supply chain in terms of introducing a concept such as *kanban* would not have been as effective if a restructure of manufacturing had not taken place at the same time. Simultaneous internal and external changes propelled Global's performance forward in terms of product development, cost and lead-time reduction, as shown in Table 2.4.

The performance improvements shown in Table 2.4 were achieved through the efforts of both supplier and buyer alike. Integration of supply chain activities and information flows accelerated the implementation of lean practices such as *kanban*, which in turn reduced the uncertainty in demand and improved relationships. Operational improvements followed a consistent and deliberate strategy of developing confidence, trust and openness between Global and its suppliers. Those who were prepared to work in partnership to develop improvements gained additional sales volumes, which in turn increased the interdependence of both parties.

Improvements in relational as well as operational performance developed a virtuous circle for both parties. Implementing pull scheduling in the supply base necessitated the simultaneous implementation of a partnering strategy. The demise of the traditional 'arm's length' approach to managing the buyer–supplier exchange helped both parties to improve their business volumes and performance over this period.

Questions

1 Make a table listing the customer service elements that Global required from its customers both pre-1996 and post-1996.

Customer service elements	
Pre-1996	Post-1996

Discuss the contrast between these two lists with your mentor.

2 The next phase of development at Global addresses the ongoing growth in demand for customised, non-standard products. Linked to an ever-increasing demand for customisation is the driver for shorter lead times and lower costs. With increasing globalisation of the lighting market, several parts of Global's product portfolio have become commodity in nature. Customers in the UK now have the opportunity to purchase their lighting products from low labour cost countries such as China. But supplying the lowest-price product is not the answer to this problem for UK companies. Instead of competing on price, companies must find alternative ways to retain their customers. One way is through the improvement of customer service.

▶

a What actions do you think Global may take to respond to the needs of their customers?

b How will Global's own customer service priorities change as a result of this?

c What are the opportunities and threats facing suppliers in light of the likely changes to Global's customer service priorities?

References

Christopher, M. (1998) *Logistics and Supply Chain Management: Strategies for reducing cost and improving service*, 2nd edn. London: Financial Times Pitman.

Doyle, P. (1994) *Marketing Management and Strategy*. New York: Prentice Hall International.

Gattorna, J. (1998). *Strategic Supply Chain Alignment: Best practice in supply chain management*. Aldershot: Gower.

Hutter, L. (1998) *Focusing on Customers: The role of technology in business*, Introduction. London: Deloitte Consulting/Euromoney Publications.

Johnston, R. and Clark, G. (2001) *Service Operations Management*. London: Pearson.

Payne, A., Christopher, M., Clark, M. and Peck, H. (1995) *Relationship Marketing for Competitive Advantage*. Oxford: Butterworth Heinemann.

Peters, T.J. (1987) *Thriving on Chaos: Handbook for a management revolution*. New York: Harper and Row.

Stern, L.W., El-Ansary, A.I. and Brown, J.R. (1989). *Management in Marketing Channels*. Englewood Cliffs, NJ: Prentice Hall.

Suggested further reading

Payne, A., Christopher, M., Clark, M. and Peck, H. (1995) *Relationship Marketing for Competitive Advantage*. Oxford: Butterworth Heinemann.

Doyle, P. (2000) *Value Based Marketing*. Chichester: Wiley.

CHAPTER 3

Value and logistics costs

Objectives

The objectives of this chapter are to:

- explain the concept of value and its implications for managing the supply chain;
- explain how total costs can be divided up in different ways, and how they can be applied to managing the supply chain;
- identify how better cost information can be used to create more value.

By the end of this chapter you should be able to:

- understand what is meant by the term 'value creation';
- understand how logistics costs can be managed for better value creation;
- understand how activity-based management can be used to identify the cost drivers in your business.

Introduction

In section 1.3 of Chapter 1 we reviewed the way in which different products may have different logistics strategies. While the range of standard shirts compete on price and brand, and demand is relatively stable over the year, fashion blouses compete on style and brand. For a fashion product, the logistics challenge is to be able to support highly uncertain demand in the marketplace. The logistics task for the two supply chains is essentially different, and some companies refer to a 'supply chain for every product' to emphasise this difference.

This chapter probes the cost and performance implications of different logistics strategies. While it may be clear that cost must form a central plank of supply chain strategy for the dishwashing product, that's not to say that the management team in the fashion ski jacket company can ignore the cost implications of their actions. The common theme is the concept of *value*, and the extent that both management teams are creating value.

While value is based on *cost* from the point of view of the company accountant, the concept of value may have a different interpretation outside the company. From the shareholder's point of view, value is determined by the *best alternative use* of a given investment. In other words, value is greatest where the return on investment is highest.

This chapter addresses five key issues:

1 **Where does value come from?**: different views of value, and how it can be measured.

2 **How can logistics costs be represented?**: three different ways to divide up total costs.

3 **Activity-based costing**: a process based alternative to allocating overheads.

4 **A balanced measurement portfolio**: balancing the needs of all stakeholders.

5 **Supply chain operations reference model (SCOR)**: a further process-based approach to measuring supply chain costs and performance.

The chapter assumes a basic knowledge of a profit/loss account and balance sheet. If finance is not your long suit, then a helpful accompanying financial text is *Management Accounting for Non-Specialists* (Atrill and McLaney, 1999). We acknowledge the assistance from our colleague at Cranfield, Sri Srikanathan, for his help with this chapter. Figure 3.1 to 3.7 and Table 3.1 are from his lectures.

3.1 Where does value come from?

Key issues: **How can shareholder value be defined? What is economic value added, and how does it help in this definition?**

Creating shareholder value is widely used today to describe the main objective of a business. In its simplest form, shareholder value is created when the shareholder gets a better return by investing in your business than from a comparable investment. A *comparable investment* is one that has a similar level of risk. You might make the same return on €100 000 from playing roulette as you do from buying a house, but the risk profiles are very different! In order for a business to create superior shareholder value, it must have a competitive advantage. Two commonly used ways of measuring shareholder value are return on investment (ROI) and economic value added (EVA®).

3.1.1 Return on investment (ROI)

One way of looking at the creation of shareholder value is to end the year with a lot more money than when we started out. If this extra money results from profitable trading, then management has been successful in *improving the productivity of capital*. Return on investment (ROI) is measured as profit (in €) before interest and tax as a percentage of capital employed (also in €):

$$\% \text{ ROI} = 100 \times € \text{ Profit} / € \text{ Capital employed}$$

The term 'investment' is used because capital employed is equivalent to the money invested in the business. ROI can also be seen as the outcome of profitability and asset utilisation:

$$ROI = \frac{Profit}{Sales} \times \frac{Sales}{Capital\ employed}$$

Let us look at the detail behind each of these ratios, and the way they fit in with each other. Figure 3.1 gives a family tree of the way return on investment is made up. Let us look at the potential for improving each from a point of view of managing the supply chain better:

Sales

Superior customer service improves sales, and makes our company more valued to the customer in the long term.

- Improving customer responsiveness is a key goal for managing the supply chain.

Costs

The supply chain is a potential goldmine for making bottom line improvements to business performance. But directors of many businesses are impatient for cost improvement, and consider that cutting stocks and headcount is all that is needed. This may achieve short-term margin improvement, but strategic supply chain management is about improving the way things are done and hence improving long-term performance.

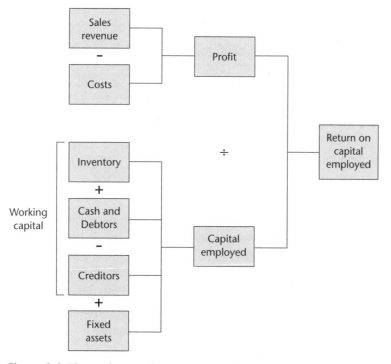

Figure 3.1 **The make-up of return on capital employed (investment)**

- Supply chain modelling shows that manufacturing and distribution costs together with inventories can be optimised while customer service is maximised.
- Studies in efficient consumer response (ECR) have shown that cutting out non-value-added products and inefficient promotional activity can reduce overall costs by 6%. (ECR is discussed in Chapter 6.)

Working capital

Note that the combination of inventory, cash and debtors *less* creditors is called working capital. Each of the elements of working capital is considered in turn.

Inventory

This is a major asset in many businesses. It is there to buffer uncertainty of supply and demand, and to permit immediate availability when replenishment times are too lengthy. However, inventory is often regarded as a hindrance rather than a help: it ties up cash, it needs resources to be stored, and it goes obsolete!

- A primary goal for supply chain management is to replace inventory with information. Try to minimise the use of forecasts and to increase the use of real demand.
- Question any means for automatically replenishing inventory.

Cash and debtors

The key task here is to make the time line between receipt of customer order and receipt of the cash as short as possible. Progress against this ideal not only makes the company more competitive by reducing lead times, but also improves its cash position. This means that business processes from sales order processing to distribution should be integrated and free from waste.

- Debtors (customers who owe us money) can be minimised by basic controls such as regular review and problem resolution. Sending out incomplete invoices is an invitation for non-payment!

Creditors

Creditors are people we owe money to. In supply chain terms, this term applies mainly to our suppliers. Many organisations think that lengthy payment terms to suppliers maximise credit and therefore improve the balance sheet. The downside of this thinking is that suppliers factor in the credit terms to their prices, and their own balance sheets become saddled with debt.

- Plan material requirements and distribution requirements to maximise flow of parts through the supply chain as needed.
- Discipline goods inwards to check delivery date, quality and correct prices. There is no point in starting the credit cycle early!

- If the supplier is a smaller company, it may be that the cost of capital is higher than it is for your company. It may be worthwhile to consider negotiating with the supplier to pay early, and therefore getting a share of the money that the supplier is paying in interest to the bank.

Fixed assets

The value-generating assets of a business that form the focus of supply chain management are a heavy drain on capital. They include manufacturing facilities, transport and distribution. They contribute to high *fixed costs* for an operation: that is, costs that do not change much with throughput. Such costs are therefore highly volume sensitive, as we shall see.

- Many organisations respond by a 'maximum variable, minimum fixed' policy. This is helped by *outsourcing* all but the key capabilities, which are retained in-house. Thus transport and warehousing are today often outsourced to specialist 'third party logistics providers' such as Exel and UPS.

Activity 3.1

1 Review the categories in Figure 3.1 and compile your own list of the way in which these categories can be influenced (made better or worse) in an organisation.
2 What are the implications for supply chain strategy?

3.1.2 Economic value added

While ROI is an important measure of how well the management of a company is performing, many people today argue that ROI does not provide the complete picture. It does not compare the ROI with the investor's required return. The required rate of return will depend on the perceived risk of the investment plus the *opportunity cost* of the capital for the investor. (The *opportunity cost* is the money that could have been earned from the next best investment.) Together, perceived risk and opportunity cost produce the 'true cost of capital'. ROI describes only the gross return on an investment, not the amount of risk that was incurred to create the return. So ROI is not a sufficient measure of whether an organisation is creating value for its shareholders. Value is created only if the ROI more than compensates for additional risk.

Economic value added (EVA®) is a measure of the return on investment less the true cost of capital employed to the investor (it has been trademarked by US consultants Stern Stewart):

$$EVA = ROI - \text{True cost of capital employed}$$

In essence, EVA measures *return* on capital employed less the *cost* of financing that capital employed. If EVA is positive, value is being added by the business. If EVA is negative, value is being drained out. In order to maximise EVA, management is being encouraged to maximise ROI while minimising the true cost of capital. In other words, the use of EVA encourages managers to generate revenue while decreasing the cost of capital employed sufficiently to satisfy shareholders' expectations.

The true cost of capital employed in effect charges the organisation for use of capital raised both by debt (bank loans, etc.) and by equity (shareholders' capital). The true cost is expressed as a *weighted average*. This additional measure puts pressure on management not only to reduce capital employed (as in ROI), but also to finance what remains in the best way. The 'best way' here means a mix of debt and equity that reduces variability of returns to shareholders without compromising the credit rating of the business.

3.2 How can logistics costs be represented?

Key issues: **What are the various ways of cutting up the total cost 'cake', and what are the relative merits of each?**

We all have a pretty good idea of what the total costs of a business are in practice. The costs of such items as materials used, power and wages are all bills that have to be paid. What is not so clear is how these costs should be allocated to supply chain processes – or even to products for that matter. Christopher (1998) states that problems with traditional cost accounting as related to logistics can be stated as follows:

- The true costs of servicing different customer types, channels and market segments are poorly understood.
- Costs are captured at too high a level of aggregation.
- Costing is functionally oriented at the expense of output.
- The emphasis on full cost allocation to products ignores customer costs.

This section reviews commonly used ways of representing costs (fixed and variable, direct and indirect), and one less commonly used way (engineered and discretionary). If you are already familiar with the concepts of variable and fixed costs and break-even charts, then start at section 3.3. Bear in mind that the total cost picture is always the same; the different ways of representing them are simply different ways of 'cutting the cake'. Let us look at the total cost as a cube instead of a cake. Then the three different ways of representing costs can be shown as different ways of cutting up the cube (Figure 3.2).

The important point here is that the total cost is constant; it is the ways we *analyse* that cost that are different. Why analyse it in different ways? To gain better information about our cost basis so that we can manage the business better. Let's look in turn at each of these ways to cut the total cost cube.

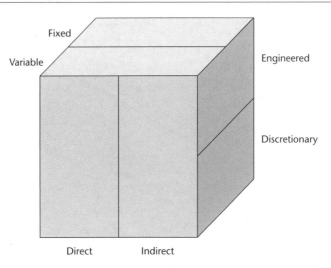

Figure 3.2 **Three ways to cut the 'total cost cube'**

3.2.1 Fixed/variable

One popular way of analysing costs is to consider the effect of *volume of activity* on them. Costs tend to respond differently as the volume changes:

- *Fixed costs* tend to stay the same as volume of activity changes, or at least, within a given volume range.
- *Variable costs* change as the volume of activity changes.

Fixed costs include things such as warehouse rental, which is charged on a time basis (€/month). As volume of activity increases, additional warehouses may be added round Europe, and we get the familiar *stepped fixed costs*, as shown in Figure 3.3. The same relationship would apply if volumes were reduced and a warehouse closed.

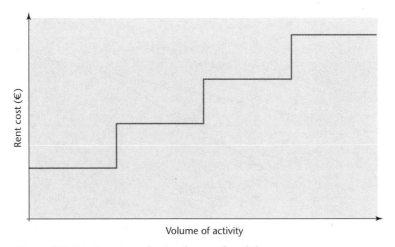

Figure 3.3 **Rent cost against volume of activity**

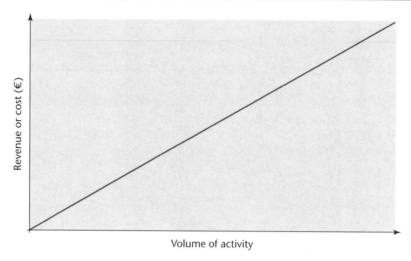

Figure 3.4 Direct material costs against volume of activity

Variable costs include things such as direct materials, which are ordered in line with demand. If demand increases, we buy more. Starting with zero cost at zero activity, variable costs increase roughly in line with volume, as shown in Figure 3.4.

If we add the variable costs to the fixed costs against a given range of volume (so that the fixed costs remain completely fixed), and add in the sales revenue (which also increases in line with volume), we arrive at the break-even chart shown in Figure 3.5. The sloping line that starts at O is the sales revenue. The total cost line starts at F, and represents the sum of fixed and variable costs. The point at which the sales revenue line crosses the total cost line is the break-even point. Below this point, a loss will be incurred; above it a profit will be made.

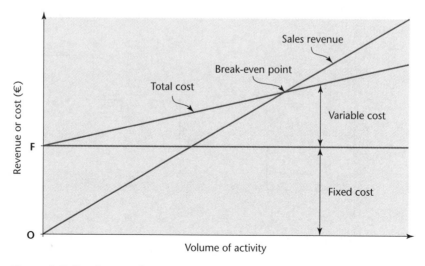

Figure 3.5 Break-even chart

A helpful concept in evaluating break-even charts is that of contribution:

Contribution = Sales − Direct costs

Therefore contribution is the fixed costs plus the profit. Contribution is useful in decision-making. High contribution per unit indicates a more volatile business: that is, one that is more risky. Therefore we should expect a business with high contribution/unit to provide a higher return on investment in the longer term. Look at the two break-even charts in Figures 3.6 and 3.7. What are the differences

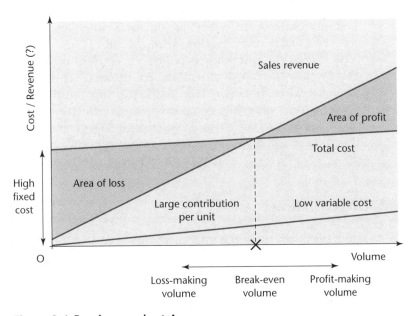

Figure 3.6 Break-even chart A

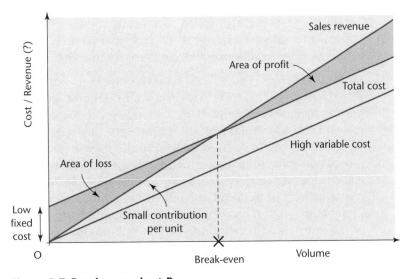

Figure 3.7 Break-even chart B

between the two situations? What has happened to the break-even point, and why?

Chart A shows a situation with high variable costs and low fixed costs. In chart B, the situation is reversed. The break-even point has moved well to the right: that is, chart B requires a higher volume to break even than A. This is because a much higher volume of sales is needed to cover the high level of fixed costs.

Furthermore, additional volume has a small impact on chart A, whereas it has a much higher impact on chart B. So high fixed costs and low variable costs lead to greater volume sensitivity. Accordingly, profitability (the area above the break-even point) is affected much more by volume changes in chart B. In terms of contribution, chart A represents a situation with low contribution/unit, and therefore low risk in comparison with chart B.

The supply chain implications of such considerations are that we are most often faced with chart B situations. For example, core resources such as warehousing and distribution systems create little opportunity to reduce investments in line with reducing sales volumes other than the step changes shown in Figure 3.3. We are back to the advice for increasing ROI given in section 3.1.1 above: to increase sales and reduce costs. The reassuring point is that every 1% increase in sales or 1% reduction in costs has a leveraged effect on profits.

3.2.2   Direct/indirect

Another way to cut up the total cost 'cube' is to analyse costs in terms of whether or not they can be directly allocated to a given product. Two further categories emerge:

- *Direct costs* can be tied to specific products. The most obvious examples are direct labour and direct materials. Thus we can allocate exactly the cost of bought-in parts to the products into which they are built.

- *Indirect costs* are whatever is left over after direct costs have been allocated. Indirect costs are also called 'overheads', and include everything from the managing director's salary to the rent rates paid for the distribution centre – anything that cannot be allocated directly to a given product.

Directness of costs is concerned with the extent to which costs can be allocated directly to given products. This is a completely different concept from that of fixed/variable costs. While there is a tendency to associate fixed costs with indirect and variable with direct, there is no necessary relationship at all. Thus direct labour costs tend to be fixed, at least in the short term.

As stated above, the reason for analysing costs differently is *to gain better information about our cost basis so that we can manage the business better.* Direct and indirect costs help us to decide the full cost of a product or service when more than one are offered. If there were just a single product, life would be easy, because all of the costs could be allocated to that one product. Most businesses are much more complex than that, and are faced with the issue of how indirect costs should be apportioned to products. The most popular way to spread indirect costs is on the basis of direct labour. This is not the 'correct way', nor is it the only way.

One way in which to get a closer view of how fixed costs behave by product is to use a method called *direct product profitability (DPP)*. This method has been widely used in the retail industry to understand the way in which logistics costs behave for each product. The understanding is achieved by allocating fixed costs by making assumptions about how these are incurred by a product as it moves through the logistics system.

A good DPP system should take account of all the significant differences in the ways products are developed, sourced, produced, sold and distributed. In order to make this analysis practical, products will normally need to be grouped together. Product groups need to recognise shared technologies, processes, fixed assets, raw material inputs and packaging methods. The key objective of product groupings is to remove the need for apportioning costs, and thereby not to apportion profit across the products.

An example DPP is shown for a manufacturing company in Table 3.1. Note that not all of the fixed costs have been assigned. DPP assumes that only those costs that can rationally be allocated may be deducted. Thus DPP may be viewed as a development of direct/indirect costing in that it attempts to convert into direct costs logistics costs that would otherwise have been regarded as fixed. In this way, DPP seeks to provide more accurate information about which products are contributing most to profitability – and which are contributing least.

Table 3.1 Direct product profitability (DPP)

Gross sales for product group ● Less product specific discounts and rebates		X X
Net sales by product ● Less direct costs of product		X X
Gross product contribution ● Less product-based marketing expenses	X	X

Product-specific direct sales support costs
● Less product-specific direct transportation costs:
  – Sourcing costs
  – Operations support
  – Fixed assets financing
  – Warehousing and distribution
  – Inventory financing
  – Order, invoice and collection processing
	X
	
	X
	X
	X
	X
	X
	X
		
		X

● Less product-attributable overheads		X
Direct product profitability		X

The principle at stake here is that good accounting and financial analysis force us to ask more questions about what is going on in our business. DPP can have a role to play here: it attempts to allocate logistics costs more specifically to products (and, in this case, orders as well) than is possible by spreading 'fixed' costs on the basis of an assumption such as direct labour. The assumption would otherwise be that direct labour actually 'drives' the overheads, which is highly doubtful.

CASE STUDY
3.1

DPP

Filmco makes two thin film (gauge = 12μm) products for packaging applications in the food industry. Product A is coated so that it can subsequently be printed on; product B is uncoated. There is no changeover time on the production line, because all that needs to happen is that the coating drum is switched on or off. Once produced on the film-making lines, the film is slit to width and to length to customer order. Roughly 40% of Filmco's output is A, and 60% B, and film-making takes place 360 days/year on a continuous basis because of the high capital cost of the process.

A DPP study was carried out at Filmco to determine the relative profitability of the two products A and B by major customer. The method was adapted from that shown in Table 3.1 because this Filmco is a manufacturing environment. Here's how it was done:

a *Invoice price*: This was the total sales value invoiced to the customer.

b *Cost of placing orders*: The total cost of the sales office (salaries, etc.) was divided by the number of orders dispatched that month. This cost per order (€150) was allocated to each order placed by each customer.

c *Manufacturing cost*: A variable cost for each product was found by collecting raw material, labour, power, packaging and waste costs. Manufacturing overheads (fixed costs) were allocated on the basis of direct labour. Because of the small difference in manufacturing methods, the manufacturing costs for the two products were similar. They were €2107 for A and €2032 for B.

d *Storage costs*: The total cost of the warehousing operation is €800k/year. There are 8300 pallet locations, and the cost/day for a pallet was calculated as €0.30 assuming 360 working days. The storage cost for a given order was calculated as the number of pallets × the number of days × €.30.

e *Opportunity costs*: Orders must wait in the warehouse until the last reel has been produced. An order with a value of €3000 that stays for 7 days in the warehouse with an interest rate of 14% is said to have an opportunity cost of €8.20.

f *Transport cost*: This was based on a price per tonne delivered to a given customer.

g *Total cost*: This was the sum of b to f for a given order.

h *DPP*: This was sales price less total cost g.

Table 3.2 gives a sample of the DPPs for four orders for customer P. The average DPP for customer P over all orders shipped over a given month was 19.6%, while that for customer Q was 23.1% and customer R was 33.0%.

Table 3.2 DPP for customer P for a sample of four orders in a given month

Order no.	Film	Weight (t)	a	b	c	d	e	f	g	h
186232	A	482	1210	157	876	1.08	1.88	79	1115	0.08
185525	A	2418	5997	157	4344	7.83	9.33	190	4709	0.215
185187	B	4538	13000	157	8402	20.8	30.33	343	8954	0.311
185351	B	2615	7576	157	4897	14.58	17.68	198	5284	0.303

Question

What can we tell from the above analysis in Table 3.2 and the average DPPs per customer? (Consider in particular the differences in DPP between the four orders shown, and between the three customers P, Q and R.)

3.2.3 Engineered/discretionary

A third way of analysing costs is to consider *the ease of allocating* them. Some things are easy to cost; others may require considerable thought and analysis because they are difficult to cost under current methods. This line of thinking creates a third way of cutting the total cost cube:

- *Engineered costs* have a clear input–output relationship. In other words, the benefit of a given cost is measurable. For example, if it takes 10 hours to produce 10 boxes of product A in the factory, then we have a clear output benefit (1 box) for the cost of each hour of input.

- *Discretionary costs* do not have a clear input–output relationship. Here, the input cost is clear but the output benefit is unclear. For example, the cost of the contract cleaners who clean the factory is clear, but the benefit they produce is not easily quantifiable.

The challenge is to convert discretionary costs into engineered costs, so that we can quantify better the competitive impact of a given course of action. A classic example of converting discretionary costs into engineered costs has been the conversion of 'quality' as a discretionary concept into engineered 'quality costs' (Dale and Plunkett, 1995). This was achieved by breaking down the concept of quality into three cost drivers:

- *Prevention.* This comprises the costs of measures to prevent defects from taking place, such as training and process capability studies.

- *Appraisal.* This comprises the costs incurred in detecting defects, which would include testing and inspection.

- *Internal and external failure.* Internal costs are scrap, rework, and the associated costs of not getting it right the first time. External failure costs are rectification after products have reached the final customer, such as warranty claims, returns and repairs.

In this case, it was argued, greater investment in prevention would result in the overall cost of quality being reduced over time.

The principle is to convert discretionary costs into engineered costs where possible. As indicated in the above examples, it is usually possible to make an estimate of what the engineered costs are, perhaps accompanied by a sensitivity or risk analysis. Without such guidelines, decisions would have to be taken on 'gut feel' – or, as usually happens, not taken at all! In other words, the logistics team may have an excellent project for increased flexibility in the distribution centre, but because they have not quantified the savings (outputs) the application for funding is rejected.

Glup SA

Glup SA supplies a range of household soaps to supermarkets in northern Europe. There are 12 stock-keeping units (sku's) in the range. The logistics manager has determined that an investment of €0.5 m on improved material handling equipment would convert the main distribution centre into a more flexible facility. A number of benefits in improved product availability have been identified – but current information is largely in the form of discretionary costs. Glup's assessment of the benefits and its plans to convert the justification into engineered costs are outlined below.

Improved in-store availability

This the percentage time for which a product is available on the shelf. If the product is not available on the shelf, then it will lose sales to competitive products that *are* available, such as supermarket own brands. (Availability is a classic 'order losing sensitive' qualifying criterion as described in section 1.3, Chapter 1.) Current available data at Glup are scant, but suggests that average in-store availability is as low as 85% for a given stock-keeping unit (sku). In order to convert this discretionary benefit into an engineered cost, Glup intends to measure the time for which each of the 12 product lines is unavailable each week. One way to do this is to use a market research agency to conduct sample studies of product availability in selected stores at random times across the working week. This will yield an availability guide, such as the 85% figure referred to. The new system will, it is believed, reduce this unavailable time. Glup then plans to model the new material-handling equipment methods using simulation, and to calculate the new in-store availability. The reduced non-availability time could then be converted into additional contribution for each sku to give an engineered cost saving.

Reduced transportation costs

The new equipment would also allow lower transportation costs, because trays of different sku's could be mixed together on the same pallet. Glup again intends to use simulation modelling to identify the opportunities for savings using this method. It is considered that this will offer the opportunity to reduce overall transport costs by more flexible loading of the trailers used to distribute the products to Glup's customers.

Promotions and new product launches

It is considered that the new equipment will enable promotions and new product launches to be delivered to selected stores more accurately and more quickly. Demand uncertainty in such situations is very high: for example, a recent 'three for the price of two' promotion created a fivefold increase in sales. In order to launch a new product it is first necessary to drain the pipeline of old product, or to 'write it off' as obsolete stock. If the more flexible warehouse system can reduce the length of the pipeline from factory to supermarket, it is argued, then a real saving in time or obsolete stock is possible. Glup again intends to measure this by simulation. It will then be necessary to determine by how much sales will increase as a result of the new product advantages. This will be estimated by Glup marketing people, who will use experience of previous promotions and new product launches. The engineered cost will be the additional time for which the new product is available multiplied by the additional estimated sales volume multiplied by the contribution per unit. Alternatively, it will be the reduction in obsolete stocks multiplied by the total cost per product plus any costs of double handling and scrapping.

Question

Comment on Glup's plans to create engineered costs from the perceived benefits of the new material-handling equipment.

3.3 Activity-based costing

Key issues: **What are the shortcomings of traditional cost accounting from a logistics point of view? How can costs be allocated to processes so that better decisions can be made?**

The driving force behind activity-based costing (ABC) is that the traditional way of allocating indirect costs by spreading them to products on the basis of direct labour is becoming difficult to manage. While direct labour used to constitute a substantial portion of product costs, today that rarely applies. Therefore overhead rates of 500% on direct labour are not uncommon. Just a small change in direct labour content would lead to a massive change in product cost.

Cooper and Kaplan (1988) explain the problem by referring to two factories: Simple and Complex. Both factories produce 1 million ballpoint pens each year; they are the same size, and have the same capital equipment. But while Simple produces only blue pens, Complex produces hundreds of colour and style variations in volumes that range from 500 (lavender) to 100 000 (blue) units per year. A visitor would notice many differences between the factories. Complex has far more production support staff to handle the numerous production loading and scheduling challenges, changeovers between colours and styles, and so on. Complex would also have more design change issues, supplier scheduling problems, and outbound warehousing, picking and distribution challenges. There would be much higher levels of idle time, overtime, inventory, rework and scrap because of the difficulty of balancing production and demand across a much bigger product range. Because overheads are allocated on the basis of direct labour, blue pens are clobbered with 10% of the much higher Complex overheads. The market price of blue pens is determined by focused factories such as Simple, so the blue pens from Complex appear to be unprofitable. As a result, the management of Complex considers that specialist products such as lavender – which sell at a premium – are the future of the business, and that blue pens are low priority. This strategy further increases overheads and costs, and perpetuates the myth that the unit cost of each pen is the same. Traditional cost systems often understate profits on high-volume products and overstate profits on low-volume, high-variety products. ABC principles would help the management of Complex to make more informed product decisions. The management of Simple has no need for another costing system; the current one works will for them.

ABC recognises that overhead costs do not just happen, but are caused by activities, such as holding products in store. ABC therefore seeks to break the business down into major processes – such as manufacture, storage and distribution – and then breaks each process into activities. For example, the distribution process would include such activities as picking, loading, transport and delivery. For each of these activities, there must be one *cost driver*: what is it that drives cost for that activity? For example, the cost driver for the storage activity may be the volume of a case, whereas the transport activity may be driven by weight. Once we know the cost driver, we need to know how many units of that cost driver are incurred for that activity, and the cost per unit for the cost driver. For example, the cost driver for the transportation activity may be the number of kilometres driven, and the cost per kilometre would be the cost per unit of the cost driver. This yields the cost of the activity and, when summed across all of the activities in a process, the total cost of that process.

ABC is difficult to implement because we need first to understand what the discrete processes are in a business where the existing links between functions are not well understood. There is then the issue of identifying the cost driver, which requires a fresh way of looking at each activity. For example, the cost driver for a warehouse fork-lift operator would be the number of pallets moved. The cost driver for stocking shelves would be the number of pieces that must be stacked in a given time period. A further problem occurs if there is more than one cost driver for a given activity. You are then faced with the same problem as with overhead allocation: on what basis should the cost drivers be weighted? Usually, this problem shows that activities have not been broken down into sufficient detail, and that more analysis is needed. ABC can therefore become complex to implement.

In spite of the implementation challenges, logistics and ABC go hand in hand (van Damme and van der Zon, 1999). It is a very rational way to analyse costs, and logistics practitioners recognise that providing a service is about managing a sequence of activities. Logistics or supply chain managers are particularly well placed to understand, analyse and apply ABC. They understand business processes and the activities that go with them. Theirs is a cross-functional task. The value chain stares them in the face!

The procedure of determining cost drivers is often considered to be more valuable than the ABC system itself. Activity-based management enables the cost structure of a business to be examined in a new light, allowing anomalies to be resolved and sources of waste highlighted. It may also help in better targeting investment decisions.

3.3.1 ABC example

Complex Ltd has four production lines, which each operates for 8000 hours a year. Each line makes a number of products, which are based on size and colour. Many changeovers are therefore required, each incurring set-up and mainten-

Table 3.3 Different ways of allocating maintenance costs

Production lines	A	B	C	D	Total
Machine hours	8 000	8 000	8 000	8 000	32 000
No. of changeovers	50	30	15	5	100
Equal allocation	250 000	250 000	250 000	250 000	1 000 000
Allocation by activity	500 000	300 000	150 000	50 000	1 000 000
Difference	250 000	50 000	−100 000	−200 000	0

ance costs. Traditionally the maintenance costs have been allocated on the basis of machine hours, so each production line is charged equally. This year, the maintenance budget of €1 million has been divided into four, so each line is charged with €250 000.

Sales and marketing are concerned that certain products are losing market share, and this is due to price relative to the competition. All departments have been instructed to investigate costs and to suggest improvements. How can activity-based costing (ABC) improve this situation? By identifying the key cost driver for maintenance, in this case the number of changeovers, costs can be allocated to each production line on this basis. Costs are then matched to the activity that generates them, so avoiding cross-subsidies.

The results are illustrated in Table 3.3. Maintenance costs have now been transferred to the production lines that incur the activity. For example, costs on line A have doubled to €500 000, while costs on line D have reduced to €50,000. ABC in this example has not taken cost out of the process, but has reallocated the costs to give a better understanding of the cost base. Complex is now in a better position to make decisions that affect the cost competitiveness of the product range.

3.4 A balanced measurement portfolio

Key issues: Who are the key stakeholders in a business, and what needs to be achieved in order to satisfy them? How can a balanced set of measures of performance be developed in order to address stakeholder satisfaction and stakeholder contribution?

Many organisations in the past have suffered from undue emphasis on particular measures of performance within the firm. For example, a preoccupation with labour productivity may lead to excessive stocks of inbound parts ('Don't run out of raw materials otherwise bonuses will suffer'). Such a preoccupation may also lead to excessive stocks of outbound products, because the most important priority is to keep workers busy, whether the product can be sold or not! While this priority may be good for productivity, it may well disrupt flow in the supply network: inbound parts are ordered too early, and outbound products are made too early. What is good for one measure (productivity in this case) is bad for others (inventories and material flow).

In reality, management today is faced with the challenge of performing across a whole range of objectives. Different groups of stakeholders in a firm include shareholders, employees, customers, suppliers, the local community and government. This is not a comprehensive list, and industries such as pharmaceuticals have other important stakeholders, including regulators such as the Drug Enforcement Agency (DEA, *www.usdoj.gov/dea/*). The challenge for the directors of a firm is to *balance* the diverse interests of these groups of stakeholders. We review the interests of each group in turn:

- *Shareholders*: typically have a passing interest in a firm in which they invest. They will keep their shareholding as long as it provides a return that is competitive with other investments. Shareholders are impressed by high dividends and share appreciation resulting from profitability and growth of the business. Failure to deliver adequate returns often turns shareholders against the management of the day!

- *Employees*: often have a long-term commitment to a firm, and are concerned with employment stability, competitive wages and job satisfaction. Failure to deliver on such goals may create negative reactions such as loss of motivation and loyalty, difficulty in recruitment, and various forms of industrial action.

- *Customers*: are in theory the most important stakeholder in a free market economy. It is their demand that draws material through the supply network. Failure to keep customers satisfied creates the risk of loss of business.

- *Suppliers*: are interested in such benefits as long-term business, involvement in new product development, and of course payment on time. Failure to meet such benefits leads to sanctions such as disruption of supply and higher prices.

- *Local community*: here, the interests are in the firm as a local employer, with a reputation for civic responsibility and long-term commitment to the region as an employer and as a ratepayer. Failure to deliver against such interests may lead to environmental disputes and difficulty in obtaining planning permission.

- *Government*: is interested in the firm as a contributor to employment and value creation in the economy, and as a source of revenues. Failure to meet government laws, on the other hand, may lead to prosecution or even closure of the business.

Thus the directors of a business are faced with the need to manage the potentially conflicting interests of the stakeholders, keeping each within what Doyle (1994) refers to as a *tolerance zone*. Each stakeholder has a limit beyond which the risk of disruption to the business increases rapidly. An upper limit exists as well. For example, a preoccupation with profits may please shareholders for the time being, but may result in negatives from labour exploitation and low levels of investment. While bumper profits appear in year 1, these are rapidly eroded as the negatives cut in during later years. In the end, the whole business suffers. The challenge for the directors is to keep all stakeholders just satisfied, keeping each within the tolerance zone.

3.4.1 Balanced measures

While balance between stakeholders is one issue, another is the balance between financial and operational measures of performance, and between history and the future. Kaplan and Norton (1996) point to the shortcomings of traditional cost accounting systems. Traditional systems are geared to the needs of the stock market, and are essentially historical and financial in emphasis. Modern systems, they argue, need to be balanced between financial and operations, and between history and the future. A way of showing the relative emphasis between traditional measures and balanced measures is to show relative priorities by means of circles, where larger circles imply a greater priority and number of measures in use, as shown in Figure 3. 8.

In developing a modern performance measurement system it is necessary to take all of these factors into account, and to create a balanced performance measurement system. That is the objective of the 'performance prism'.

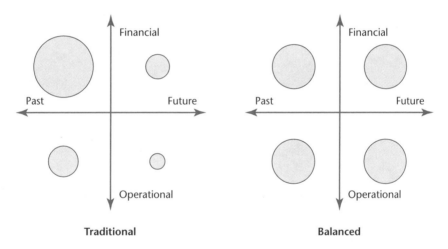

Figure 3.8 **Traditional and balanced priorities**

3.4.2 The performance prism

The performance prism (Neely *et al.*, 2000; Neely and Adams, 2000) is a framework that helps in dealing with the problem of deciding what performance measures to select for use within organisations. The framework is in the form of a prism with five facets. It adopts a 'stakeholder-centric' view of performance measurement: that is, a view that the purpose of the firm is to satisfy stakeholder requirements and to receive contributions from the stakeholder in return. Thus stakeholder satisfaction occupies the top facet of the prism (Figure 3.9), and stakeholder contribution occupies the bottom facet. In between are three facilitating mechanisms: strategies, processes and capabilities.

The five facets of the performance prism can be described as follows:

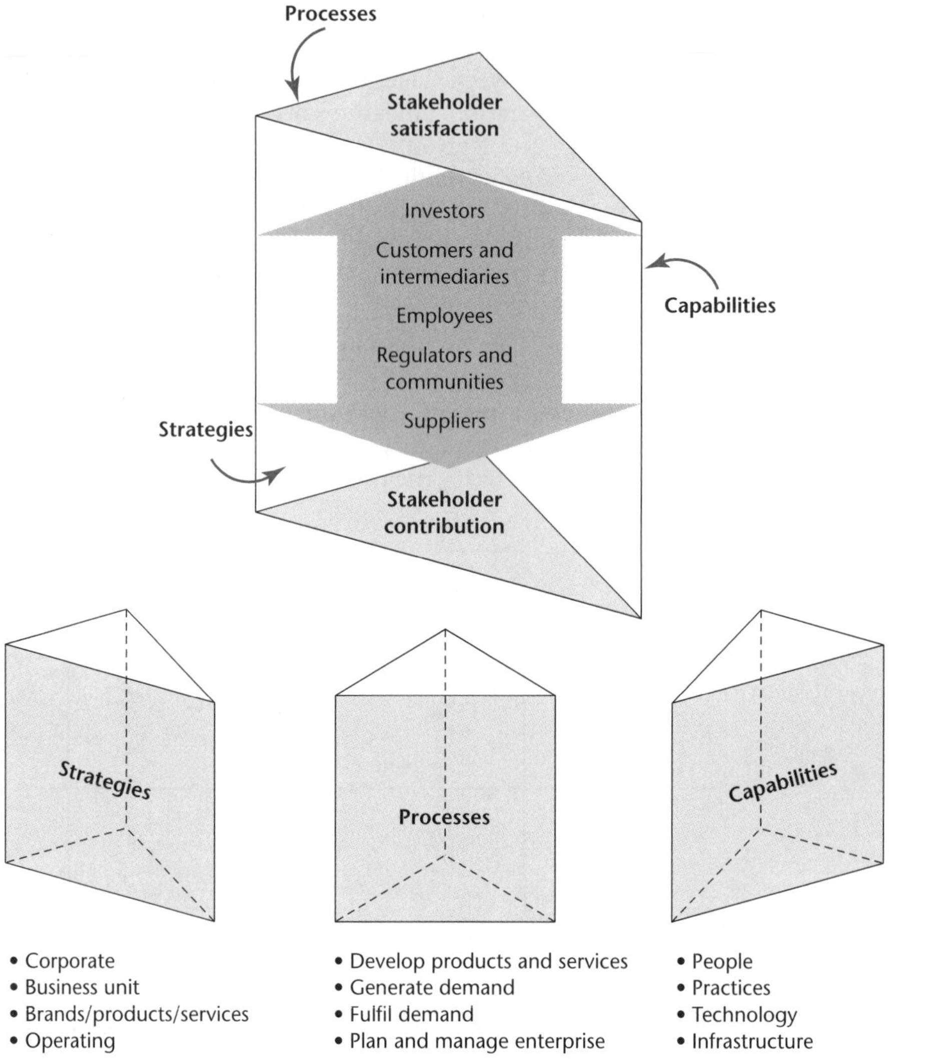

Figure 3.9 **The five facets of the performance prism**

- Facet 1 is labelled 'stakeholder satisfaction', and addresses the question 'Who are the stakeholders and what do they want and need?
- Facet 2 is labelled 'strategies', and addresses the question 'What are the strategies we require to ensure that the wants and needs of the stakeholders are satisfied?'
- Facet 3 is labelled 'processes', and asks the question 'What are the processes we have to put in place in order to allow our strategies to be delivered?' By 'processes' is meant the business processes needed to drive the organisation, including developing new products and services, generating demand, fulfilling demand, and managing the enterprise.
- Facet 4 is labelled 'capabilities', which are defined as the combination of

people, practices, technology and infrastructure that together enables execution of the organisation's business processes. Capabilities address the question 'What are the capabilities we require to operate our processes?'

● Facet 5 is labelled 'stakeholder contribution'. An organisation's relationship with stakeholders is not limited to satisfying them (facet 1); stakeholders should also contribute to the organisation. Thus an organisation may satisfy employees in terms of salary, recognition, long-term employment and so on. But it wants in return such things as improvement suggestions, loyalty, and keeping up to date with knowledge and expertise. The prism therefore recognises a reciprocal relationship between stakeholder and organisation.

Each step of the performance prism, represented by the five facets listed above, demands that performance measures be established to harmonise all aspects of the way the organisation is run. At facet 1, for example, the competitive criteria explained in Chapter 1, section 1.3 are listed alongside stakeholder needs under the same headings. For example, delivery speed could be identified as the top order-winning criterion. The implications to stakeholder needs are then analysed in such terms as:

● *Employees:* awareness and training. Communication of time-related performance measures such as throughput efficiency.

● *Customers:* agreement of time-based performance objectives. Clearly understood monitoring system put in place. Agreed improvement objectives for the next 3 years.

● *Suppliers:* agreement of time-based targets for delivery and flexibility. Improvement objectives in line with customer objectives, etc.

A similar process is used to extend performance measures across the other four facets of the prism. For example, the employee satisfaction measures drill down into the capabilities needed (facet 4). The performance prism therefore sets out to balance and integrate performance measures across key aspects of the management of the business.

3.5 Supply chain operations reference model (SCOR)

Key issues: How can process thinking be applied to measures across the supply chain? What is the supply chain reference model (SCOR), and how is it constructed?

The previous two sections looked at process-based performance measures within an organisation. This section reviews a model that places an organisation in the context of the supply chain. In order to help companies to understand their supply chain performance and opportunities for improvement, a cross-industry framework has been developed by the Supply Chain Council. You can visit the Council web site at *www.supply-chain.org* This section gives an introduction to SCOR based on publicly available material; in order to obtain

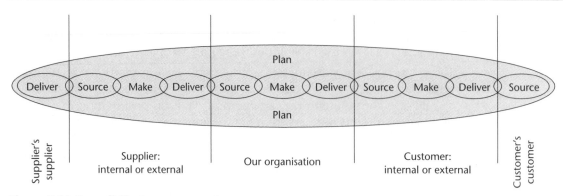

Figure 3.10 Four distinct management processes

(Source: After Supply Chain Council www.supply-chain.org)

detailed benchmarking data from the model, your organisation would need to become a member. In common with ABC, the SCOR model uses a process-based approach to the supply chain.

The supply chain operations reference model (SCOR) is founded on four distinct management processes. The supply chain is viewed in terms of overlapping management processes – source, make and deliver – within an integrated planning framework that encompasses all of the organisations in the chain, as shown in Figure 3.10.

It is a process-based version of Figure 1.1 in Chapter 1. The management processes of 'our organisation' are seen as linked with corresponding processes within supplier and customer organisations. The four distinct management processes can be described as follows:

- *Plan*: the tasks of planning demand and supply set within an overall planning system that covers activities such as long-term capacity and resource planning.

- *Source*: the task of material acquisition, set within an overall sourcing system that includes activities such as vendor certification and vendor contracting.

- *Make*: the task of production execution, set within an overall production system that includes activities such as shop scheduling.

- *Deliver*: the day-to-day tasks of managing demand, orders, warehouse and transportation, and installation and commissioning. These tasks are set within an overall delivery management system that includes order rules and management of delivery quantities.

There are four levels to the SCOR model:

- *Level 1*: a broad definition of the plan, source, make and deliver management processes, which is used to set competitive objectives.

- *Level 2*: defines core process categories that are possible components of a supply chain.

- *Level 3*: provides the information needed to plan and set goals for each element that comprises the level 2 categories.

- *Level 4*: the implementation plan needed to put improvements into play.

Table 3.4 Supply chain performance is tied to measurements that can be benchmarked

SCOR level 1 Supply chain management	Customer-facing		Internal-facing	
	Supply chain reliability	Flexibility and responsiveness	Cost	Assets
Delivery performance	●			
Order fulfilment performance	●			
Fill rate				
Order fulfilment lead time				
Perfect order fulfilment	●			
Supply-chain response time		●		
Production flexibility		●		
Total logistics management cost			●	
Value-added productivity			●	
Warranty cost or returns processing cost			●	
Cash-to-cash cycle time				●
Inventory days of supply				●
Asset turns				●

Table 3.4 shows the 11 metrics at level 1 in the SCOR model. The intention is that an individual company should not attempt to be 'best in class' in all areas. Rather, a given company should target its strength in four to six selected areas to create differentiation in the marketplace. The company will also need to ensure that it stays competitive in the other areas. Note that the customer-facing measures are what we referred to in section 3.2 as 'discretionary costs', while the internal-facing measures are 'engineered costs'. By drilling down into levels 2 and 3 of the SCOR model, the aim is to identify the cost drivers and so convert discretionary costs into engineered costs: that is, to convert supply chain performance directly into revenue, cost and margin. Also note that the internal-facing metrics encourage improvement of ROI (section 3.1) by reducing costs and maximising asset turns. Participating companies in the Supply Chain Council may obtain benchmarking information on how their organisation's performance compares with others: see the web site given above.

In order to illustrate how such concepts could be applied in practice, Table 3.5 is adapted from the SCOR web site. It shows actual performance against the SCOR level 1 metrics for a given company. It also shows how those metrics compared with the SCOR database in terms of what was needed to achieve parity with the 'competitive population', what was needed to gain advantage, and what was needed to show superior performance. Where is this supply chain positioned in terms of its competitive performance? Not very well, it seems! *All* of the level 1 metrics are below parity with the exception of order fulfilment lead times. External metrics such as delivery performance and perfect order fulfilment are seriously adrift. Production flexibility is way behind the competitive population, suggesting that the master schedule is 'fixed' for too long a period – and there will no doubt be underlying causes of that. Internal measures are not in good shape either, with a poor cost performance and a seriously uncompetitive asset utilisation record.

Table 3.5 **Supply chain performance evaluated within the context of the competitive environment**

		Supply chain scorecard v. 3.0			Performance versus competitive population		
	Overview metrics	SCOR level 1 metrics Delivery performance to commit date	Actual 50%	Parity 85%	Advantage 90%	Superior 95%
External	Supply chain reliability	Fill rates	63%	94%	96%	98%
		Perfect order fulfilment (on time in full)	0%	80%	85%	90%
		Order fulfilment lead times (customer to customer)	7 days	7 days	5 days	3 days
	Flexibility and responsiveness	Production flexibility (days master schedule fixed)	45 days	30 days	25 days	20 days
Internal	Cost	Total logistics management costs	19%	13%	8%	3%
		Warranty cost, returns and allowances	NA	NA	NA	NA
		Value added per employee productivity	$122K	$156K	$306K	$460K
	Assets	Inventory days of supply	119 days	55 days	38 days	22 days
		Cash-to-cash cycle time	196 days	80 days	46 days	28 days
		Net asset turns (working capital)	2.2 turns	8 turns	12 turns	19 turns

Summary

What is 'value' in the context of the supply chain?

- Two commonly used methods of measuring shareholder value are return on investment (ROI) and economic value added (EVA). ROI focuses logistics management onto controlling costs, working capital and fixed assets. EVA balances ROI with the true cost of financing that capital.

- Logistics is concerned with material flow and information flow (Chapter 1). It is therefore a cross-functional concept that addresses management processes of plan, source, make and deliver. These processes are repeated across the supply chain.

- Traditional cost accounting is unhelpful in making logistics-related decisions because it is insensitive to processes and to cost drivers. Traditional cost accounting tends to understate profits on high-volume products and to overstate profits on low-volume/high-variety products.

How can logistics costs be better represented?

- Logistics costs can be better described by using a variety of methods of allocating costs to products. The purpose of such variety is to gain better information about the cost base of logistics operations, and hence to take better decisions. For example, direct product profitability (DPP) attempts to allocate logistics costs more specifically to products by considering how they use fixed resources. Another principle is to convert discretionary costs such as product availability into engineering costs such as profit contribution from increased sales.

- Activity-based costing (ABC) seeks to understand what factors drive costs, and how costs are incurred by logistics processes that span the organisation and the supply chain in general. It is essentially a process-based view of costing, and again seeks to enhance the quality of logistics decision-making.

- Financial measures that are rooted in the past are insufficient for taking rational logistics decisions. A balanced measurement portfolio is called for, one that takes into account the needs of different stakeholders in a business. The performance prism aims to link shareholder satisfaction with shareholder contribution by considering strategies, processes and capabilities. The balanced measurement portfolio is extended into the supply chain by means of the supply chain operations reference model (SCOR).

Discussion questions

1 Explain what is meant by the term *value* in a supply chain. How can value best be measured in a supply chain context?

2 Why are processes important in terms of managing logistics? Suggest how the processes of plan, source, make and deliver might differ in the case of the two factories Simple and Complex described in section 3.4.

3 What are the advantages of cutting the 'total cost cube' in different ways? Summarise the different perspectives on logistics costs provided by fixed/variable, direct/indirect and engineered/discretionary costs, and by activity-based costing.

4 Suggest balanced measurement portfolios for the two factories Simple and Complex described in section 3.4. In particular, suggest key performance measures in the areas of strategy, process and capability.

References

Atrill, P. and McLaney, E. (1999) *Management Accounting for Non-Specialists*, 2nd edn. London: Prentice Hall Europe.

Christopher, M. (1998) *Logistics and Supply Chain Management: Strategies for reducing cost and improving service*, 2nd edn, p. 8. London: Financial Times Pitman.

Cooper, R. and Kaplan, R.S. (1988) Measure costs right: make the right decisions. *Harvard Business Review*, Sept/Oct, 96–105.

Dale, B.G. and Plunkett, J.J. (1995) *Quality Costing*, 2nd edn. London: Chapman & Hall.

Doyle, P. (1994) *Marketing Management and Strategy*. New York: Prentice Hall.

Kaplan, R. and Norton, D. (1996) *The Balanced Scorecard.* Boston: Harvard Business School Press.

Neely, A. and Adams, C.A. (2000) *Perspectives on Performance: The performance prism.* Centre for Business Performance, Cranfield School of Management.

Neely, A., Mills, J., Platts, K., Richards, H., Gregory, M., Bourne, M. and Kennerley, M. (2000) Performance measurement system design: developing and testing a process-based approach. *International Journal of Operations and Production Management,* **20**(10), 1119–45.

van Damme, D.A. and van der Zon, F.L. (1999) Activity based costing and decision support. *International Journal of Logistics Management,* **10**(1), 71–82.

Suggested further reading

Atrill, P. and McLaney, E. (1999) *Management Accounting for Non-Specialists,* 2nd edn. Harlow: Financial Times Prentice Hall.

Neely, A. (1998) *Measuring Business Performance.* London: Economist Books.

Part Two

LEVERAGING LOGISTICS OPERATIONS

Part Two uses the basic understanding of logistics strategy and management developed in Part One to focus in on critical roles for logistics operations. This covers the centre panel of our model of logistics: the flow of materials, lead times and the network in a global context.

Despite its role in corporate success, the logistics task ultimately boils down to moving goods and coordinating the flow of materials and information. The aim is to support products and services in the marketplace better than competitors are able to do. You could say that the logistics task is about making strategic objectives a reality by executing against demand and making value propositions to customers a reality.

Chapters 4 and 5 look at the basic dimensions of logistics operations: their global reach and their contribution to a timely response to demand. Chapters 6 and 7 then take that one level of complexity higher by introducing key managerial concepts that play a role in logistics operations. Just-in-time (or 'lean thinking'), explained in Chapter 6, has been a pillar of management thinking for some time, and has proved to be an important way of coordinating the manufacturing and upstream part of the supply chain in an efficient manner. The agile supply chain (Chapter 7) is a more recent concept that focuses on leveraging responsiveness to customer demand. Here, logistics plays a crucial role in aligning the supply network with customer demand, and in ensuring execution in a flexible and customised manner.

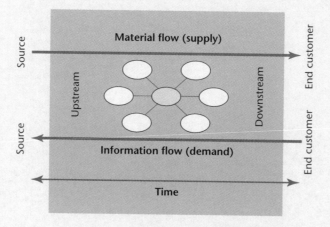

CHAPTER 4

Managing logistics internationally

Objectives

The objectives of this chapter are to:

- identify the challenge that globalisation presents to logistics management;
- consider the structure and management of a global logistics network.

By the end of this chapter you should be able to:

- understand the trend towards international logistics;
- understand the challenge of international logistics networks;
- understand how to begin to organise for international logistics.

Introduction

The early roots of logistics are in international transport, which became a central element in business modelling. In traditional location theory, for example, transport costs were optimised in relation to distance to market and production locations. The origins of globalisation can be traced back to the expanding trade routes of early civilisations. Discoveries made in excavations from Europe, Asia, Africa and the Americas reveal artefacts made hundreds or even thousands of miles away from the site, at the edges of their respective known worlds. Developments in transport, navigation and communication have progressively expanded horizons. Measured in transport time and costs the world has shrunk to the dimensions of a 'global village'. Many take for granted the availability of products from around the world and safe, fast inter-continental travel on container carriers and aircraft. It is in this context that a clear link exists between logistics and economic development. The connectivity of all regions of the world is essential for international trade. As a result, many projects aimed at supporting regional economic development focus on the infrastructure needed to support integration into the global economy. Much of the infrastructure to support international trade and business is founded on logistics operations.

The logistics dimension of globalisation conjures up a vision of parts flowing seamlessly from suppliers to customers located anywhere in the world, and a supply network that truly spans the entire globe. Often basic products such as deep-freeze pizzas combine a multitude of locations from which ingredients are sourced, and an international transport network that links production locations to warehouses and multiple stores. The enormous geographical span of this logistics system cannot be recognised in the price of the product. This can be explained by transport having become just a commodity in the global village. At the micro level of the individual company, however, the reality is that there are few examples of truly global supply chains. There are many barriers to such a vision. For example, local autonomy, local standards and local operating procedures make the integration of information flow and material flow an uphill task. Local languages and brand names increase product complexity. Global supply chains are made more complicated by uncertainty and difficulty of control. Uncertainty arises from longer lead times and lack of knowledge over risks and local market conditions. Coordination becomes more complex because of additional language and currency transactions, more stages in the distribution process, and local government intervention through customs and trade barriers. Additionally, there are many instances in which a truly globalised logistics system is not necessary, and where 'internationalisation' is a more accurate description. Internationalisation certainly is an increasing feature of the majority of supply chains. International sourcing of component parts and international markets for finished goods are extending as world trade increases.

As part of that process location factors used in positioning logistical operations around the globe are changing. Figure 4.1 ranks international location factors from a Cranfield survey among 300 companies in Europe (van Hoek, 2000). Interestingly, important as physical distribution still is, the traditional domain of logistics is no longer the most important factor. In today's digital world, information infrastructure is more important – as is the availability of qualified personnel. Information and communication technology, if used properly, can

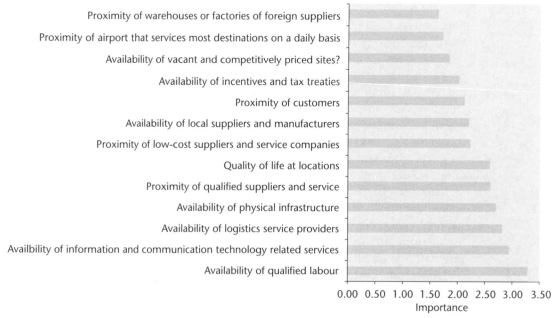

Figure 4.1 Ranking of international location factors

(Source: van Hoek, 2000)

enable global, instant connectivity and coordination of transport flows. The inclusion of qualified personnel reflects the changing roles and responsibilities of logistics personnel. They have become far more focused on brains than on boxes!

Within the context of this changing global landscape for logistics the overall aim of this chapter is to analyse the internationalisation of logistics, and to explore the impact this is having on supply networks.

Key issues   *This chapter addresses five key issues:*

1 **Drivers and logistics implications of internationalisation:** the trade-off facing internationally operating businesses.

2 **The trend towards internationalisation:** three strategies for improving the transition to global supply chains.

3 **The challenge of international logistics and location:** barriers to international logistics.

4 **Organising for international logistics:** proposes principles by which international logistics should be organised.

5 **General tendencies:** current trends in international logistics.

4.1 Drivers and logistics implications of internationalisation

Key issue: **What are the trade-offs between responsiveness to local markets and economies of scale?**

Despite the general trend towards internationalisation, the business approach is not taking place by means of any universal patterns. In assessing the nature of cross-border interfaces in logistics, three questions can be asked:

● Does internationalisation imply a universal global approach of the supply network?

● Does internationalisation require a 'global' presence in every market?

● Does internationalisation distinguish between the companies that globally transfer knowledge and those that do not?

The answers presented in this section suggest that the answer to each of these questions is 'no'.

The 'single business' concept of structuring the supply network in the form of uniform approaches in each country is losing ground. 'McColonisation' has recently been abolished, when McDonald's announced localisation of its business in such areas as marketing and local relations. In response to local crises in quality, and suffering from local competition, the corporate headquarters were downsized to help empower the local organisation. The same applies to the Coca-Cola Company, which has abandoned 'CocaColonisation' – based on a universal product, marketing, and production and distribution model – for the same reasons. In favour of local brands and product varieties, Procter & Gamble is doing the same. In supply chains we find regional variations in the application of international principles.

This does not mean to say that localisation is the new mainstay. Unilever, a traditionally localised competitor of Procter & Gamble, has announced a decrease in the number of brands, and has rationalised operations away from strict localisation over the past decade, and probably will continue to do so for a while. Somewhere between local and global extremes, Procter & Gamble and Unilever will meet each other in a new competitive area.

Looking at the different drivers of internationalisation, three basic global shifts in international investment and trade have been identified, with a possible fourth coming to the forefront in modern markets, as listed in Table 4.1. Such shifts of course have an impact on international trade and the flow of goods. In particular, destinations change as well as logistics requirements. The 'fourth generation' recognises the logistics trade-off between responsiveness to local markets and internationalisation.

At a company level, generic drivers of internationalisation include:

- a search for low factor and supply costs (land, labour, materials);
- the need to follow customers internationally in order to be able to supply locally and fast;
- a search for new geographical market areas;
- a search for new learning opportunities and exposure to knowledge (such as by locating in Silicon Valley – a 'hot spot' in development of international electronics, software and internet industries).

The importance of these drivers varies by company and with time. Considering the sequence of global shifts, proximity to production factors such as labour and low material costs can be considered more basic than market- or even knowledge-

Table 4.1 The fourth-generation global shift in Europe?

Generation	First	Second	Third	Fourth
Period	1950s–60s	From 1960	From 1980	Emerging now
Primary drivers	Labour shortage	Labour costs and flexibility	Market entrance	Responsiveness to customer orders
Shift of labour and investment towards	European countries without labour shortage	NICs, low labour cost countries	Eastern Europe, China, Latin America	Western Europe
Transport routes	Still significantly continental	Increasingly intercontinental	Adding additional destination regions	Beginning to refocus on continental
Nature of international flow of goods	Physical distribution of finished products from new production locations	Shipping parts to production locations and exporting finished products	Physical distribution towards new market regions	Shipping semi-finished products to Europe, where they are finalised in response to customer orders, while within the logistics system

Table 4.2 **Dimensions of different internationalisation strategies**

Dimension	Setting in a pure multi-domestic strategy	Setting in a pure global strategy	Setting in an integrated network strategy
Competitive moves	Stand-alone by country	Integrated across countries	Moves based on local autonomy and contribution of lead subsidiaries, globally coordinated
Product offering	Fully customised in each country	Fully standardised worldwide	Partly customised, partly standardised
Location of value-adding activities	All activities in each country	Concentration: one activity in each (different) country	Dispersal, specialisation, and interdependence
Market participation	No particular pattern; each country on its own	Uniform worldwide	Local responsiveness and worldwide sharing of experience
Marketing approach	Local	Integrated across countries	Variation in coordination levels per function and activity
Logistical network	Mainly national; sourcing, storage and shipping on a national level and duplicated by country	Limited number of production locations that ship to markets around the globe through a highly internationalised network with limited localised warehouses and resources	Balanced local sourcing and shipping (e.g. for customised products and local specialties) and global sourcing and shipping (for example for commodities)

Source: Based on Yip (1989) and Bartlett and Ghoshal (1989)

related drivers. Furthermore, the importance of the respective drivers is dependent upon the internationalisation strategy of the company involved. Table 4.2 provides examples of strategic contexts, and – in the bottom row – the logistics implications of those strategies. The multi-domestic and global strategies represent two extremes, while the integrated network strategy represents a balance between them. The consequences of this 'balancing act' for logistics are analysed below.

4.1.1 Logistical implications of internationalisation

Internationalising logistics networks holds consequences for inventory, handling and transport policies.

Inventory

Centralising inventories across multiple countries can hold advantages in terms of inventory-holding costs and inventory levels that are especially relevant for high-value products. On the other hand, internationalisation may lead to product proliferation due to the need for localisation of products and the need to respond to specific local product/market opportunities.

Handling

Logistics service practices may differ across countries as well as regulation on storage and transport. Adjusting handling practices accordingly is a prerequisite for internationalisation. Furthermore, the opportunity to implement best practice across various facilities may also be possible. Both of these practices assist the process of internationalisation.

Transport

Owing to internationalisation logistics pipelines are extended and have to cope with differences in infrastructure across countries, while needing to realise delivery within the time to market. This may drive localisation. On the other hand, the opportunity for global consolidation may drive international centralisation. Within this final, central, consideration in the globalise–localise dimension of logistics, global businesses face a challenge that can be summarised in terms of a simple trade-off between the benefits of being able to consolidate operations globally on the one hand, and the need to compete in a timely manner on the other.

4.1.2 Time to market

Time to market has particular significance for the management of the global logistics pipeline. This subject is considered in depth in Chapter 6, although we shall touch on the following issues here:

● product obsolescence;
● inventory-holding costs.

Product obsolescence

The extended lead time inherent in international logistics pipelines means that products run the risk of becoming obsolete during their time in transit. This is especially true for products in industries with rapid technological development, such as personal computing and consumer electronics, and for fashion goods such as clothing and footwear.

Inventory-holding costs

Lead time spent in the supply pipeline increases the holding cost of inventory. In addition to the time spent in physical transit, goods travelling internationally will incur other delays. These occur at consolidation points in the process, such as in warehouses where goods are stored until they can be consolidated into a full load, such as a container. Delay frequently occurs at the point of entry into a country while customs and excise procedures are followed.

4.1.3 Global consolidation

Global consolidation occurs as managers seek to make the best use of their assets and to secure the lowest-cost resources. This approach leads to assets such as facilities and capital equipment being used to the fullness of their capacity and economies of scale being maximised. Resources are sourced on a global scale to minimise cost by maximising purchasing leverage and again to pursue economies of scale. The types of resource acquired in this way include all inputs to the end product, such as raw materials and components, and also labour and knowledge.

Familiar features of global consolidation include:

- sourcing of commodity items from low-wage economies;
- concentration at specific sites;
- bulk transportation.

Sourcing of commodity items from low-wage economies

Two sourcing issues are used by internationally operating organisations:

- consolidation of purchasing of all company divisions and companies;
- sourcing in low-wage economies.

Internationally operating organisations seek to consolidate the purchasing made by all their separate divisions and operating companies. This allows them to place large orders for the whole group, which enables them to minimise costs by using their bargaining power and seeking economies of scale. At its extreme, a company may source all of its requirements from its range of a given commodity, such as a raw material or component, from a single source.

Internationally operating companies are on a constant quest to find new, cheaper sources of labour and materials. This trend led to the move of manufacturing from developed industrial regions to lower cost economies. Examples of this are:

- Western Europe to Eastern Europe;
- USA to Mexico;
- Japan to the 'Asian Tigers' of South Korea, Taiwan, Hong Kong and Singapore.

These developing economies have seen impressive growth over recent years. This has led to increased prosperity for their people and rising standards of living. However, these advances in social standards raise the cost of labour and other resources. Therefore, the relentless search for the lowest production cost has led to some companies resourcing commodity items to lower-wage countries in Asia, North Africa and South America.

In some cases this movement of facilities around the globe has come full circle, with Asian companies setting up plants in the UK not only to gain access to the EU market but also to take advantage of low wages.

Concentration at specific sites

Consolidation of purchasing applies not only to commodity goods but also to high-value or scarce resources. Research and development skills are both-high value and scarce. Therefore there is an incentive to locate at certain sites to tap into specific pools of such skills. Examples of this are 'Silicon Valley' in California and 'Silicon Fen' near Cambridge as centres of excellence in IT. Companies originally located in these areas to benefit from research undertaken in the nearby universities.

Companies become more influential in directing such research and benefiting from it if they have a significant presence in these locations. This is helped if global research is consolidated onto a single site. While this may mean missing

Activity 4.1

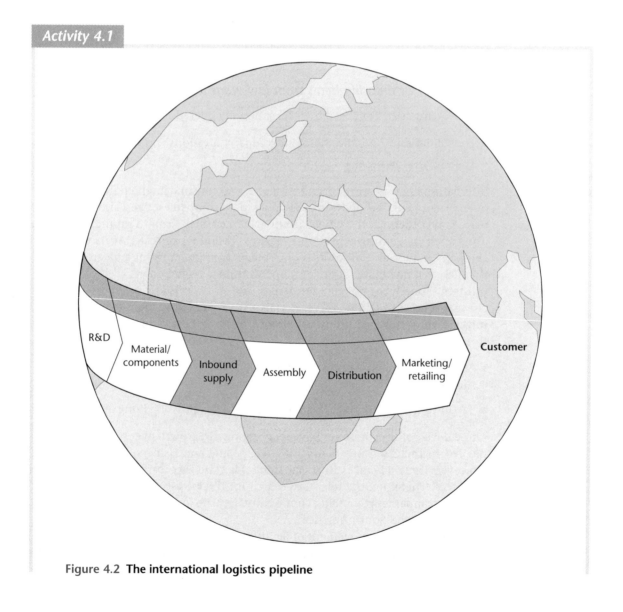

Figure 4.2 **The international logistics pipeline**

The international logistics pipeline is made up of the same basic elements as any other pipeline, as shown in Figure 4.2. However, this pipeline has a number of special characteristics. Use Table 4.3 to make a list of the characteristics that you believe make a global logistics pipeline different from one that operates only nationally.

Table 4.3 Characteristics of the international pipeline

Elements of the pipeline	Special characteristics of the international pipeline
Research and development	
Material/component sourcing	
Inbound supply	
Assembly	
Distribution	
Marketing/retailing	

out on other sources of talent, consolidated R&D gives a company a presence that helps to attract the bright young things who will make their mark in these industries in the future, and it allows synergies to develop between research teams.

Bulk transportation

One of the more obvious advantages of operating a company in a global manner is the cost advantage of consolidated transportation. Taking Procter & Gamble as an example, 350 ship containers, 9000 rail car and 97 000 truck loads are transported every day. The opportunity for cost saving by coordinating these movements and maximising utilisation is significant.

4.2 The trend towards internationalisation

Key issue: **How can we picture the trade-offs between costs, inventories and lead times in international logistics?**

In order to remain competitive in the international business environment, companies seek to lower their costs while enhancing the service they provide to customers. Two commonly used approaches to improve the efficiency and effectiveness of supply chains are focused factories and centralised inventories.

4.2.1 Focused factories: from geographical to product segmentation

Many international companies, particularly in Europe, would have originally organised their production nationally. In this situation, factories in each country would have produced the full product range for supply to that country. Over time, factories in each country might have been consolidated onto a single site, which was able to make all the products for the whole country. This situation, in which there is a focus on a limited segment of the geographical market, is shown in Figure 4.3(a).

The focused factory strategy involves a company's consolidating production of products into specific factories. Each 'focused factory' supplies its products internationally to a wide market and focuses on a limited segment of the product assortment. This situation is shown in Figure 4.3(b).

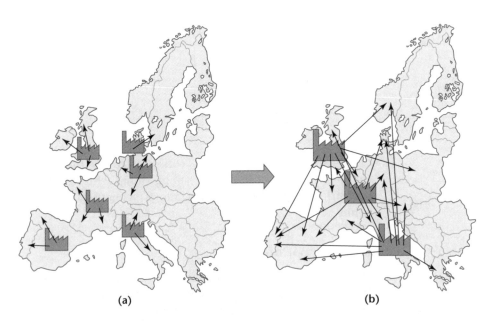

(a)   (b)

Figure 4.3 **(a) Focused markets: full-range manufacture for local markets
(b) Focused factories**

Traditional thinking is that this organisation strategy will deliver cost advantages to a global company. While this is true for production costs, the same is not necessarily true for inventory-holding costs and transport costs.

Activity 4.2

Focused factories have an impact on the important trade-off between cost and delivery lead time. Make a list of the advantages and disadvantages of focused factories. One example of each has been entered in the table below to start you going.

	Cost	Lead time
Advantages	*Lower production costs through economies of scale*	*Specialised equipment may be able to manufacture quicker*
Disadvantages	*Higher transport cost*	*Longer distance from market will increase lead time*

4.2.2 Centralised inventories

In the same way that the consolidation of production can deliver cost benefits, so can the consolidation of inventory. Rather than have a large number of local distribution centres, bringing these together at a small number of locations can save cost. Saving can be achieved in this way by coordinating inventory management across the supply pipeline. This allows duplication to be eliminated and safety stocks to be minimised, thereby lowering logistics costs and overall distribution cycle times. Both may sound contrary to the fact that the transport pipeline will extend, owing to the longer distribution legs to customers from the central warehouse, in comparison with a local warehouse. Nevertheless, through centralising inventory major savings can be achieved by lowering overall speculative inventories, very often coupled with the ability to balance peaks in demand across regional markets from one central inventory. Figure 4.4 characterises the different operating environments where centralised inventory may be a more relevant or a less relevant consideration, based upon logistics characteristics.

In product environments where inventory costs are more important than the distribution costs, centralised inventories are a relevant concern. This is typically the case for products of high value (measured in costs per volume unit). Microchips are an extreme example: these products are of such high cost per volume unit that distributing from the moon could still be profitable! Distribution costs have a marginal impact on logistics costs per product, assuming of course that transport costs are mainly a function of volume and weight. Products that require special transport, such as antiques, art, confidential documents or dangerous chemicals, may represent a different operating environment.

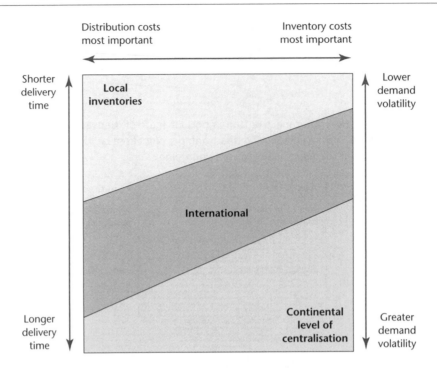

Figure 4.4 Inventory centralisation against logistics costs and service dimensions

A second dimension that needs to be taken into consideration is that of distribution lead times.* Where service windows to customers are very compressed there may not be sufficient time to ship products from a central warehouse and allow for the required transit time within the service window. This is why, for example, hospitals and pharmacies retain in-house stocks of products, almost irrespective of their inventory costs. Critical medicines and surgical appliances need to be available instantly and locally, regardless of inventory costs.

In general transport costs have continued to decline over time as a relative cost item because of innovations in transport technology, the commoditisation of transport (such as container ships), and the oversupply of transport capacity for basic transport. These factors in themselves contribute to the increasing internationalisation of logistics: physical distance becomes less important, even for bulky products. However, the lead time dimension loses some of its relevance, from a transport point of view. Customer demand can be very volatile and unpredictable. *Accuracy* of delivery (the right quantity) can therefore be a more demanding challenge than *speed* (the right time). Speed is available through different transport modes (container ship, air cargo, express, courier, for example) at reasonable prices. In very volatile markets, control over international inventories by means of centralised inventories can be crucial. Overall delivery reli-

*Note that the discussion focuses on physical distribution from warehouse to customer. The inbound pipeline from factory to warehouse is not considered. Centralising inventory may lead to lower factory-to-warehouse distribution costs because shipments can be consolidated into full container loads.

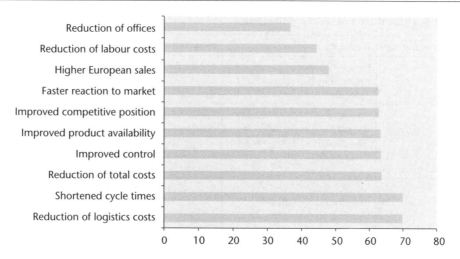

Figure 4.5 Realised benefits of centralised inventories in Europe
(Source: Buck Consultants International, 1997)

ability ('on time in full') tends to increase significantly, much to the benefit of an organisation's performance in terms of service requirements. The ability to balance peaks across market regions from a central inventory is among the additional advantages. Different levels of inventory centralisation can be applied according to different dimensions. Taking the European market as an example, the range is from local inventories (by country or even by location) through international (a selection of countries) to the complete continent. Several companies now include the Middle East and Africa as a trading bloc (Europe, Middle East and Africa – EMEA).

Figure 4.5 lists commonly stated advantages of centralised inventories as reported in a late-1990s study by companies with experienced benefits in this area. So the research population here is companies that fall in the bottom-right quadrant of the previous figure.

Centralised inventory management and focused factories enable different delivery strategies to be combined. Figure 4.6 depicts a simple distribution network that enables three different delivery strategies (listed in Table 4.4) to be applied as appropriate. For example, an opportunity to think globally arises

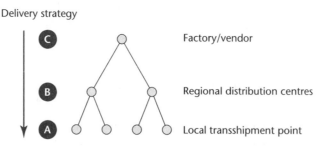

Figure 4.6 Delivery strategies in a global network

Table 4.4 Three different delivery strategies

Delivery strategy	Description	Pros	Cons
A	Direct shipment of fast-moving, predictable lines. Held locally, probably pre-configured	Short lead time to customer	Multiple inventory points leading to duplication of stocks
B	Inventory of medium velocity, less predictable demand lines held at generic level awaiting final configuration	Lower overall levels of inventory, consolidated shipments to distribution centres and concentrated handling	Longer lead time to customers
C	Slowest-moving lines, least predictable. Perhaps one shared global inventory or make to order	Low overall inventory levels	Long lead time to customers

where the key product relies more on the designer label and its promotion and marketing and less on its manufacturing origins. The key to success in clothing is often about fashionable design and labelling. Low labour costs (rather than material costs) of production can then be achieved by outsourcing to low-wage economies, often in the Far East.

CASE STUDY 4.1

Nike's central warehouse operation

Nike consolidated its European warehousing in the early 1990s by reducing the number of its warehouses in Europe from 22 to just one, based at Laakdal in Belgium. Laakdal receives Nike products – such as sports footwear and clothing – from all over the world, and serves retail stores across Europe.

In Europe, Nike initially worked through distributors, selecting local partners in each country. By the 1980s the market had grown to the point where the company decided to gradually buy up its distributors. Nike then converted them into wholly owned subsidiaries. To a large extent, however, each distributor operated autonomously. Each local warehouse had its own logistics infrastructure and its own salesforce. They ordered products individually and controlled their own stock. As a result, a range of service levels evolved, which differed from country to country. There was virtually no coordination of inventory allocation. Thus unused stock stored in one country was often needed in another country, and vice versa. Continued growth in the early 1990s soon created a shortage of warehouse capacity. In response to these bottlenecks, the distribution centres focused most of their efforts on solving distribution problems; but their real priority should have been sales and marketing.

In the light of a strategic evaluation conducted in 1991, Nike decided to centralise its European activities. The first step was to set up a European headquarters in the Netherlands. The second step was to centralise all of its European distribution operations. The main reasons for centralising distribution were as follows:

● There were major problems in getting apparel to the retailer by the due date. Long lead times on advance orders and unreliable suppliers were blamed for this.

- Local management was not adequately informed about the arrival date of shipments. This led to a corresponding failure to keep customers informed of when they might expect to receive their orders.
- It was difficult to keep collections together. When retailers wanted to put together a special collection, it often proved impossible to have that order sent as a single delivery.
- It was difficult to ensure consistent value-added services. It was recognised that labelling, adding price tags, repacking, and other services were potentially an important part of the package. However, not all countries were equipped to provide these services.
- Computer systems had been developed autonomously in each country. Most of these systems had serious deficiencies. As a result, communication within the distribution network was very difficult.

In 1992, Nike decided to build a European Distribution Centre (EDC) in Laakdal, Belgium. The first high bay for apparel was opened in September 1994, and the first high bay for footwear was opened a year later.

The centralised operation works as follows. When the apparel arrives in Laakdal, it goes through seven steps:

1 *Receiving and palletising.* The containers are taken off the river barges and opened, and the boxes, which are taken out of the containers, are given a bar code. With this barcode, the computer assigns a storage location to the boxes. Next, the boxes are placed on a pallet. All the handling cranes are manually controlled. They can handle both boxes and pallets. Each crane has an on-board computer, which informs the driver where to stock the pallets or boxes. This procedure is more efficient and flexible than a fully automatic system.

2 *Quality control.* After receiving the products, they are taken to quality control (QC), a 12 unit with 12 people. Colours and sizes are checked. Also, the employees look for defects, and conduct washing trials. QC is an important activity. Without it, Nike cannot guarantee the quality of its products to its customers. This goes back to Nike's policy of switching among various suppliers to get cost benefits. Because there is no long-term relationship between Nike and the supplier, Nike has to control the quality of products received in Europe. Another reason for QC is that Nike's quality standards may differ from those of its suppliers.

3 *Storage.* As soon as the goods pass QC, the products are stored. The storage bays form an immense warehouse. For example, a high bay for apparel is 28 m high, 125 m long, and 42 m wide.

4 *Picking (apparel) and sorting (shoes).* At the unit for picking and sorting, the products are sorted by order. A computer terminal, using radio frequency, lets the pickers know exactly which product is needed and where it is stored. Most of the footwear is sorted on an automatic conveyor system by a machine that can handle orders for up to 160 customers at a time. The automated process makes this a paperless warehouse. The products are transported to a pick pool when the date of delivery approaches.

5 *Value-added services.* From the picking and sorting unit, most of the products are transported to the processing division. Here, the products are finished in accordance with client-specific orders. For example, this is where labelling and special packing are done. Offering value-added services and high quality was one of the major goals

▶

of the Customer Service Group. These activities are very labour intensive, and liable to human error. For that reason, value-adding activities are performed for only one order and type of product at a time.

6 *Packing (apparel) and checking and sealing (shoes).* After a computer-controlled check, the apparel is packed in boxes. This is done at a packing station. But prior to packing the goods, operators check the apparel, which was delivered at their station by the conveyor belt against the order specifications. For footwear, a scanner checks whether the boxes contain the correct shoes. After a confirmation, the boxes are sealed automatically.

7 *Shipment.* Boxes are consolidated automatically by order and country of destination. Then they are ready to go.

The steps of (1) receiving and palletising, (2) quality control, (5) value-added services, and (6) packing, checking and sealing are done in a low-bay area; for the others high-bay areas are also used.

Questions

1 How does the seven-step logistics process at Laakdal provide competitive advantage for Nike?

2 Can you identify any logistics issues that are not adequately covered in the above description?

4.3 The challenge of international logistics and location

Key issues: **What are the risks in international logistics in terms of time and inventories, and how can they be addressed?**

International logistics is complex, and different from localised logistics pipelines. The main differences that need to be taken into consideration are:

● extended lead time of supply;
● extended and unreliable transit times;
● multiple consolidation and break points;
● multiple freight modes and cost options.

Information technologies can help to circumvent these challenges in general, and the proper location of international operations in particular can help to resolve some of these challenges.

4.3.1 Extended lead time of supply

In an internationally organised business most products produced in a particular factory will be sold in a number of different countries. In order to manage the interface between the production and sales teams in each territory, long lead times may be quoted. This buffers the factory, allowing them to respond to the local variations required in the different markets.

4.3.2 Extended and unreliable transit times

Owing to the length and increased uncertainty of international logistics pipelines, both planned and unplanned inventories may be higher than optimal. A comparison of the length of domestic and international product pipelines and their associated inventories is shown in Figure 4.7. Variation in the time taken to undertake international transport will inevitably lead to increased holding of inventory with the aim of providing safety cover.

4.3.3 Multiple consolidation and break points

Consolidation is one of the key ways in which costs in pipelines can be lowered. Economies of scale are achieved when goods produced in a number of different facilities are batched together for transport to a common market.

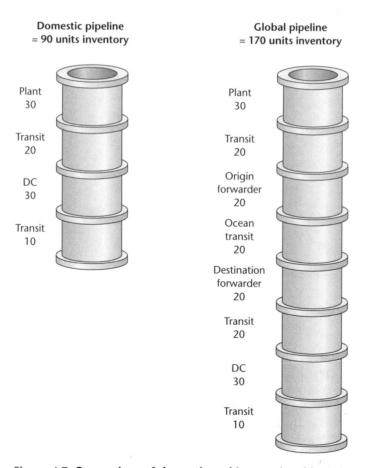

**Domestic pipeline
= 90 units inventory**

Plant
30

Transit
20

DC
30

Transit
10

**Global pipeline
= 170 units inventory**

Plant
30

Transit
20

Origin
forwarder
20

Ocean
transit
20

Destination
forwarder
20

Transit
20

DC
30

Transit
10

Figure 4.7 **Comparison of domestic and international logistics pipelines**

A footwear company has a number of manufacturing facilities around Asia, as shown in Figure 4.8. There are five manufacturing sites in China, three in India, and one each in Thailand, Singapore and Taiwan. Singapore and Hong Kong also have the facility to act as regional consolidation sites.

Draw arrows on the map showing where the flow of exports to the North American market could be consolidated. Write a brief description that explains your reasons for choosing these consolidation points and the flows between them.

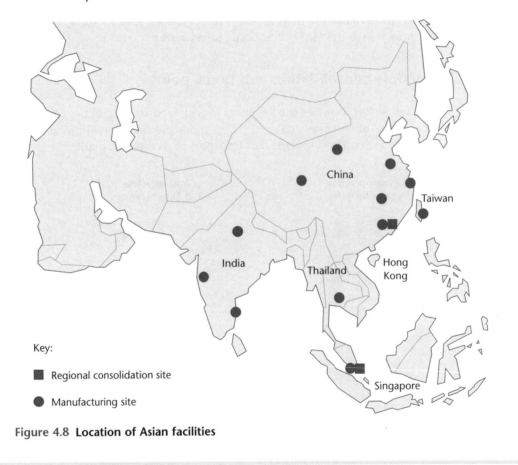

Figure 4.8 Location of Asian facilities

The location of consolidation points depends on many factors that are not really appropriate to consider in a simple assignment such as this. That said, here is one solution. Products manufactured in India should be consolidated at the site on the east coast (near Madras) for shipping to Singapore. Here they are consolidated with the output from the Thai and Singapore factories and shipped to Hong Kong.

To the north of China, products are consolidated at one of the northern ports, possibly Shanghai, and transported by either rail or sea to Hong Kong. All the other manufacturing sites deliver direct to Hong Kong, where products from all the various facilities are consolidated and shipped to Los Angeles.

It is worth noting that, after arrival in LA, this process runs in reverse. The consignment will be broken down at various 'break points' throughout North America and the goods distributed to market via hubs.

4.3.4 Multiple freight modes and cost options

Each leg of a journey between manufacture and the market will have a number of freight mode options. These can be broken down in simplistic terms into air, sea, rail and road. Within each of these categories lies a further range of alternative options. Each of them can be assessed for their advantages and disadvantages in terms of cost, availability and speed. When the journey along the supply chain involves multiple modes, the interface between them provides further complication.

Consider each of the four freight modes in terms of their cost, speed and availability, and write in the respective box in the table 'high', 'medium' or 'low'. Explain your answers in the 'Rationale' box on the right.

Freight mode	Cost	Speed	Availability	Rationale
Air				
Sea				
Rail				
Road				

Note that these comparisons are fairly subjective, and your answers will reflect your experience of the different freight modes in your industry, product type and geographic location.

4.3.5 Location analysis

A structural component of international logistics pipeline design is the location design. As demonstrated, for example, in the Nike case example, selecting an operating format for the pipeline and locations for the operations represents longer-term commitments to underlying operating formats. As Figure 4.9 shows, there is a sequence to the decision-making process involved that incorporates the business (left-hand side) and geographical decision-making (right-hand side). The business decision-making evolves from a strategic commitment through a decision support analysis project to implementation of the resulting plan as a selected location. In parallel the location analysis starts at the level of relevant continent (Europe in the case of Nike), through relevant countries and regions to

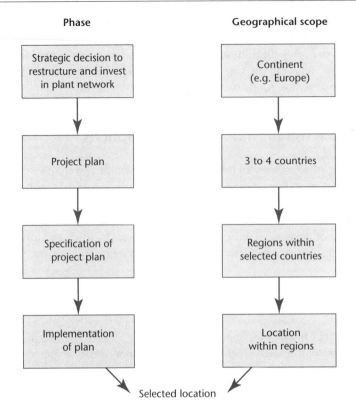

Phase   **Geographical scope**

Strategic decision to
restructure and invest
in plant network

Continent
(e.g. Europe)

Project plan

3 to 4 countries

Specification of
project plan

Regions within
selected countries

Implementation
of plan

Location
within regions

Selected location

Figure 4.9 Phases in the location selection process

consider in the plan, to the selection of a location (Laakdal, Belgium, in the case
of Nike).

In the location decision-making process location factors such as those listed in
Figure 4.1 play a crucial role. The typical four-phase decision-making process can
be structured using the following steps:

1 Deciding upon the appropriate level of centralisation–decentralisation using
   for example Figures 4.4 and 4.9. In the case of Nike it was decided that a
   threshold had been reached that made centralisation of inventories in Europe
   relevant.

2 Selecting relevant location criteria: in Nike's case these included factors such
   as the availability of physical infrastructure including sea, road and rail connections, the availability of warehouse sites, and a central position in the
   European market where relevant.

3 Selecting criteria weightings. In Nike's case infrastructure and proximity to
   market, where key, keeping short delivery timetables in mind.

4 An economic trade-off analysis of structures and relevant locations.

Table 4.5 displays a representative trade-off table for two locations by relevant
weighted criteria.

Table 4.5 **Trade-offs between two locations**

Location criteria	Weight	Score region A	Score region B
Railways	1	4	1
Water connections	1	4	1
Road connections	2	2	4
Site availability	2	2	3
Central location	3	1	2
. . .	. . .		
Total		19	22

Key: Score on a five-point scale ranging from poor to excellent

4.4 Organising for international logistics

Key issue: How can supply chains be better organised to meet the challenges of international logistics?

There are at least three elements in organising for international logistics. These are:

- layering and tiering;
- the evolving role of plants;
- reconfiguration processes.

These will be outlined in the following subsections.

4.4.1 Layering and tiering

Internationalisation is often looked at from the point of view of asset centralisation and localisation; but the wider organisational setting needs to be taken into consideration as well.

A commonly used maxim is *global coordination and local operation*, which relates to laying out the flow of information and coordination differently from the map of the physical operations. For example, Hewlett-Packard operates a globally consistent and coordinated structure of product finalisation and distribution in contrast to its continental operations. The company runs a final manufacturing and central distribution operation in Europe, the United States and Asia for each continent. The operations are structured and run exactly the same, with the only difference being the regions and customers. Furthermore, including tiers of players in the supply chain, these operations are largely outsourced. Facilities are often owned and operated on a dedicated basis by a contract manufacturer and third parties. Hewlett-Packard only brings in some management to assure global coordination. Thus, although HP operates in a globalised way, its products are tuned to local markets by means of local logistics operations. Therefore developments in ICT do not eliminate the need for such local operations.

Another example can be found in the automotive industry. In this industry, major OEMs structure their plant networks globally, while making suppliers build their plants in the immediate vicinity of the OEM plant. The distance or broadcasting horizon between the two plants is defined by the time between the electronic ordering of a specifically finalised single module on the on-line system and the expected time of delivery in sequence along the assembly line. Time horizons for order preparation, finalisation, shipment and delivery tend to be in the area of an hour and a half or less. This causes localisation of the supplier or co-location, while the OEM plant services a continental or even global market.

4.4.2 The evolving role of individual plants

Ferdows (1989) projects the theories by Bartlett and Ghoshal (1989) on the role of individual plants/factories in achieving the targeted international capabilities of global efficiency, local responsiveness and worldwide learning, or a combination of the three. Using the same type of approach, with location considerations on the horizontal axis and performed activities on the vertical axis, van Hoek (1998) adjusted the model for distribution centres. The model indicates the way in which the growth of performed activities changes the demands placed on the capabilities of the plant and changes the location requirements. Location is concerned with the response of governments to globalisation: adjusting local taxes, incentives and infrastructure to favour selection of their territory.

In Figure 4.10 a traditional warehouse is projected to possibly develop into a semi-manufacturing operation with product finalisation among its responsibilities and added value. This also contributes to the creation of a flexible facility for responding to local markets. The model also indicates a possible downgrading of the plant, with its two-way arrows showing development paths. These developments could be driven by poor location conditions, an inability to reach supply chain objectives, or the ability to reach the supply chain objectives more easily at other plants in the company's network. This suggests that the role of individual plants could be seen as an internal competitive issue for plant management. Most relevant, the evolutionary roles and functions of individual plants within the evolving supply chain are specific issues of concern for the realisation of global objectives.

4.4.3 Reconfiguration processes

Related to this last point, the achievement of the required changes in international logistics pipelines is a central issue. In the research presented in Figure 4.8 (van Hoek, 1998), it was found that, across companies, large differences can be found in reconfiguration paths. This was found even in cases where the same supply chain structure (a traditional factory warehouse, as displayed in Figure 4.8) was targeted.

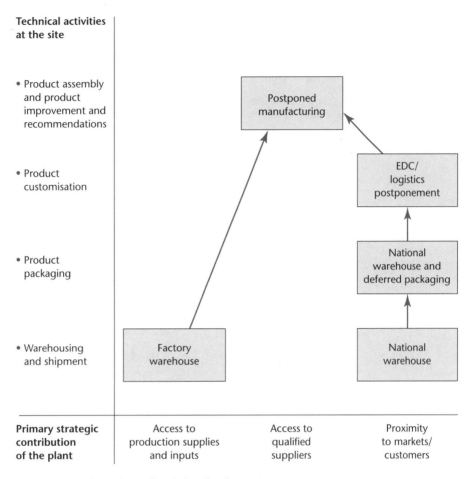

Technical activities at the site

- Product assembly and product improvement and recommendations

- Product customisation

- Product packaging

- Warehousing and shipment

Postponed manufacturing

EDC/ logistics postponement

National warehouse and deferred packaging

Factory warehouse

National warehouse

Primary strategic contribution of the plant

| Access to production supplies and inputs | Access to qualified suppliers | Proximity to markets/ customers |

Figure 4.10 Changing role of distribution centres

Differences included:

- *Supply chain scope/activities involved.* Was only final manufacturing relocated, or did sourcing undergo the same treatment?
- *Focus.* Were activities moved into the market, e.g. localised or centralised within the market? Did the move have a single or multiple focus?
- *Tendency.* Were activities moved out of the (European) market or vice versa, with single or multiple tendencies?
- *Timetable.* Was it a single-step process or did it involve various steps spanning out the process over a longer period of time?
- *Pace.* Was it an overnight change or the result of a gradually changing process?
- *Authority.* Was it directed from a global base (top down) or built up region by region (bottom up)?

The differences can be explained through differences in the supply chain characteristics of companies, among which are:

- *Starting point*: Is the base structure localised or globalised?

- *Tradition*: Does the company have a long preceding history with the baseline in the market, or can it build up from scratch, in supply chain terms (brownfield or greenfield)?

Table 4.6 summarises the differences found in companies implementing post-

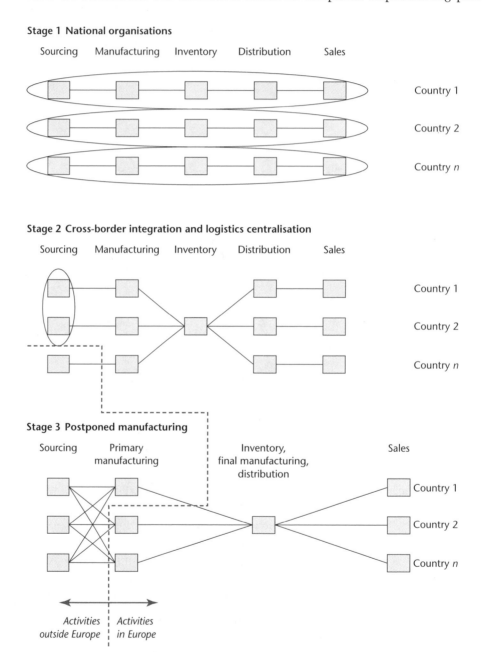

Stage 1 National organisations

Sourcing   Manufacturing   Inventory   Distribution   Sales

Country 1

Country 2

Country *n*

Stage 2 Cross-border integration and logistics centralisation

Sourcing   Manufacturing   Inventory   Distribution   Sales

Country 1

Country 2

Country *n*

Stage 3 Postponed manufacturing

Sourcing   Primary   Inventory,   Sales
            manufacturing   final manufacturing,
            distribution

Country 1

Country 2

Country *n*

Activities   *Activities*
outside Europe   *in Europe*

Figure 4.11 Stages in the implementation of postponed manufacturing: local starting point

poned manufacturing as an example of a reconfiguration process. The same argument could be applied to the difference between a central European warehouse and a country-based, localised distribution network.

Figures 4.11 and 4.12 represent the reconfiguration process from local distribution through logistics centralisation to postponed manufacturing (final manufacturing in the warehouse). The differences in the implementation path

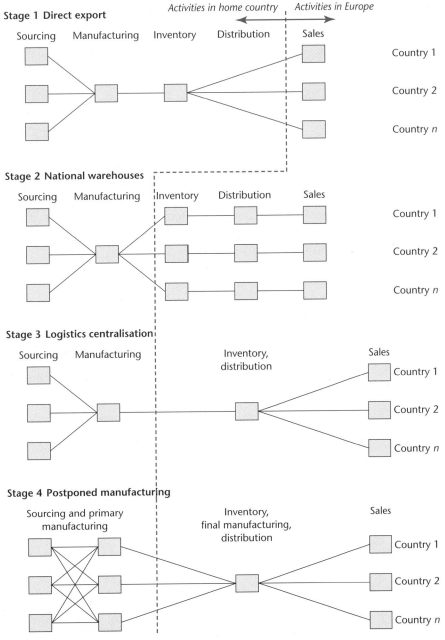

Figure 4.12 **Stages in the implementation of postponed manufacturing: global starting point**

Table 4.6 Differences in reconfiguration processes for companies depending upon starting point (global or local)

Starting point	Global structure	Localised structure
Heritage in market	Little, greenfield approach	Extensive, brownfield approach
Supply chain scope	Narrow, involving inventory and final manufacturing	Broad, involving inventory, manufacturing, and sourcing
Focus	Decentralising final manufacturing and inventory into market	Centralising inventory and final manufacturing at continental level and globalising manufacturing and sourcing
Tendency	Single, placing activities into market	Multiple, relocating within market and moving outside market
Timetable	Short (1–10 months)	Long (number of years)
Authority	Global, top-down directions	Local, bottom-up iterative process

are based upon the different starting points. The path with a localised starting point goes through centralisation within Europe starting from autonomous, duplicated local structures. The path with a global starting point builds a small European presence and then migrates through the increase of European presence centrally (representing a further location into Europe, rather than a further centralisation from within Europe).

4.5 General tendencies

Key issue: **What are the current trends in international logistics?**

Current thinking uses a number of principles to determine where the appropriate balance lies between global and localised supply chains. These are as follows:

- Control over logistical flows must be centralised in order to optimise costs.
- Control and management of customer service must be localised.
- Outsourcing must be coordinated at a global level.
- Logistic information systems must be global in order to link the globally organised logistics systems with the locally organised customer service systems.

4.5.1 Structure and control

Key to the success of a global strategy is the rationalisation of sourcing, production and distribution. This can be achieved only through the centralised planning, application and management of this policy. At this level decisions are made on where to invest in manufacturing facilities, where to source subcontracting and components, and where to establish consolidation facilities. These decisions will need ongoing review in the light of currency movements, and demographic changes in the countries where goods are made and where they are sold. This is necessary when low-wage economies develop to create new markets and sources of advanced capabilities but lose their former advantage as low-cost resources.

4.5.2 Local marketing

Local markets have their local characteristics. In these situations one size does not necessarily fit all. This is true for consumer products, where all manner of factors must be accommodated, from colour preferences to the size of the typical family. The same is also true of industrial markets. Local customs and cultural practices must be observed for a company to be considered as a potential supplier. Similarly, local preferences need to be understood so that a service can be tailored to the customers' requirements.

4.5.3 Outsourcing and partnership

Outsourcing is one of the most significant elements of internationalisation. The major multinational companies are tending to increase their levels of outsourcing. This trend has extended beyond the manufacture of components to encompass all non-core activities, including services. Outsourcing can be undertaken in a range of alternative ways, one of which is through partnership. This topic is discussed in detail in Chapter 9, but it is worth touching upon it here.

Partnerships allow companies to plan beyond the short term, which allows them to understand each other's needs better and to align themselves in a more coordinated manner. This allows waste in the supply chain to be removed, and opportunities to add value to be identified and applied.

By their nature, internationally organised supply networks are complex and have added potential for things to go wrong. Working in partnership with other companies along the network helps in identifying and resolving potential problems before they happen. Should problems occur, then partnerships (Chapter 9) are more likely to overcome those problems, while keeping the relationship intact.

CASE STUDY 4.2

Cranfield AeroSystems Ltd

Cranfield AeroSystems Ltd (CAS) is part of an increasingly competitive aerospace industry whose customers are demanding reduced product cost and increased responsiveness. Internal change and supply chain improvement is now an ethos firmly rooted in CAS in order to improve the 'bottom line'.

This case study presents an investigation into the CAS supply chain in order to determine the effect of its policy of global sourcing. It follows the production of a sidestay bracket. This aluminium assembly connects an aircraft undercarriage to the fuselage. Its approximate dimensions are 1 m × 0.5 m, and the price is €15 000.

▶

The bracket starts life as a forging made by AeroForge Ltd in Orange County, California. It is then transported to CAS in Bedford, England, before travelling to MechAero Français in Northern France, who perform some initial machining. From here the forging returns to AeroForge in California for heat treatment and testing. After completion of this work the bracket goes back to MechAero Français, who finish the machining. The component is chrome plated at TopPlate of Liverpool, after which MechAero Français assembles the bracket and tests it. Production concludes with the brackets returning to TopPlate in Liverpool for painting, after which it is delivered to CAS. The final step in the process is to deliver the bracket to the aircraft production line in the Western USA.

This supply chain has evolved over time in order to make use of the specific capabilities of particular companies. Separate decisions have been made over the sourcing at each step without regard for the overall process. The consequence is a process with a cumulative lead time of 78 weeks, and €678 000 of work in progress. Physically, the part makes eight journeys and travels around 15 000 miles during its manufacture.

Questions

1 Assess how well CAS has done at the globalisation challenge of balancing consolidation and access to expertise against time-based competition.

2 What steps do you think the company should take in order to ensure that it takes a more holistic view of its logistics pipeline in the future?

Summary

Why international logistics?

- A major driver of the internationalisation of business has been labour shortages and costs in established markets, and the availability of low-cost production in newly industrialised regions. A further driver has been the need to follow customers into new local markets, and to create new learning opportunities.

- This has created phases in internationalisation of operations, and hence of the logistics pipelines that are associated with them. Logistics pipelines differ from market to market and from company to company over time.

- Global sourcing can create economies of scale for transportation through multiple consolidation as organisations orchestrate their global networks, and focus key areas such as manufacturing and R&D.

What are the logistics implications of global sourcing?

- The localisation of products and services to meet specific market needs creates implications for inventory, handling and transport.

- Time to market can be extended by the additional distances and complexity of the network. Product obsolescence and inventory holding costs need to be managed in different ways.

● Manufacturing focus needs to be re-thought to cover new markets, along with new delivery strategies.

How do we organise for international logistics?

● New solutions for layering and tiering the supply network are being tried out, such as co-location of suppliers with OEM plants in the auto industry. Meanwhile, the role of individual plants may be modified to allow more flexible response to local markets, for example by carrying out final assembly in local distribution centres.

● The key to success of internationalisation strategies is the rationalisation of sourcing, production and distribution. At the same time, the organisation needs to be sensitive to local markets and preferences. Most internationally operating organisations are extending the degree of outsourcing so that they focus only on 'core' activities.

Discussion questions

1 What are the benefits and limitations of international logistics? Illustrate your response by referring to the sourcing of standard shirts and fashion blouses (shown in Table 1.1 in Chapter 1) from manufacture in the Far East.

2 Tiering of the supply network is referred to in section 4.4.1 above, and also in Chapter 1, section 1.1, and in the Global Lighting case study at the end of Chapter 2. Describe the advantages of tiering in terms of globalisation, touching on areas such as outsourcing and the focused factory.

References

Bartlett, C.A. and Ghoshal, S. (1989) *Managing Across Borders*. Boston: Harvard Business School Press.

Buck Consultants International (1997) *Europese distributie en waardetoevoeging door buitenlandse bedrijven*. Nijmegen: BCI.

Ferdows, K. (1989) Mapping international factory networks. In Ferdows, K. (ed.), *Managing International Manufacturing*, pp. 3–22. Amsterdam: Elsevier Science.

Van Hoek, R.I. (1998) Reconfiguring the supply chain to implement postponed manufacturing. *International Journal of Logistics Management*, 9(1), 95–110.

Van Hoek, R.I. (2000) *Postponement in European Supply Chains*. Cranfield University.

Yip, G.S. (1989) Global strategy . . . in a world of nations? *Sloan Management Review*, Fall, 29–41.

Suggested further reading

Dicken, P. (1992) *Global Shift*. London: PCP Publishing.

CHAPTER 5

Managing the lead-time frontier

Objectives

The objectives of this chapter are to:

- introduce time-based competition definitions and concepts;
- show how lead time needs to be managed to serve customer expectations;
- explain how organisations compete through responsiveness.

By the end of this chapter you should be able to:

- understand how organisations compete through managing lead time;
- understand how time can be used as a performance measure;
- understand P-times and D-times and the consequence when they do not match;
- understand different solutions to reduce P-times;
- understand how to apply a methodology for implementing these solutions.

Introduction

Chapter 6 will show how an important starting point for analysing the supply network is creating visibility of the sources and causes of waste – including wasted time. This chapter takes a more strategic view of time, and the impact of time on logistics performance. It provides an introduction to the nature of time-based competition and how competing on time can be used in logistics. As we saw in Chapter 1, section 1.3, logistics supports competitiveness of the supply chain as a whole by meeting end customer demand through the supply of what's needed, when it's needed, at low cost. Because logistics supports time and place commitments in the supply chain, you could argue that the lead-time frontier accounts for at least half of logistics success. This leads to the notion of lead times for delivery and service *windows*, which are essentially the timeframes within which logistics operations need to be completed. The basic operating formula is thus:

> Cumulative cycle time for supply chain operations to be performed after an order has been placed ≤ Service window to customer.

Competing on time is the principle of taking timely completion of supply chain tasks to a higher level: that of compressing cycle times for supply chain operations for internal and external benefits. External benefits include:

- lowering overall cycle time and providing services faster;
- outrunning the competition.

These benefits are especially important in the context of improving responsiveness to customers and volatile markets. Chapter 7 will return to these points. Internal benefits include:

- shorter cash to cash cycles, thereby freeing up working capital and reducing asset intensity of the supply chain;
- lowering inventories in the pipeline and storage by speeding up turnover times for work in progress and inventory.

These benefits are especially important within lean or waste elimination approaches, as will be developed in Chapter 6. The overall aim of this chapter is to show how time-based strategies link with the way a business competes.

Key issues	*This chapter addresses five key issues as follows:*

1 **Introduction to the role of time in competitive advantage**: using time in logistics management and strategy.

2 **P:D ratios and the lead time gap**: the gap between the time it takes to get the product to the customer (P-time) and the time the customer is prepared to wait (D-time).

3 **Time based mapping**: how to create visibility of time across the network.

4 **Managing timeliness in the logistics pipeline**: strategies and practices for coping when P-time is greater than D-time.

5 **A method for implementing time-based practices**: implementing time-based practices across the network.

5.1 Introduction to the role of time in competitive advantage

Key issues: **What is time-based competition, how does it link to other initiatives, and what is the purpose of it?**

5.1.1 Time-based competition: definition and concepts

Many attempts at business improvement focus on cost reduction and quality improvement. While a great deal of benefit has been achieved by many organisations through these efforts, most of the obvious opportunities for improvement have now been taken. This has led to the emergence of time as a fresh battleground in the search for competitive advantage. A working definition of competing on time is:

the timely response to customer needs.

The emphasis in this definition is on 'timely'. This means responding to a customer's needs on time – neither early nor late. The implication of this definition is that the organisation must focus its capabilities on being responsive to the customer.

Traditional thinking states that you cannot have low cost *and* high quality, or low cost *and* fast delivery, or fast delivery *and* high quality. Some kind of trade-off is at work, meaning that more of one advantage means less of another. For example, better quality means putting in more inspectors, which increases costs. Such thinking was shown to be flawed when the quality movement showed that good quality actually *reduces* costs (Crosby, 1979). The trade-off between cost and quality can be altered by preventing defects from happening in the first place. Spending more on the *prevention* of defects through such measures as

- designing the process so that defects cannot occur (error proofing);
- designing products so that they are easy to make and distribute;
- training personnel so that they understand the process and its limitations.

leads to savings in *detecting* defects (inspection) and in the *failures* that result (scrap costs and the like). Overall quality costs (prevention + detection + failure) can be reduced by spending more on prevention. Changes in trade-offs can be worked to advantage:

- Costs do not have to increase in order to improve quality; they can reduce.
- Costs do not have to increase when lead times are reduced; they can also reduce.
- Costs do not have to go up as product variety increases and times reduce; they can also reduce.

These new understandings have important links with strategy. Organisations that put responsiveness to the customer first need to change the way they go about their business. This involves redesigning systems and processes to allow these goals to be achieved.

5.1.2 Time-based initiatives

When a company attacks time directly, the first benefits to emerge are usually shorter cycle times and faster inventory turns. Lower overhead costs usually follow, as the costs of dealing with breakdowns and delays begin to disappear from the system. So by seeking time reduction, both time reduction *and* cost reduction are often the rewards.

Attacking the sources and causes of delays helps to reduce quality defects in product and service. Thus not only does focusing on time make customers happier by having their needs met more quickly, but a quality benefit also often accompanies the time benefit.

5.1.3 Time-based opportunities to add value

There are several ways in which a company can use time to help meet customer needs better, thus adding more value. The most common examples of this are:

- increased responsiveness to customer needs;
- increased variety;
- increased product innovation;
- improved return on new products;
- the reduction of risk by relying less on forecasts.

We deal with each of these opportunities in turn.

Increased responsiveness to customer needs

This is the most common reason for organisations to invest in time-based approaches to performance enhancement. Many elements of customer service are dependent upon time. These include how long it takes to deliver a product or service, on-time delivery, and how long it takes to deal with customer queries, estimates and complaints.

High levels of responsiveness to customers tend to correlate with greater loyalty from them and therefore more business over time. Such responsiveness is also addictive to the customer, creating customer lock-in. Once they get used to short lead times they often reorganise their own products and services to customers to make use of responsiveness from their suppliers, such as by holding less inventory and promising their own customers shorter lead times. Once they start to do this they find it hard to accept longer times again.

With customers not having to carry as much raw material or component stock, with the cost reduction that entails, customers of time-based organisations are often inclined to pay more for their products. This requires customers to recognise that the total cost of doing business is lower, and the supplier to be able to recover some of this value by charging more.

Increased variety

Shortened lead times in manufacturing, the supply chain and product development help factories to deliver a variety of products without the traditional cost penalty of doing so. By reducing overall lead time, product complexity and process set-up times, the production of a particular product can be scheduled in more frequently with smaller production batches. This improves the variety of products available to a customer over a given time.

Increased product innovation

Time-based organisations are more likely to meet customer needs accurately by minimising product development lead times. Short product development lead times mean that products can be more closely aligned with market needs, and that innovations can be capitalised on to maximum effect. If a company innovates through product design faster than its competitors it will become increasingly competitive. Conversely, if your competitors are innovative then reducing the time to develop imitations will underpin a 'fast follower' strategy to keep up.

Improved return on new products

Reducing product development lead time means that a product can get to market earlier. This has a number of important advantages:

- The sales life of the product is extended.
- A higher price can be charged.
- New customers can be won.
- A high market share can be built through building upon the initial lead.

Each of these benefits can add to the other. Therefore being first to the market allows a higher initial price to be charged, helping to recoup development costs more quickly. This revenue will support investment into the further developments that are necessary to retain these initial customers. Meanwhile, the initial product can continue to be sold, building on its initial high market share. Being first in the market maximises the product life until the time when it becomes obsolete.

An impressive approach to the issue of obsolescence is attributed to Akio Morita, the co-founder of Sony and inventor of the Walkman. He believed that it was his job to make his own products obsolete before competitors did so. In effect, not only did Sony aim to make innovative products, it sought to build on this success in the knowledge that if it did not then someone else soon would.

The related argument here is that of *break-even time*, rather than break-even volumes as discussed in Chapter 3. Traditional break-even analysis focuses on the volume of product needed to be moved before the investment pays off. Given shortening times to market and compressed product life cycles (example: from 6 months to 45 days of shelf life for Nike footwear), the analysis shifts towards the question 'How long before break even is reached?' Figure 5.1 illustrates the point.

As product life cycles shrink, so the time window of opportunity for making profits also shrinks. This consideration means that a new product must achieve its break-even time more quickly.

The reduction of risk by relying less on forecasts

There is a saying in industry that there are only two types of forecast, wrong ones and lucky ones, and there are precious few of the latter! It is certainly true that the further ahead a company tries to forecast, the more likely the forecast is to be at least partially wrong.

One of the aims of a time-based initiative is often to minimise the amount of forecasting that is needed. By reducing the production time, the forecast period can be shorter. This results in a more reliable forecast and therefore in less risk of

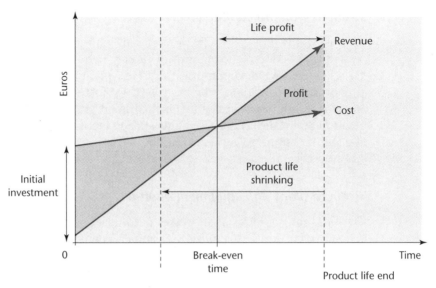

Figure 5.1 Break-even time

stock-outs or obsolete stock. It also reduces the amount of finished goods stock needed, which frees up working capital. In product development risk is also reduced. Shorter development lead times mean that the specification for a product can be fixed with more certainty, thus improving the chances of market success.

The ultimate goal is to reduce production time to within the lead time it has been given by the customer to deliver. In this scenario, no forecasting is needed and all production is done to order. The importance of reducing production time in relation to the demand time of customers means that we have devoted the whole of section 5.2 to it.

5.1.4 Time-based opportunities to reduce cost

A key element of time-based competition is to reduce cost and therefore improve productivity through the elimination of non-value-adding time in processes. This means that wasted lead time and unnecessary tasks that are not actually adding any value in the customer's eyes should be identified and eliminated. Stopping unnecessary tasks and removing wasted time from those that remain reduces cost in the following ways:

- It reduces the need for working capital.
- It reduces the need for plant and equipment capital.
- It reduces development costs.
- It reduces quality costs.

Again, we address each of these in turn.

Reduced working capital

Increasing the flow through processes by eliminating unnecessary steps and wasted time reduced the amount of money tied up in the system. In the short term the focus will be upon inventory. Here manufacturing lead time is inversely proportional to work-in-progress levels. By focusing on time we decrease raw material, work-in-progress and finished good stocks. Lowered inventory levels result in reduced working capital. As already mentioned, returns on working capital will be improved by reducing obsolescence caused by making to stack and not to order.

Reduced plant and equipment capital

Over the longer term, as processes become more visible and inventory levels reduce, opportunities to minimise capital expenses become more visible. These will include the removal of equipment not employed in value-adding activities. Initially this will focus upon the racking and pallets formerly used to store inventory, but it will extend to jigging for unnecessary operations of obsolete parts. This purge of unnecessary equipment needs to extend across offices, stores and production. Some of the equipment may be sold, and capital recovered. Other items can just be skipped. While it may seem stupid to just throw it away given how much some items may have cost, these are sunk costs. If the equipment can no longer be used to generate revenue, then all it does is incur further costs. This may involve maintenance but definitely includes floor space, which can be better used.

As a company embraces time-based competition, success in the marketplace will increase demand for products and services that the customer really values. To make way for these means that space will be at a premium in the company. This is just the driver needed to replace the old with the new.

Reduced development costs

Shortened lead times in product development are achieved in part by more effective use of development resources through the elimination of rework and the reduction of distracting superfluous projects. This leads to cost reductions as the time spent on a given project is less.

Reduced quality costs

One of the key elements in improving quality is to reduce the time between an error being made and its being detected. The sooner the error is detected the smaller the amount of product affected by it. Reducing lead times has a positive effect on the speed of feedback, and hence quality costs are reduced.

In keeping with the total quality movement, time-sensitive organisations will become consistently responsive only if they strive to maintain quality processes. This means that, as defects and errors arise, they are detected quickly, root causes are identified, and effective solutions are installed to ensure that they do not reoccur.

List six applications of responsiveness in an organisation: for example, 'external phone calls answered within five rings'. How many organisations can you think of that compete overtly on time, such as the Vision Express example given in Chapter 1?

5.1.5 Barriers to time-based approaches and their relevance

Despite the clear benefits of time-based approaches to logistics management described above there are obvious barriers to their application, as well as limitations to its relevance.

Two basic limitations to the need for time-based logistics management are the need for speed and the degree of speed needed. Not all operating environments require speed. Product orders that are easily predictable, such as high-volume, low-value commodity products, can be planned well in advance and processed without particular speed. Not all customers value speed, as they may be able to order well in advance of the actual need for delivery. Delivery that is too early also creates waiting inventories. In particular, when there are costs involved in creating speedy delivery, customers may trade that off against ordering in advance. Not all products are shipped with express carriers, for example.

A particular issue with the costs involved in speeding up logistics processes in the supply chain is the distribution of those costs between companies in the supply chain. It is well known that JIT deliveries, for example, may generate significant costs for suppliers, whereas the customer may experience most of its benefits (such as low process inventories, and rapid delivery). Toyota is capable of manufacturing a car in five days, but has decided not to do so because of the pressure it would cause on its suppliers and its distribution processes, creating costs that are not expected to be outweighed by revenue opportunities in current market circumstances. An additional issue is that time-based approaches may lead

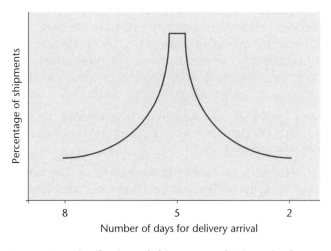

Figure 5.2 **Distribution of shipment cycle times in days**

to high performance on a limited number of occasions. What that points at is the distribution of delivery performance, as displayed in Figure 5.2. This figure plots distribution performance variation. In this example a minor portion of shipments was completed in a day, but the fact that this was in exceptional cases only means that customers cannot *depend* on shipments being consistently completed within a day. Rather customers will order 5 days in advance. Time-based approaches are not about managing exceptions but about managing for speed reliably.

5.2 P:D ratios and the lead-time gap

Key issues: What are P- and D-times, and why are they important to logistics strategy?

P-time and D-time are measures of the performance of the supply pipeline. They are explained in section 5.2.2, but let us look at the importance of time as a performance measure.

5.2.1 Using time as a performance measure

One of the major advantages of a time-based approach to managing processes over one based on cost or quality is the ease with which time is understood as a measure. While cost and quality are open to differences in interpretation, time is a universal measure that is relatively well understood.

Thus cost is a somewhat abstract, arithmetical measure that is frequently misunderstood by those without finance-based training. Many people across an organisation have a poor grasp of how accounts are built up, and do not understand how the actions they take will affect these figures. An all-too-frequent example is saving costs in one part of the supply network only to cause extra costs elsewhere. While quality is an important area for organisations to improve, there are a number of different ways to interpret 'quality'. Garvin (1988) lists eight *dimensions of quality*, which depend on the perspective taken, such as product quality (design), conformance quality (manufacturing), and fitness for use (customer). In order for quality measures to be useful they often require a statistical approach that can easily be misunderstood by those who have not been explicitly trained. Deming's famous Monte Carlo experiments with a funnel and glass marble (Deming, 1986) illustrate the perils of interfering with a stable process:

> If anyone adjusts a stable process to try to compensate for a result that is undesirable, or for a result that is extra good, the output that follows will be worse than if he had left the process alone.

Frequent interference in a stable process increases the variability of its output! Time, on the other hand, is a measure that everyone understands. Every person has access to the exact duration of a second, minute or hour, thanks to clocks using the same units of time. Time allows people across an organisation, with very little training, to measure the performance of a process or activity. Using this measure anyone can answer the key question:

Do we meet the target the customer has set for us?

By comparing this measure with one taken for the performance of competitors, we can easily answer the next key question:

How good are we compared with the competition?

If we take a key reason for measuring performance as being to understand the effect of making changes to a process, we can more easily answer the question:

Is our performance getting better or worse?

By using measures that are simple to understand, people can see the big issues more easily. They can measure and quantify the flow of activities directly, and ask themselves whether each of the steps in a process is adding real value or just adding cost. By following the flow through a process we can see where time is lost (see Chapter 3). This allows us to translate the data into time-reduction and cost-reduction opportunities. Looking at cost analyses alone does not tell anyone where to save time.

5.2.2 Using time to measure supply pipeline performance

In the same way that time can be used to measure the performance of a process within a company so it can be used to measure the supply pipeline. Two measures are presented below that are key to understanding supply pipeline performance: P-time and D-time.

P-time

The first measure of performance for the total supply process is to determine how long it takes for a product or service to pass through it. This measure is used to identify the total logistics lead time, also known as the *P-time* or production time.

Just to be clear, the P-time is a measure of the total time it takes for a product to go through a pipeline. Thus it includes procurement lead time, manufacturing lead time and distribution lead time: it is not just the time it takes to supply from stock.

The measure starts the moment a new order is raised. It includes all the time needed to take a product through all the processes necessary to make and deliver that product. It is important to be clear about when these activities start and end in order for the measure to be consistent should you want to measure performance for a number of processes, including those of competitors. For a first attempt at this measure take the starting time as the point when an order is raised. Consider the total time needed to make and deliver a new product or batch of products. This includes the time needed to procure the longest lead parts and the total manufacturing time. The end of the process is the time when you fulfil an order and send the product to the customer.

When you are competent in measuring this time and creating useful data you should improve the measure you take. Instead of measuring from when you receive the order, measure from when the person in the customer's company realises they have a need. The end point is not when you send the product but when it is received by that person. This measure incorporates the internal process of the customer's company for informing you of the order and the steps they take to receive your delivery and get it to where it is needed. Exploring this process will reveal useful opportunities where you can help the customer to help themselves, thus strengthening your competitive position.

D-time

The time for which a customer is willing to wait to have their demand fulfilled is the *D-time* or demand time. D-time varies considerably. For example, the time a customer is willing to wait for 'fast food' is quite short. Assuming you are in a city with plenty of options, once you realise you are hungry you will probably want to be eating within 10 minutes. This D-time will include the time it takes to walk to the outlet/restaurant, wait in a queue, be served and sit somewhere. By contrast, as a customer of an upmarket restaurant you may have travelled for an hour to reach it, spend 20 minutes in a reception area over an aperitif and study the menu for 15 minutes, before happily waiting half an hour for the meal to be cooked and served.

In addition to the obvious differences in grade and choice of food, the implication from a supply chain point of view is that the two restaurants must be organised in totally different ways to deliver the food within their customers' D-time. Interestingly, the same customer may visit both restaurants on the same day and accept the two different delivery systems. You do not expect to wait at a fast food counter, but you *do* expect to linger over a meal in a high-quality restaurant.

Similar examples can be found in other industries. New car buyers expect to wait a month or two for delivery when they place an order. Some people are not prepared to wait so long, but are prepared to accept a second choice of colour instead of their first, especially if the dealer gives a discount! Manufacturers of vehicles for customers with short D-times face increased supply chain challenges compared with those who have long ones. If it is not possible to make a car to order within the expected D-time, then the manufacturer is forced to carry out some or all of the logistics processes speculatively. The most risky scenario is to make the whole car for stock, hoping that the forecast mix of diesel and petrol, of left- and right-hand drive and so on is correct. But taking such a risk is necessary to cope with the customer who wants to drive away a vehicle the same day he or she enters the dealer's showroom.

It is worth pointing out the parallels in new product development. Some new product development is a race to get new ideas and innovations to market. However, others involve hitting specific customer-defined windows of opportunity for getting products to market. This is particularly true for lower-tier suppliers in supply chains.

Suppose your customer announces their intention for the launch of their new product. They usually give a number of deadlines for suppliers, including:

● date for tenders;
● date for first-off samples;
● date for volume launch.

These are their D-times for each stage of product development; you must be able to meet all of these windows.

5.2.3 Consequences when P-time is greater than D-time

P-time should be measured for each separate product group, because each will have different internal processes. D-time should be measured for each different market segment that is served, because customers may have different needs (e.g. prepared to wait/not prepared to wait).

Armed with this data, P-times and D-times should be contrasted for each product/customer group to see if there is a lead-time gap. A simple way to do this is by drawing them on a graph as time lines, as shown in Figure 5.3. The length of the two shaded bars shown in Figure 5.3 represents *time*. The bar for the P-time represents the time taken for procurement, manufacturing and delivery. The D-time bar represents the time the customer is prepared to wait for an order to be fulfilled.

Comparing the length of the two bars, it can be seen that the time it takes to respond to an order is longer than the customer is prepared to wait. Thus the P-time is longer than the D-time (P-time > D-time), resulting in a lead-time gap. The consequence is that this company is not able to make to order.

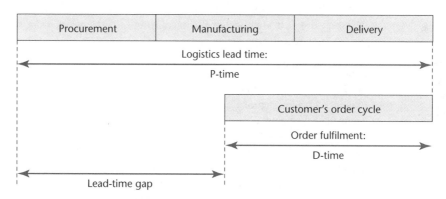

Figure 5.3 **The lead-time gap**

| CASE STUDY 5.1 | **Wiltshire Distribution Transformers** |

Sid Beckett, the Managing Director of Wiltshire Distribution Transformers (WDT), had concentrated on a new generation of simplified, modular designs that used proven US technology. He had energetically exploited the market advantages this had given. WDT now has two major product ranges:

● TR 100: 3-phase, oil-cooled transformers with a power rating from 200 to 2000 kVA;
● PS 300: packaged substations that utilise TR 100 transformers with appropriate switchgear and LV control panels.

▶

Judging by the number of enquiries, the market for both product ranges was now increasing.

The new JIT system

Each product must be individually designed to order. Formerly, this process had taken 2 weeks, because a design engineer had to develop an entirely new design from scratch based on the customer order. Designs have now been modularised as a result of the new system: that is, a new design is produced from a few hundred standard 'modules' that are held on file. This can be done by a sales engineer in a matter of hours. If a tender is accepted by a customer, it had formerly taken another two weeks to convert the tender information into specifications and drawings for manufacture. Today, it is possible simply to send the accepted tender information to the shopfloor, and to use the set of standard engineering information already held on file to act as manufacturing instructions. The following is a list of the main features of the new JIT system.

Enquiry processing

The engineer enters major design details (kVA rating, voltage ratio, product classification and quantity) into a computerised estimating program. From a list of 700 possible options, the selected ones to suit the tender requirements are added. From a library of material, labour and overhead costs, a tender price is calculated.

Should the customer accept this price, then a customer delivery date is agreed and the tender becomes the works order.

Engineering instructions

WDT's efforts had resulted in the completion of a comprehensive library of standard drawings and instructions that covered all major options. The works order simply calls these up by reference number and description. The one exception is the fabricated cubicle that houses the packaged substations. This has to be individually designed. A simple CAD/CAM system enables the design and associated manufacturing instructions to be completed quickly. Presentations of the panels can be separately worked on and designed. The output is a set of CNC tapes for the relevant machines in the fabrication shop, and a set-up schedule indicating sheet size, clamp positions, list of tools, etc.

Master production scheduling (MPS)

Standard networks are kept on file. Activity durations for each manufacturing process vary according to specific designs, and are picked up from the works order. Only bottleneck operations are scheduled, and can be loaded only up to 100% of their capacity. Given the customer requirement date, the scheduling program works backwards and loads activities to key resources so that the final assembly date will be met. The MPS acts by pulling demand through the manufacturing system (a process called *pull scheduling*).

Material requirements for each work centre for each order are calculated by means of a modular bill of material, which has been simplified as a result of the modular designs.

Shop scheduling

The MPS generates *operation release tickets* (ORTs) for each scheduled process. The type and quantity of units required by the next process are withdrawn from the previous one as they are needed. When a work square becomes empty, an ORT is passed back to the preceding work centre to trigger a manufacturing operation. This serves as a signal (*kanban*) to the previous process to produce just enough units to replace those withdrawn.

Work is performed in sequence of ORTs, and is carried out only when an output square is available. Completed operations are marked up on the hard copy of the MPS, which is pinned to the wall of the works manager's office by the supervisors at the end of each shift. The MPS is updated for completed operations and new orders each week.

A combination of four weeks' reduction in the time taken to tender and the time taken to produce a manufacturing design, and a further two weeks' reduction in manufacturing times, has placed WDT in a pre-eminent position in the marketplace. Customers want to place orders for this type of equipment later and later in their own projects, so short lead times are a major benefit to WDT in the marketplace.

Questions

1 Sketch out the main processes between a customer's placing an enquiry and receiving delivery of a WDT transformer. Where has WDT really scored in terms of reducing this time?

2 What are the potential negatives of WDT's new JIT system in terms of limiting customer choice and short-circuiting the design process?

5.3 Time-based mapping

Key issue: **How do you go about measuring time in a supply network?**

The purpose of supply chain mapping is to generate visibility of the processes within the supply chain. Once this visibility has been achieved it is possible to benchmark similar processes. The processes we need to map are the actual processes that are taking place, not what is supposed to happen. Quality standards based on ISO 9000 require processes to be documented, but within the organisation the actual process undertaken may often differ considerably. When undertaking a supply chain mapping exercise it is the *actual* process that we need to focus on. The key is to track one order, one product, or one person through the process with respect to time. A map is a snapshot taken during a given time period. Workloads may vary during the course of a month, and so may the individual process times. Record the actual times that you observe. Most processes take place in batches, so if you're mapping a trailer being filled with tyres, record the time that the median (middle) tyre waits before being moved. Use the following symbols to map the process:

Table 5.1 **Example of a process map**

Step	Description	Symbol	Time	Notes
1	Machine complete	O	1:37	
2	Inspect	□	0:45	
3	Wait transport	D	5:53	
4	Transport to heat treat	→	0:08	
5	Wait heat treat	D	3:34	
6	Heat treat	O	4:15	

Key:

→ = transport

▽ = store

O = operation

□ = inspect

D = delay

An example of a process map is shown in Table 5.1. The key operations are still visible, but the subprocesses that often consume the most time and generate the greatest inefficiencies are also revealed. This enables solutions to problems to be generated and the supply chain to be improved.

The following sections give an overview of the key stages involved in the time-based mapping process.

5.3.1 Stage 1: Create a task force

Before the mapping process can be undertaken it needs to be recognised that supply chain processes cross all functions of the organisation. It is therefore important to have all key functions represented. The task force must be assured of top management support. A project champion may also need to be appointed.

5.3.2 Stage 2: Select the process to map

It may not be feasible to map the total supply chain initially. Take an overview of the core processes within the organisation and the time they take before deciding on the priorities for detailed mapping. To get the organisation to 'buy in' to the project a subprocess may be identified in the first place. This can act as a pilot for the task force, enabling them to prove that their methods are effective within the organisation. When selecting the process, ensure that there is a generic customer or group of customers that the process serves. A clear start (or trigger) and finish to the process should also be present.

5.3.3 Stage 3: Collect data

To collect the data the most effective way is to follow an item through the process. This is often referred to as *walking the process*. An actual component or order will be followed through all the stages of the process. Identify someone who is actively involved in each part of the process and knows what is really happening within the process; interview these key individuals. Get the interviewee to describe each movement of the item with respect to time. It can be useful to ask the interviewee to describe 'a day in the life of' that product or order. Remember that the steps an item goes through is not just those where something is done: for example, items could be waiting or being moved, or may be sitting waiting for a decision to be made. Identify an appropriate level of detail at which to map the process. Initially it might be better to map at a high level to gain an overview of the process; one can always map in more detail if needed later.

5.3.4 Stage 4: Distinguish between value-adding and non-value-adding time

A rough definition of value-adding time is time when something takes place on the item that the end customer is willing to pay for. The definition of value-adding time requires much debate within the organisation, and should be aligned with the overall business strategy. The business strategy should define the markets that the organisation operates in and thus the order qualifiers and order winners for those markets (see Chapter 1). Once an understanding of the value-adding criteria at the strategic level has been defined these can be translated into value-adding criteria at an operational level. The time data collected in stage 3 can then analysed to identify the value-adding time.

Value-adding time is characterised using three criteria:

- whether the process (or elements of the process) is physically changing the nature of the consumable item (i.e. the customer's product);
- whether the change to the consumable item produces something that the customer values or cares about and may be willing to pay for;
- whether the process is right first time, and will not have to be repeated in order to produce the desired result that is valued by the customer.

Non-value-adding activity can be split into four categories: delay, transport, storage and inspection.

5.3.5 Stage 5: Construct the time-based process map

The purpose of the time-based process map is to represent the data collected clearly and concisely so that the critical aspects of the supply network can be communicated in an easily accessible way. The ultimate goal is to represent the process on a single piece of paper so that the task force and others involved in

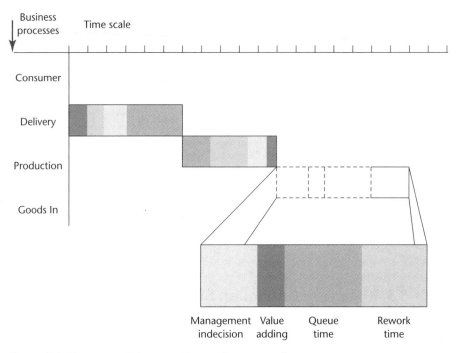

Figure 5.4 **Process activity mapping and sources of waste**

the project can easily see the issues. A simple Gantt chart technique can be used to gain visibility of the process, and different categories of non-value-adding time can be represented on this. These categories will be dependent on the nature of each process. Figure 5.4 shows three operations processes (delivery, production and goods in), with the last one magnified to show four types of waste.

From the interviews and data from walking the process, extract the relevant data. It is sometimes useful to sketch a flow diagram so that linkages and dependences between steps can be clarified before constructing the map. This flow diagram can be used to approximate the total time that the business process consumes.

5.3.6 Stage 6: Solution generation

Once the time-based process map has been produced, the opportunities for improvement are generally all too obvious. The task force can collect ideas and categorise causes of non-value-adding activity using problem-solving approaches such as cause-and-effect diagrams. (A helpful condensed guide to problem-solving tools and techniques will be found in Bicheno (2000).)

The next case study describes how the above principles were applied to an organisation that produces electroplated parts for the automotive industry.

CASE STUDY
5.2

Electro-Coatings Ltd

Electro-Coatings Ltd electroplates parts for the automotive industry: for example, the marquee badges fitted to the front of prestige cars. Customers were becoming increasingly demanding, resulting in Electro-Coatings' undertaking a review of their internal supply chain. The initial analysis by walking the process identified 12 key processes, shown in Figure 5.5.

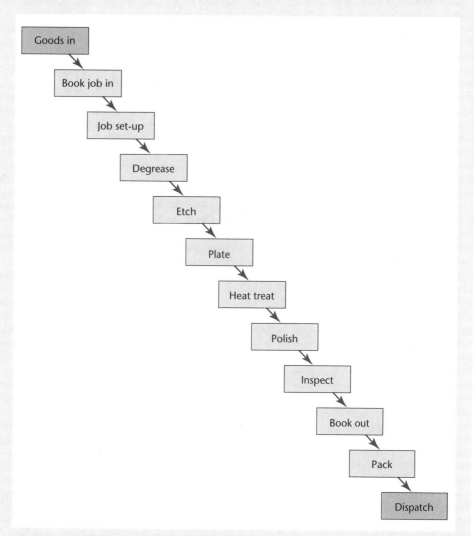

Figure 5.5 Walk the process (12 steps)

Once this initial map has been produced, each step was mapped in detail, and some 60 steps were identified. These steps have been summarised as a flow diagram in Figure 5.6, showing *every* process step.

An initial analysis of value-adding and non-value-adding time was undertaken. This is

▶

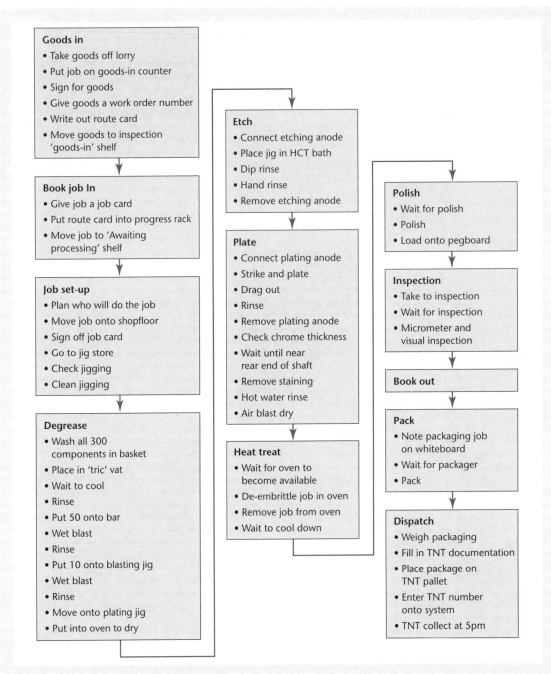

Figure 5.6 Identify every process step

shown in Table 5.2, which summarises the total time, wasted time and value-adding time for each of the 12 steps. These data were then used to produce a map with the value-adding (activity) time and non-value-adding (wasted) time shown as the series of 12 steps against total elapsed time in hours (Figure 5.7).

Table 5.2 Time-based analysis data

	Total time (hours)	Wasted time (hours)	Activity time (hours)
Goods in	0.00	3.91	0.41
Book job in	4.32	20.00	0.41
Job set-up	24.73	5.50	1.77
Degrease	32.00	1.00	0.60
Etch and plate	33.60	8.75	2.20
Heat treat	44.55	0.00	4.50
Polish	49.05	1.95	1.95
Inspect	52.95	9.50	1.00
Book out	63.45	0.00	0.40
Pack	63.85	4.00	0.85
Dispatch	68.70	0.00	0.40

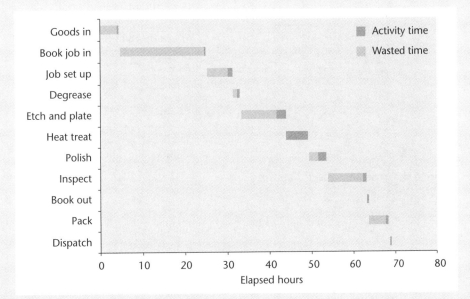

Figure 5.7 Time-based process map: current

The total process took approximately 70 hours. The project team held an afternoon meeting with those involved in the process, and the results of this brainstorming session produced the cause-and-effect diagram shown in Figure 5.8. This was then used to identify opportunities for improving the process. For example, the analysis revealed that jobs arriving goods inwards at 9.00 am might not be input into the system until 5.00 pm because the operator would undertake the computer inputting in one go at the end of the day. This resulted in manufacturing not having visibility of the updated order book until 9.00 am the following morning. This was easily addressed by combining the booking-in process with the good inwards process, removing a further lead time. Figure 5.9 depicts the re-engineered process.

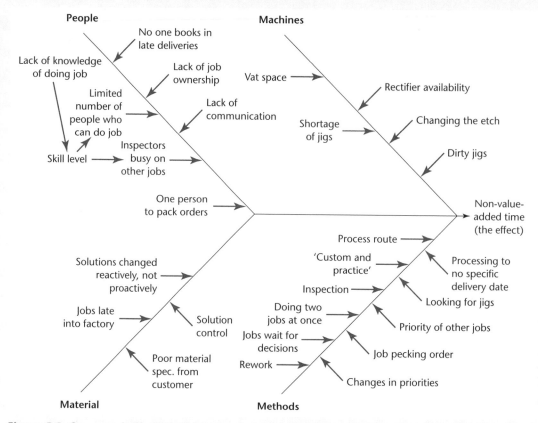

Figure 5.8 Cause and effect diagram

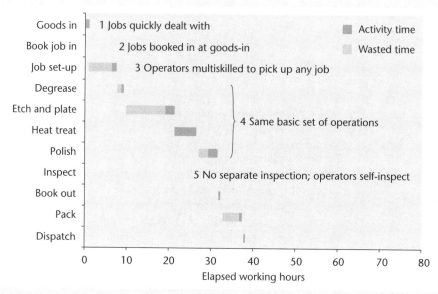

Figure 5.9 Time-based process map: re-engineered

The simple actions undertaken by the company resulted in the total process taking 37 hours. This resulted in a more responsive service being offered to its customers, and increased business.

(Source: Based on a study by Dr Paul Chapman and Dr Richard Wilding, Cranfield Centre for Logistics and Transportation.)

5.4 Managing timeliness in the logistics pipeline

Key issue: When P-time is greater than D-time, what time-based strategies and practices can help to improve competitiveness?

5.4.1 Strategies to cope when P-time is greater than D-time

When faced with a D-time shorter than the P-time a company has a number of options. In the short term it can attempt to make to order or forecast demand and supply from stock.

Making to order in these circumstances is likely to dissatisfy customers. If competitors exist that can deliver within the customer's D-time, or there are substitute products available that will, then the customer is likely to select them. If there are no alternatives then it may be possible to continue supplying to order for the short term. In the longer term it is likely that the customer will seek to develop alternative suppliers, or re-engineer its products to remove the need for yours.

The more common solution is to forecast customer demand, make products to stock, and supply from there. This stock may be held as finished goods if the D-time is very short, or it could be work-in-progress held in the manufacturing process that can be finished in time. This option incurs a number of penalties. The stocks of goods will need to be financed, as will the space needed to store them. There is also the risk that the customer may not order those goods already made within their shelf life, causing them to become obsolete.

Both make to order and make to stock have associated costs and risks, so a company should look at ways to reduce these costs and risks in the longer term. Reducing risks can be grouped into three interlinked areas:

● marketing;
● product development;
● process improvement.

Detail on each is provided below.

Marketing

There are various ways in which you could reduce risk, with customer help. For example, ask the customer to cooperate by supplying more detailed demand information at an earlier stage. Speed up the access to demand data, perhaps by locating one of your people in the customer's scheduling process. Perhaps the customer is prepared to wait longer than stated, if you can guarantee delivery on time.

Product development

There are only so many improvements to the reduction of production time that can be made when a process is based around existing products. With time-based thinking in mind, next-generation products can be designed for 'time to market'. Such thinking aims for products that can be made and distributed quickly, and which offer product variety without unnecessary complexity.

Process improvement

Time-based organisations come into their own by changing the way they go about their business. They engineer their processes to eliminate unnecessary steps, and take wasted time out of those that remain. Engineering your key processes means focusing on those things the customer cares about and getting rid of all the rest. Having done this once, the best organisations go on to do it again and again as they learn more about their customers and grow in confidence in what they can change.

5.4.2 Practices to cope when P-time is greater than D-time

There are a number of ways to reduce P-time. These can be summarised as follows:

- *Control* by optimising throughput and improving process capability.
- *Simplify* by untangling process flows and reducing product complexity.
- *Compress* by straightening process flows and reducing batch sizes.
- *Integrate* by improving communications and implementing teams.
- *Coordinate* by adding customer-specific parts as late as possible.
- *Automate* with robots and IT systems.

Control

In any process, lead time depends on the balance between load and capacity. If demand rises above available capacity, lead times will increase unless resource is also increased, for example through overtime or subcontracting work. Therefore in order to maintain or reduce lead time it is necessary to balance this equation effectively by optimising throughput. Similarly, if a process is out of control, and we are never sure whether conforming product will be produced, the focus will be on improving the capability of that process.

Simplify

Simplification is concerned with cutting out sources of process complexity and of product complexity. Process complexity is often caused by many different products *sharing the same process*. This process becomes a bottleneck, and process flows become tangled because they all have to go through this single, central process. In manufacturing, the solutions are based on cellular manufacturing: in distribution, the solutions are based on different distribution channels. Product complexity is often related to the *number of parts*. The more parts there are in a product the more difficult it is to plan, to make and to sell. One way to reduce product complexity is to reduce the number of parts, by integrating several components into one. The other is to reduce the number of parts by standardising them between products.

Compress

Compressing P-time is concerned with squeezing out waste in each process step. There are two main ways to achieve this. First, straighten the process flow by making a linear flow for each product. Second, reduce the batch size so that flow is improved and queuing time is minimised.

Integrate

Integrating different value-adding activities so that they work more closely together helps to reduce P-time. Integration is in turn helped by improving the speed and accuracy of information to the process owner. Important issues are demand information (what to do next?), product information (what is it?) and process information (how is it done?). Ways of speeding up information range from simple, paperless systems such as *kanban*, through simple IT systems such as e-mail, to more complex systems such as making EPOS data available in real time through the Internet. Integration is also helped by forging relationships between departments or organisations that need to communicate. Teams and partnerships help to integrate activities that are otherwise disconnected.

Coordinate

Other approaches to reducing P-time aim to reorganise value-adding activities so that they are done in parallel and/or in the best order. Thus running activities at the same time (in parallel) instead of one after another (in series) will reduce lead times. Sometimes it is possible to reduce lead times by doing the same activities in a different order. This may make it possible to combine activities or allow them to be done in parallel. It may also make better use of resource by fitting an extra job into a shift, or by running long tasks that need no supervision overnight.

Automate

This approach should be used last, once all the others have delivered their improvements (Don't automate waste!). Chiefly it is concerned with reducing lead time through the use of robots and IT systems to speed up processes. Such approaches are best focused on bottleneck steps in the overall process. The aim is to improve process capability and reliability as well as speed.

5.5 A method for implementing time-based practices

Key issue: How can time-based practices be implemented?

Becoming a time-based company means that a systematic approach is essential to improve all three measures of cost, quality and time. This approach means identifying and removing the sources and causes of waste in the supply network, rather than merely treating the symptoms. The method shown here will give you a starting point for implementing a time-based strategy.

First, you need to understand the ways in which customers value responsiveness. Then the method (shown in Figure 5.10) takes you through a series of steps that help you to change your processes to be able to deliver what the customer wants.

5.5.1 Step 1: Understand your need to change

The first step in implementing a time-based strategy is to understand whether you *need* to change. This need to change depends on how important responsiveness is to your customers. Here are five key questions that will help to identify the strategic importance of time:

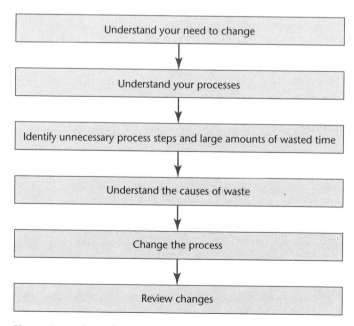

Figure 5.10 **A methodology for time-based process improvement**

- Is supply responsiveness important to your customers?
- How important is it to them?
- What is the supply D-time target that customers have officially or unofficially set?
- What happens if you did not meet this target?
- What is the total P-time, i.e. the lead time time taken from an order's arriving in the company until it is fulfilled and finally leaves the company?

5.5.2 Step 2: Understand your processes

While you may think you already know your current processes, the only way to make sure is to walk the process in the way described in section 5.4 above. Mapping a process involves creating a very simple flow chart. This is best done with a pad of paper, a pencil – and a smile. Start at the point where a customer order comes into the company. This could be with a salesman in the field, over a phone, through the fax or via a computer. Write down the name of this step and draw a box around it. Ask whoever picks this order up what happens next. Very probably it gets reviewed, logged in or put on someone's desk. Any of these options is a step. Write this down on your pad of paper below the first step. Draw a box around it too, then join the boxes with an arrow. Keep going, throughout the company, following that order until a product is finally delivered to the customer. Write down every step you encounter.

During your expedition following the process through the company ask the people who undertake each step how long it takes to work on a single, typical order. You need to find out the *activity time* – the time they spend physically working on it, not the time it spends on their desk or next to their machine.

When you have mapped the whole process, compare the total lead time (the P-time) with the time in which your customers are demanding you respond to them (their D-time). How well do you do? If the P time is greater than the D-time you have a challenge.

Now add up the activity times for all of the steps in the process. How does this compare with the overall lead time (the P-time)? It is likely to be considerably smaller. How does it compare with the D-time? Possibly it is also smaller. If so, you have a real opportunity to improve your responsiveness and get your lead time within that demanded by the customer through applying the ideas listed above, and without the need for extensive investment in technological solutions.

5.5.3 Step 3: Identify unnecessary process steps and large amounts of wasted time

Using your process flow chart you should work with the other members of the company involved in the process to identify those steps that do not add value to the customers. Also, identify where large amounts of wasted time are added to the overall lead time.

5.5.4 Step 4: Understand the causes of waste

Once again, work with your colleagues and identify the causes of the unnecessary process steps and wasted time. Why do they exist?

5.5.5 Step 5: Change the process

Having understood the process, and the causes of waste in it, choose from the generic solutions described above approaches that will make the process more responsive. Apply these solutions with vigour, going for easy ones that deliver early results first to give everyone confidence that you are doing the right thing.

5.5.6 Step 6: Review changes

Having made changes to the way you go about your operations measure the performance of the process again and find out whether there have been any changes to your performance. Have you become more responsive? If not, why not? Find out and try again. If you have, tell as many people as you can, and have another go to build on your success.

5.5.7 Results

The likely result of the above change programme is a situation such as that graphically displayed in the basic four-step supply chain shown in Figure 5.11 Through the implementation of time-based practices or initiatives, cycle times are compressed throughout the supply chain. As a result, delivery can take place in a timely manner more reliably and faster, while more operations can be performed to order within the service window. As a result, lower asset intensity is coupled with enhanced delivery service as possible input to both lean thinking and agility efforts (see Chapters 6 and 7 respectively).

Note that this approach assumes a supply chain point of view, not just a focus on manufacturing or any other segment of the supply chain. A well-known illustration of the importance of this point is that lean approaches have resulted in automotive manufacturing cycle times being compressed to a matter of hours. After manufacture, however, cars are stored in the distribution pipeline or in dealer outlets for weeks, if not months. Lack of supply network thinking results in all of the cycle time investments in manufacturing being wasted.

This does not mean to say that all operations in the supply chain need to be subject to time compression. In the example shown in Figure 5.11, the new delivery cycle times (shown with a dotted line) actually increase in the new structure. But this sub-optimisation is allowable, as traditional distribution from local warehouses here is replaced with direct delivery from the factory, where products are made to order. The transition to make to order replaces the need for inventory-holding points, where goods typically are stored for extensive periods of time. Of

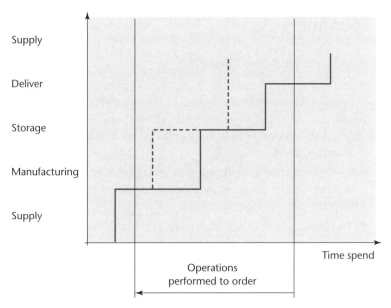

Figure 5.11 Results of time-based change initiatives

course this basic example also indicates how time-based initiatives can require structural supply chain redesign, such as the reconfiguration of distribution channels and the adjustment of manufacturing systems and policies.

5.6 When, where and how?

There are several tactical considerations to be made when planning a time-based strategy. We have grouped these in the form of three questions to be asked:

When?

Time-based competition is only as relevant as the customer perceives it to be. Speed for the sake of speed can create unnecessary costs, and can cut corners, leading to poor quality.

Where?

D-times are a measure of the importance of speed as a competitive factor, while P-times measure the ability to deliver. The integration of the two measures the point at which the customer order penetrates the supply chain. In Chapter 7 we develop this issue in terms of the customer order decoupling point.

How?

The more predictable and lower-priority products and components can be delivered from inventory with less priority given to speed. Shipments of customised products can be assembled from stocks of standard components and modules within the D-time demanded.

Summary

What is the lead-time frontier?

- Competing on time demands a fast response to customer needs. Time-based approaches to strategy focus on the competitive advantage of speed, which helps a network to cope with variety and product innovation, while also improving returns on new products. Speed also means less reliance on long-term forecasts.

- Speed of response also helps to lower costs by reducing the need for working capital, and plant and equipment. It also helps to reduce development costs and the cost of quality.

- The lead-time frontier is concerned with reducing P-time (time needed to produce a product or service) to less than D-time (time for which the customer is prepared to wait).

- Differences between P-times and D-times times are referred to as the lead-time gap. The gap has strategic implications for marketing, product development and process development. P-time can be reduced by a six-stage process: control, simplify, compress, integrate, coordinate, automate.

How do we measure and implement time-based strategies?

- Time-based mapping aims to generate visibility of time in the supply network. A six-step approach to mapping involves creating a task force, selecting the process, collecting data, distinguishing between value-adding and non-value-adding activities, constructing the time-based process map, and generating a solution.

- Implementing time-based practices can be accomplished using another six-step process involving understanding the need to change, understanding the processes, identifying non-value-adding processes, understanding the causes of waste, and reviewing what has been done.

Discussion questions

1 Why is time important to competitive advantage? Identify and explain six key contributions that speed can make to logistics strategy.

2 Explain the significance of P:D ratios. How can the production lead time be reduced?

3 Sections 5.3, 5.4 and 5.5 all contain step-by-step models for reducing waste and implementing improved logistics processes. Why are such models useful in implementing logistics strategy?

References

Bicheno, J. (2000) *Lean Toolbox*, 2nd edn. Buckingham: PICSIE Books.

Crosby, P.B. (1979) *Quality is Free: The art of making quality certain*. New York: McGraw-Hill.

Deming, W.E. (1986) *Out of the Crisis*, p. 327. Cambridge, MA: MIT.

Garvin, D.A. (1988) The multiple dimensions of quality. In *Managing Quality*, Ch. 4. New York: Free Press.

Suggested further reading

Galloway, D. (1994) *Mapping Work Processes*. Milkwaukee: ASQC Quality Press.

Rother, M. and Shook, J. (1998) *Learning to See*. Brookline: The Lean Enterprise Institute.

Stalk, G. and Hout, T.M. (1990) *Competing Against Time*. New York: Free Press.

CHAPTER 6

Just-in-time and lean thinking

Objectives

The objectives of this chapter are to:

- explain the philosophy of just-in-time and how that philosophy relates to managing the supply chain;
- identify two methods of applying just-in-time philosophy to the supply chain (vendor-managed inventory and quick response);
- explain how lean thinking can be used to avoid the build-up of waste in supply chain processes.

By the end of this chapter you should be able to:

- distinguish between 'push' and 'pull' scheduling;
- understand how companies can compete by using vendor-managed inventory and quick response methods of controlling material flow;
- understand how lean thinking can be used to improve performance of the supply chain in meeting end customer demand with no waste;
- identify different ways of reducing waste in supply chains.

Introduction

The discipline of doing things just-in-time – neither too early nor too late – has had a profound influence on the way supply chains are managed. The ideal of materials flowing at a controlled and coordinated rate through the supply network in line with end customer demand has been widely adopted across many industrial sectors. While the origins of just-in-time are somewhat shrouded (Slack, 1997), the company that has made JIT famous across the world is Toyota Motor Company of Japan. Toyota adopted just-in-time as one of the pillars of its production system. The lead in productivity and quality that leading Japanese auto producers in Japan opened up over Western producers led to the term *lean production* being coined (Krafcik and McDuffie, 1989). Lean production sought to describe a radically different approach to running the business from the traditional *mass production* – characterised by higher stocks, lower productivity and poor quality. Researchers on the International Motor Vehicle Program (IMVP; Womack *et al.*, 1990) described lean production as cutting needed resources in half:

It uses less of everything compared with mass production – half the human effort in the factory, half the manufacturing space, half the investment in tools, half the engineering hours to develop a product in half the time. Also, it requires keeping far less than half the needed inventory on site, results in many fewer defects, and produces a greater and ever-growing variety of products.

In other words, a lean producer can use its advantages to reduce costs, or to increase product variety, or a combination of both. The concept of 'lean' in the automotive industry has been extended into other sectors using the term *lean thinking* (Womack and Jones, 1996). And instead of lean production, today we refer to the *lean enterprise* to emphasise that lean concepts spread organically from production into design and development and into logistics. The concepts of 'JIT' and 'lean' essentially come from the same stable. This chapter provides an introduction to just-in-time and lean thinking, and shows how these concepts have been extended to the supply network through techniques such as quick response and vendor-managed inventory.

The overall aim of this chapter is to introduce you to methods of coordinating material movements in the supply chain in line with end customer demand.

Key issues   *This chapter addresses four key issues:*

1 **Just-in-time:** pull and push scheduling. Different ways of scheduling materials.

2 **Lean thinking:** the seven sources of waste, cutting out waste in business processes

3 **Vendor-managed inventory:** delegating to the supplier the responsibility for controlling inventories and replenishments.

4 **Quick response:** improving communications between retailers and the rest of the supply network.

6.1 Just-in-time

Key issues: **What are the implications of just-in-time for logistics? How can just-in-time principles be applied to other forms of material control such as reorder point and material requirements planning?**

Just-in-time is actually a broad philosophy of management that seeks to eliminate waste and improve quality in all business processes. JIT is put into practice by means of a set of tools and techniques that provide the cutting edge in the 'war on waste'. In this chapter, we focus on the application of JIT to logistics. This limited view of JIT has been called *little JIT* (Chase and Aquilano, 1992): there is far more to this wide-ranging approach to management than we present here. Nevertheless, little JIT has enormous implications for logistics, and has spawned several logistics versions of JIT concepts.

This limited view of JIT is an approach to material control based on the premise that a process should operate only when a customer signals a need for more parts from that process. When a process is operated in the JIT way, goods are produced and delivered just-in-time to be sold. This principle cascades upstream along the supply network, with subassemblies produced and delivered just-in-time to be assembled, parts fabricated and delivered just-in-time to be built into subassemblies, and materials bought and delivered just-in-time to be made into fabricated parts. Throughout the supply network, the trigger to start work is governed by demand from the customer – the next process (Schonberger, 1991). The network can be conceived of as a *chain of customers*, with each link coordinated with its neighbours by JIT signals. The whole network is orchestrated by demand from the end customer. Only the end customer is free to place demand whenever he or she wants; after that the system takes over.

The above description of the flow of goods in a supply chain is characteristic of a *pull* system. This contrasts with a *push* approach, in which products are made whenever resources (people, material and machines) become available. The two systems of controlling materials can be distinguished as follows:

- *pull scheduling*: a system of controlling materials whereby the user signals to the maker or provider that more material is needed. Material is sent only in response to such a signal.
- *push scheduling*: a system of controlling materials whereby makers and providers make or send material in response to a pre-set schedule, regardless of whether the next process needs them at the time.

The push approach is a common way for processes to be managed, and often seems a sensible option. If some of the people in a factory or an office are idle, it seems a good idea to give them work to do. The assumption is that those products can be sold at some point in the future. A similar assumption is that building up a stock of finished goods will quickly help to satisfy the customer. This argument seems particularly attractive where manufacturing lead times are long, if quality is a problem, or if machines often break down. It is better and safer to make product, just in case there's a problem in the future. Unfortunately, this argument has severe limitations. Push scheduling and its associated inventory do *not* always help companies to be more responsive. All too often, the very things the organisation wants to sell are unavailable, while there is too much stock of things that are not selling. And building up stock certainly does not help to make more productive use of spare capacity. Instead it can easily lead to excess costs, and hide opportunities to improve processes.

6.1.1 The just-in-time system

Companies achieve the ability to produce and deliver just-in-time to satisfy actual demand because they build a production system that is capable of working in this way. Such a production system can be envisaged as a number of elements that interact with each other, as shown in Figure 6.1. This shows JIT as being underpinned by two layers of elements that interact to form a system. The six points on the pyramid refer to the relative effectiveness with which JIT material control can be achieved: that is, how easy it is to get to the top of the pyramid:

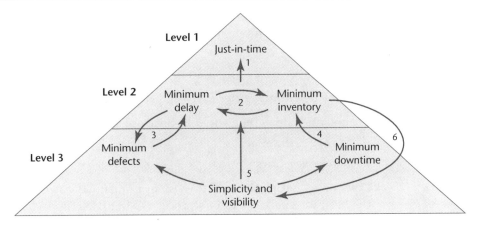

Figure 6.1 **The pyramid of key factors that underpin JIT**

Point 1

The top of the pyramid is full capability for just-in-time supply. This is the level at which an organisation can produce and deliver according to demand. The relationships operating within and between levels 2 and 3 form the system that ultimately underpins the achievement of JIT. They are complex, and in some cases there is a long time delay between taking actions and seeing the effects.

Point 2

The two factors *delay* and *inventory* interact with each other in a system of positive amplification: that is, as one changes so the other does in the same way. This interrelationship results in either a virtuous cycle, where things keep getting better, or a vicious cycle, where they keep getting worse. For example, extra delay in a process will result in extra inventory being held to compensate for the delay. Adding more inventory causes further delays as products take longer to flow through the process, which leads to the need for more inventory. Conversely if delays are reduced then less inventory is needed, which results in fewer delays, meaning that inventory can be further reduced. Making sure this relationship operates as a virtuous cycle of reducing delay and inventory instead of a vicious one where they increase depends on the underpinning factors in level 3.

Point 3

Defects lead to delays, either through requiring rework or necessitating increased production to compensate for scrap. The likelihood of defects leads to safety stocks being held as a buffer against potential problems. This thinking amplifies quality problems by increasing the time between a defect's occurring and its discovery. Not only is the cause harder to identify, but more production will be affected. The attitude that holding inventory can mitigate the effect of quality problems is fundamentally flawed. It stands in opposition to the only successful approach to defect minimisation, where problems are quickly identified, their causes are traced, and permanent solutions are devised and applied.

Point 4

Machine downtime relates to a number of issues:

- unplanned downtime – that is, breakdowns;
- planned maintenance;
- changeover times.

Downtime, and particularly the risk of unplanned downtime, is a key cause of the need for safety stocks in a process. Other JIT tools and techniques can help to minimise the problems here. For example, *total productive maintenance* (TPM; Nakajima, 1989) seeks to answer the question 'What can everyone do to help prevent breakdowns?' Regular planned preventive maintenance, closer cooperation between production and maintenance personnel, and equipment sourcing for ease of maintenance are some of the actions that can be taken in response. In other words, increasing planned maintenance costs often results in reduced overall costs of machine downtime. Minimising changeover time is a JIT tool that can be used not only to reduce lost production time but also to raise production flexibility. Inflexible facilities delay the rapid production of customer orders.

Point 5

Where the flow through a process is easily seen, people in the process will have a better understanding of their colleagues' work and how they themselves affect others. A simple process results from having first focused operations around a family of compatible products. Layout is then organised to bring together all the people and equipment needed to undertake the process. These are arranged so that there is a logical flow between the process steps. Arranging the process so that the stations for undertaking the steps are close together not only helps to reduce inventory but also will itself be made easier when inventory is low. A simple process will be more visible, allowing it to be better maintained. Not only should there be fewer things to go wrong, they will be more obvious when they do, and will be easier to fix. This attribute helps to minimise both machine downtime and product defects.

Maintenance of the process is underpinned by housekeeping and cleanliness. This starts with designing processes and facilities to create order. There is a place for everything, and everything is in its place. Orderliness depends on a thinking workforce that has accepted ownership and responsibility for organising the work place. Attention to detail in terms of 'respect for human' issues is an essential part of JIT philosophy (Harrison and Storey, 2000).

Point 6

The levels of work in progress and other types of inventory have a significant impact upon the visibility of a process. It becomes increasingly difficult to see the flow of a process as inventory increases. This may be literally true on a shopfloor or in a warehouse, where piles and stacks of goods can isolate workers. The same is true in offices when the process flow becomes lost in assorted piles of work on people's desks.

In order to highlight the inadequacies of push production we next consider the case of how a company took a rather traditional approach to responding to new demands being placed on their production process.

**CASE STUDY
6.1**

Smog Co.

The Smog Co. production system

This is the case of Smog Co., a small supplier of well-engineered components. Smog produces a range of products grouped into families. Production of one of the higher-volume product families has been organised into a flow process made up of four steps, which follow one after the other in sequence. Changeover from one product to another is relatively simple, but takes around 10 minutes per machine. To minimise delays caused by changeovers, products tend to be made in batches. These batches move from one step to the next, where they queue on a first in, first out basis to be worked on, after which they move to the next step. This process is shown in Figure 6.2.

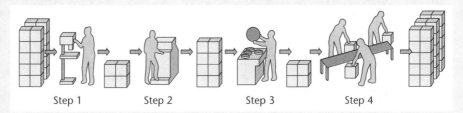

Step 1   Step 2   Step 3   Step 4

Figure 6.2 The Smog Co. production process

Key measures of the performance of this process are the utilisation of people and of machines. The objective is to keep utilisation of both as high as possible. In this situation, if people or machines are idle – and material is available – they are used to make something. Naturally it wouldn't make sense to make *anything*. Instead the production manager has a feel for what is needed, and uses a forecast from the sales department to make an early start on products that it is considered will be required in the near future.

Fred Hollis, the Smog production manager, felt pleased with performance as he looked out across the factory. He was pleased because his machines and people were busy, there were plenty of finished goods on hand, which the sales team could use to supply customers, and there was stock to call upon if product demand increased. Everything seemed to be under control.

Changes to customer requirements

The motivation to change from the current system has been low in the past, as the process at Smog Co. is a reliable one, which has worked well for the company. The 'big three' customers, who take three-quarters of sales, tend to order the same things in similar quantities one week in advance of delivery. With a production lead time of three weeks Smog Co. uses a forecast to schedule production and make sure that finished goods stocks will be available to meet predicted demand. Consistent demand means that forecasts are often close to real demand, so stockouts are rare. In fact the only time this occurred was an incident a couple of years ago, when a key machine went down and a spare part took a long time to source. Current inventory levels now include safety stock to provide cover against a similar problem in the future.

When the company found that certain finished goods were selling slowly, the sales team was particularly good at finding a way to move them. Sometimes prices were cut; at other times sales used special promotions. If production was too high, or the forecast was a bit optimistic, then there were ways of selling surplus stock, and the sales team seemed to enjoy the challenge.

Recently, however, this well-understood position has begun to change. The main customers have started to use a number of new strategies to compete with each other. First one and now a second of them has announced that it will be reducing the call-off time for its products from one week to two working days. At the same time they are all looking for a 5% cost reduction, and are demanding quality improvements.

A 'traditional' reaction to customer demands for better service

The combination of demands for better services caused Smog management some concern. The obvious response to the changes in ordering patterns was to increase stock levels to cater for unexpected variations in demand. This approach had worked before, when it was used to justify the safety stocks that covered production problems. It seemed worth trying again, so stocks were increased.

Things went well over the first few months, during which time delivery performance remained good, while the customers went ahead with their plan to reduce the order lead time. Keeping up with these orders provided the production manager with a few headaches. Preventing stockouts led to an increase in the number of batches being expedited through the factory. This disrupted the production plan, increased the number of machine changeovers, and lowered productivity. As a result, overtime increased in order to maintain output.

The higher level of inventory meant that quality problems were harder to detect. In one case a new operator missed a drilling operation. By the time the first customer discovered the error, nearly two weeks' worth of production had to be recalled and reworked.

The higher inventory levels were also taking up more space. Fred Hollis had submitted a requisition to the finance director to pay for more storage racking. The extra racks were necessary because existing ones were full, and parts stored on the floor were suffering occasional damage in an increasingly cramped factory. Some parts were recently returned by a customer, who felt that damaged packaging indicated damaged products. Naturally, Fred was concerned when his request for more storage space was turned down owing to spending reductions imposed in response to price cuts imposed by customers.

Reflecting on what had happened at Smog, the increase in stock levels had badly affected competitiveness. Smog Co. was experiencing the consequences of trying to forecast demand and using the forecast to determine what to make. Their 'make to stock' approach was responsible for:

- removing the company's ability to be responsive to changes in either quantities or product mix;
- increasing costs and making quality problems worse;
- burying underlying production problems under inventory, and thereby preventing efforts to uncover and resolve them.

In conclusion, while the company had been motivated to change by its customers, the direction it took seemed to have caused many problems.

(Source: after an original by Paul Chapman)

Questions

1 List the actions that Smog Co. took to respond to the new demands being placed on it by customers. Group your responses under the headings of stock levels, level of expediting, and storage space. Briefly describe the effects that these actions had on production performance.

2 Use the 'Pyramid of key factors that underpin JIT' to describe the factors that caused these actions to affect the company's ability to respond to the demands being placed on it by customers.

6.1.2 'Economic' batch sizes and order sizes

One of the key contributions of just-in-time to logistics thinking has been the understanding of *how many* to order and *when* to order. The question of how many parts to make at a time has traditionally been answered by reference to a longstanding concept called the *economic batch quantity* (EBQ) formula. Similar principles are used to determine how many parts at a time to order from suppliers in *economic order quantities* (EOQs). Both EBQ and EOQ assume that parts are used up at a uniform rate, and that another batch of parts should be ordered when stock falls below the *reorder point*. The principle behind the reorder point, which sets out to answer the question 'When to order', is shown in Figure 6.3. A buffer stock line is shown below the reorder level. Buffer stock acts as a safety net in order to cushion for the effects of variability in demand and in lead times. Buffer stock is a function of the service level (risk of stockouts), lead time variability and demand variability. The reorder point is therefore defined as the sum of demand during the lead time and the buffer stock. There are various ways of calculating buffer stock (for a detailed coverage, and for details of EBQ and EOQ calculations, see Vollman *et al.*, 1997).

In manufacturing, the EBQ is determined by means of a calculation of the trade-off between changeover cost and inventory-carrying cost:

- *changeover cost*: the cost associated with changing a given machine over from the last good part from the preceding batch to the first good part from the succeeding batch
- *inventory-carrying cost*: the opportunity cost of holding stock of a given part.

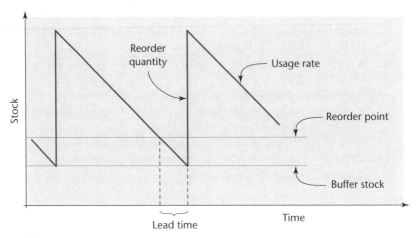

Notes:

1. Reorder point = demand during lead time + safety stock
2. Reorder quantity = economic order quantity
3. Buffer stock = f(service level. lead time variability. demand variability)

Figure 6.3 **When: the reorder point**

It is the product of the unit cost of the part and the percentage annual inventory-carrying cost rate.

Calculation of this trade-off shows the EBQ increasing in line with the square root of the changeover cost, and reducing by the square root of the inventory-carrying cost. The higher the changeover cost, the higher the EBQ. The key point here is that the trade-off can be changed. If a given changeover can be simplified so that it can be carried out in seconds rather than in hours, the changeover cost becomes negligible, and the EBQ becomes 1. Given zero changeover costs, the EBQ formula obeys the JIT ideal of pull scheduling: make only in response to *actual* demand. We return to the issue of small batch production in section 6.4 of this chapter. Actual demand is, of course, likely to vary from one day to the next, unlike the assumption for demand rate shown in Figure 6.3 above. Pull scheduling is more sensitive to demand changes, because only what is needed is made.

Similar considerations have resulted in the concept of the economic order quantity (EOQ). Here, the calculation addresses the question 'How many parts shall we order?' The trade-off this time is between the cost of placing an order and inventory-carrying cost:

● *cost of placing an order*: the notional cost of raising an order, including purchase department costs, transportation costs from the supplier, and goods-in inspection and receiving.

EOQ again increases in line with the square root of the cost of placing an order, and reduces in line with the inventory-carrying cost. Again the trade-off can be changed. If the cost of placing an order can be simplified to a routine basis whereby parts are ordered by paperless systems such as cards, and collected on regular pick-up routes called *milk rounds*, the EOQ can again be reduced towards the JIT ideal. Note that EOQ principles are still widely used for ordering 'independent demand' items that are not directly used to manufacture products, such as spare parts and office supplies.

6.1.3 Periodic order quantity and target stock levels

EOQ models a fixed order size placed whenever stock falls below the reorder level. This is not 'supply chain friendly' when the demand is difficult to forecast. Suppliers are faced with a known order quantity, but the time when that order is placed can vary enormously. An EOQ system finds it very difficult to cope if demand goes up or down rapidly. If demand goes up rapidly, then an EOQ system would tend to make replenishments lag behind the demand trend.

To illustrate, let us assume a sequence of 10 weeks where demand fluctuates between 100 and 1000 units. The economic order quantity (EOQ) has been established as 1000 units, and the safety stock at 100 units. Inventories at the start and end of each week can then be calculated, as shown in Table 6.1.

A more satisfactory way to deal with variable demand is to use the periodic order quantity. Here the reorder quantities are revised more frequently. The method uses mean time between orders (TBO), which is calculated by dividing the EOQ by the average demand rate. In the above example, the EOQ is 1000 and the average demand 410. The economic time interval is therefore approximately 2. An example shown in Table 6.2 illustrates the same situation as in Table 6.1 in terms of demand changes and safety stock level. However, the reorder quantity is based on total demand for the immediate two weeks of history. This reorder method is called *periodic order quantity* (POQ).

Table 6.1 Economic order quantity example

Week no.	Demand	Order quantity	Inventory end	Inventory start	Inventory holding
1	100	1000	900	1000	950
2	100	0	800	900	850
3	200	0	600	800	700
4	400	0	200	600	400
5	800	1000	400	200	300
6	1000	1000	400	400	400
7	800	1000	600	400	500
8	400	0	200	600	400
9	100	0	100	200	150
10	200	1000	900	100	500
SUM	4100	5000	5100	5200	5150
AVERAGE	410	500	510	520	515

Table 6.2 **Periodic order quantity example**

Week no.	Demand	Order quantity	Inventory end	Inventory start	Inventory holding
1	100	200	100	200	150
2	100	0	0	100	50
3	200	600	400	600	500
4	400	0	0	400	200
5	800	1800	1000	1800	1400
6	1000	0	0	1000	500
7	800	1200	400	1200	800
8	400	0	0	400	200
9	100	300	200	300	250
10	200	0	0	200	100
SUM	4100	4100	2100	6200	4150
AVERAGE	410	410	210	620	415

POQ normally gives a lower mean inventory level than EOQ in variable demand situations. In this example, the average inventory holding has fallen from 5150 to 4150. The same number of orders (Chase and Aquilano, 1992) have been used, but the order quantity varies from 200 to 1800.

A widely used model for inventory control in retailing is *periodic review*. This works by placing orders of variable size at regular intervals – the *review period*. The quantity ordered is enough to raise stock on hand plus stock on order to a target level called the *target stock level* (TSL):

Order quantity = Target stock level − Stock on hand − Stock on order

The TSL is the sum of cycle stock (average weekly demand over the review period and replenishment lead time) and the safety stock. An example of the way the TSL is calculated is:

$$\text{TSL} = \text{Cycle stock} + \text{Safety stock}$$
$$= D(T + LT) + Z\sigma\sqrt{(T + LT)}$$

where D = average weekly demand per sku, T = review period in weeks, LT = lead time in weeks, Z = number of standard deviations from the mean corresponding to the selected service level, and σ = standard deviation of demand over $(T + LT)$.

6.1.4 JIT and material requirements planning

Material requirements planning (MRP) was conceived in order to answer the questions *how many?* and *when?* in ordering parts that are directly used to manufacture products (dependent-demand items) simultaneously. MRP systems are widely used in manufacturing companies for materials planning, and MRP logic is one of the pillars of current *enterprise resource planning* (ERP) systems. A detailed description of MRP is given in Vollman *et al.* (1997), but the basic principles are as follows:

- Demand information for finished products (orders and forecasts) is collated by means of a *master production schedule* (MPS). The MPS covers a given *time horizon* (e.g. the next 6 months), and allocates demand for each product into *time buckets* (e.g. days or weeks).

- The structure for each finished product, called the *bill of materials* (BOM), is held on file. The BOM for a given finished product details how each part and subassembly fits together, level by level, in the form of a family tree.

- Starting at the top level of the BOM (level 0, the finished product itself), MRP calculates the *gross* requirements. It then takes into account quantities that are already on order or in stock, and calculates *net* requirements for that part. Then MRP takes into account any batching rules such as EBQ. Finally, MRP allows for manufacturing lead times (made-in parts) or purchased order lead times (bought-out parts), and brings forward the scheduled make-or-buy dates accordingly. Then it carries out the same routine for all of the parts at level 1, then level 2, and so on to the lowest level of the BOM.

- The output from MRP is a set of *time-phased materials requirements* that show how many of each part should be made or bought, and in which time bucket the action should be taken.

MRP is a logical and systematic way of planning materials. It links downstream demand with manufacture and with upstream supply. It can handle detailed parts requirements, even for products that are made infrequently and in low volumes.

On the other hand, MRP is based on a centrally controlled, bureaucratic approach to material planning. Although it is based on a pull scheduling logic, it instructs processes to make more parts whether or not the customer (the next process) is capable of accepting them. Typically, MRP adopts push scheduling characteristics. It remains insensitive to day-to-day issues at shopfloor level, and continues to assume that its plans are being carried out to the letter. In other words, MRP is good at planning, but weak at control.

Meanwhile, JIT pull scheduling is good at handling relatively stable demand for parts that are made regularly. It is sensitive to problems at shopfloor level, and is designed not to flood the next process with parts that it cannot work on. On the other hand, JIT pull scheduling is not good at predicting requirements for the future, especially for parts and products that are in irregular or sporadic demand. JIT is good at control, but weak at planning. There are clear opportunities for putting together the strengths of both systems, so that the weaknesses of one are covered by the strengths of the other. For example, even in systems with great variety, many of the parts are common. So JIT can be used to control those parts, while a much downsized MRP plans what remains.

Honda production system

A striking example of the application of Japanese methods was the introduction of the Honda production system in the UK. Planning and control of the thousands of parts that go to make up a motor vehicle is a complex and difficult task, which often creates chaos in the supply network. Frequent schedule changes have a disastrous effect on suppliers, and the final build programme at the assembler is often governed by what parts are available rather than by what was planned.

Honda devised a production system that was much more logistics-friendly than that of any other motor manufacturer. The basic principle was simple: make the car in batches of 30 at a time. Tell your suppliers what you want five months in advance, and don't change your mind under any circumstances. Five months' notice is long enough for any supplier to get it right, and to ensure that – when build day approaches – parts are delivered just-in-time. In fact, some of the early challenges revolved around the problem that suppliers didn't believe that Honda meant what it said. Other manufacturers were forever chopping and changing right up to and including build day. Once the disciplines had been explained and put into practice, suppliers found that the Honda production system was better than the others: you could actually rely on the schedules, and were given a whole 5 months' notice to plan your production schedules.

The Honda production system was put into practice using standard pallets, which ensured that parts were delivered to the production lines in multiples of 30 at a time. This created a rhythm in the production process whereby empty pallets were removed after each batch, and the fresh ones that replaced them were exactly what was needed for the next batch. It was unnecessary to perform the usual gross to net conversion in MRP because everything was delivered and built in exact quantities of 30 at a time. The only complication to this rule was due to paint defects. If a body was rejected after paint (and paint is the most variable process in a final assembly plant), the parts that would have been fitted were placed in temporary storage at the side of the line. They were fitted when the reject body had been rectified and added to a subsequent batch. A small emergency parts store was maintained for troublesome parts supplies, but this was a last resort, and its presence was frowned upon.

The Honda production system ensured that the principle of *heijunka* was enforced in the inbound material flow. *Heijunka* seeks to level and balance the flow of materials, so that parts arrive at assembly in a coordinated fashion. Unbalanced flow results in unnecessary waste as parts that cannot be used in the current time bucket clog up the factory. The Honda factory appeared a model of orderliness and tidiness: pallets of parts arrived in a seamless flow from the inbound supply network. The longest lead parts were engines and other parts that were sourced from the Japanese parent in Japan: these had several weeks in transit on the high seas before they arrived in the UK. But again, the five-month lead time gave plenty of notice for these parts to arrive just-in-time at the assembly plant located at Swindon.

The downside of the five-month notice period for inbound parts was that it was necessary to forecast the market a corresponding distance ahead. Changes in product mix as a result of increased demand for left-hand drive vehicles, or for diesel rather than petrol engines, could result in an unbalanced flow of finished vehicles coming to the dealers. While both of these factors could be difficult to get right, Honda had a solution for the other options that complicated the model mix. Basically, the solution was: Don't offer many different options. Honda had relatively few painted body colours and just two trim colours. Other options, such as air conditioning and ABS, were unavailable separately. Instead, they were lumped together into options packages, which greatly reduced finished product variety and simplified customer choice.

Questions

1 Identify the advantages of the Honda Production System in terms of material flow. Sketch out a bar chart to show trigger points for production of long-lead items such as engines (made in Japan) and short-lead items such as pressed panels for the car body (made in Rover Body and Pressings in Swindon). Suggest how *heijunka* works in practice.

2 The Honda production system was initially conceived for the US market, where the customer likes to select a car on the dealer forecourt, put down his or her money, and drive it away. In the European market Honda found it more difficult to educate customers to behave this way. Further, the model mix of sales was not always as forecast. What trade-offs are apparent in the Honda production system?

6.2 Lean thinking

Key issues: **What are the principles of lean thinking, and how can they be applied to cutting waste out of supply chains?**

As stated in the introduction to this chapter, *lean thinking* (Krafcik and MacDuffie, 1989) developed as a term used to contrast the just-in-time production methods used by Japanese automotive manufacturers with the mass production methods used by most Western manufacturers. Suffering shortages and lack of resources, Japanese car manufacturers responded by developing production processes that operated with minimum waste. Gradually the principle of minimising waste spread from the shopfloor to all manufacturing areas, and from manufacturing to new product development and supply chain management. The term *lean thinking* refers to the elimination of waste in all aspects of a business.

Lean thinking is a cyclical route to seeking perfection by eliminating waste (the Japanese word is *muda*) and thereby enriching value from the customer perspective. The end customer should not pay for the cost, time and quality penalties of wasteful processes in the supply network. Four principles are involved in achieving the fifth, seeking perfection (see Figure 6.4):

● specifying values;

● identifying the value stream;

● making value flow;

● pull scheduling.

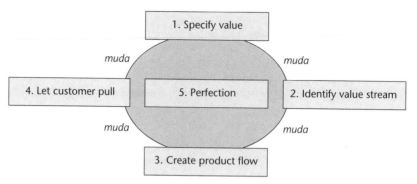

Figure 6.4 Principles of lean thinking
(Source: After Womack and Jones, 1996)

Specify value

Specify value from the customer perspective. In Chapter 3 we discussed value from the shareholder perspective. From the customer perspective, value is added along the supply network as raw materials from primary manufacture are progressively converted into finished product bought by the end customer, such as the aluminium ore being converted into one of the constituents of a can of coke (see Chapter 1, section 1.1). From a marketing and sales perspective the can of coke should be 'always within reach of your thirst'. That is an attempt to define value from the customer perspective. Another is Porter's concept of the *value chain* (Porter, 1985), which sees two types of activity that are of value to the customer. The first is the primary value activities of transforming raw materials into finished products, then distributing, marketing and servicing them. The second is support activities, such as designing the products and the manufacturing and distribution processes, needed to underpin primary activities.

Identify the value stream

Following on from the concept of value, the next principle is to identify the whole sequence of processes along the supply network. The principles of time-based mapping are discussed in sections 5.4 and 5.5 of Chapter 5.

Make value flow

In essence, this means applying the pyramid of key factors that we outlined in section 6.1. Minimising delays, inventories, defects and downtime supports the flow of value in the supply network. Simplicity and visibility are the foundations to achieving these key factors.

Pull scheduling

Enforce the rules in section 6.1: make only in response to a signal from the customer (the next process) that more is needed. This implies that demand information is made available across the supply chain. Where possible, supply from manufacturing, not from stock. Where possible, use customer orders not forecasts.

While some of these concepts may be distant from current practice, lean thinking shares the philosophy of 'big JIT': seek perfection. This is the fifth principle, and is achieved by gradually getting better at everything we do, squeezing waste out at every step. We continue this section by considering the sources of waste, and the way in which lean thinking can be applied to enriching value in business processes.

6.2.1 The seven wastes

In Chapter 5 we saw how any activity that does not add value is a form of waste. By mapping processes through the supply chain, it is possible to sort value-adding and non-value-adding activities (transport, store, inspect and delay). Lean thinking goes further by adding three more types of 'waste' to make seven in all. They are as follows:

- *The waste of overproduction:* making or delivering too much, too early or 'just in case'. Instead, the aim should be to make 'just-in-time' – neither too early nor too late. Overproduction creates unevenness or lumpiness of material flow, which is bad for quality and productivity. It is often the biggest source of waste.
- *The waste of waiting:* takes place whenever time is not being used effectively. It shows up as waiting by operators, by parts or by customers.
- *The waste of transporting:* moving parts around from one process to the next adds no value. Double handling, conveyors and movements by fork lift truck are all examples of this waste. Placing processes as close as possible to each other not only minimises the waste of transport but also improves communications between them.
- *The waste of inappropriate processing:* using a large, central process that is shared between several lines (e.g. a heat treatment plant) is an example of this type of waste. Another example is a process that is incapable of meeting quality standards demanded by the customer – so it cannot help making defects.
- *The waste of unnecessary inventory:* inventory is a sign that flow has been disrupted, and that there are inherent problems in the process. Inventory not only hides problems, it also increases lead times and increases space requirements.
- *The waste of unnecessary motions:* if operators have to bend, stretch or extend themselves unduly, then these are unnecessary motions. Other examples are walking between processes, taking a stores requisition for signature, and decanting parts from one container into another.
- *The waste of defects:* producing defects costs time and money. The longer a defect remains undetected (e.g. if it gets into the hands of the end customer),

the more cost is added. Defects are counteracted by the concepts of 'quality at source' and 'prevention, not detection'.

Lean thinking invites us to analyse business processes systematically to establish the baseline of value-adding processes and to identify the incidence of these seven wastes. The aim is to get parts and data to flow through business processes evenly and in harmony. The more detailed analysis prompted by the concept of seven wastes encourages a greater analysis and understanding of processes and their relationships than is made by supply chain mapping. This analysis should first start with key business processes such as the supply pipeline. Working back from the customer, a business should consider the following processes in the first instance:

- order to replenishment;
- order to production;
- product development.

In each of these processes, the application of lean thinking involves examining the process, quantifying waste within it, identifying root causes of the waste, and developing and implementing of solutions. Examining the process involves mapping it using a variety of techniques such as flow charting, depending on the nature of the process. Performance is quantified by taking measures of the different kinds of waste. For a first attempt, using the time-based measures of lead time and value-adding time often reveal the main incidences of waste. Having identified waste, lean thinking applies the problem solving tools associated with total quality control (TQC) to identify root causes and develop solutions.

The application of lean thinking is the means by which many companies bring their processes under control. Following a systematic approach to tackling waste, they seek to:

- minimise defects;
- minimise downtime;
- maximise simplicity and visibility.

6.2.2 Application of lean thinking to business processes

Order to replenishment

The order replenishment cycle concerns the time taken to replenish what has been sold. Lean thinking seeks to manage the order replenishment cycle by replacing only what has been sold within rapid replenishment lead times. These points are taken up in the next two sections of this chapter, on vendor-managed inventory and on quick response.

Order to production

The order to production cycle is the series of steps that are followed to respond to an order, organise and undertake production, and deliver the product to the customer. This 'make to order' process may be contained within a company or can extend down the supply chain.

Product development

Product development delivers new products or services that can be sold. This process is essential if an organisation is to have future success. Lean thinking can be applied to this process to make it more effective by supporting the development of products with desirable attributes and features and achieving this on time. It can also make the process more efficient and ensure that products are developed to cost.

6.2.3 Role of lean practices

Lean thinking is associated with a number of operational practices that help to deliver the aim of waste minimisation. Two of the most significant are:

- small-batch production;
- rapid changeover.

These two practices are closely associated with each other, but are considered separately here to aid clarity.

The target in small-batch production is a batch size of 1. The traditional logic behind large batches is to take advantage of reduced costs through economies of scale (see EBQ in section 6.1 above). This approach is often flawed, as batch size decisions generally consider only production costs, and overlook costs of inventory and the lack of flexibility caused by large batches. The rationale behind small batches is that they can reduce total cost across a supply chain such as removing the waste of overproduction. They help to deliver products that the end customer wants within the expected lead time (D-time – Chapter 5, section 5.2).

The contribution of rapid changeover was graphically shown by the changeover of press tools used to make car body panels. These cumbersome pieces of equipment can weigh up to 10 tonnes, and historically took up to 8 hours to change within the large presses. The consequence of these long changeover times was that component production runs were long, often going on for days before the press tools were changed so that another component could be made. Extensive work, again led by Toyota, was undertaken on press design, tooling design and component design over a number of years to help to reduce changeover times. The effect has been to reduce changeover times for tools for large pressed parts to around 5 minutes. Consequently, practices that reduce changeover times are often known as single minute exchange of dies (SMED) (Shingo, 1988). The ability to undertake rapid changeovers allows a batch of each different body panel to be produced each day in line with current demand instead of having to produce to forecast.

The lesson from the automotive industry is that even very large pieces of equipment can be developed to allow rapid changeovers. This effort may take a number of years, and is reliant upon developments in machinery and product design, but it can be done. The effect is to provide the flexibility to make possible small-batch production that responds to customer needs.

Small-batch production associated with rapid changeover allows productivity to be maintained by taking advantages of economies of scope. Instead of economies of scale, where quantities of the same thing are made, economies of scope lower costs when quantities of similar things that use the same production resources are made.

6.2.4 Design strategies

Underpinning the application of lean thinking is the need to influence design. Many of the wastes uncovered in the replenishment, make to order and product development cycles cannot be removed because they are inherent in the design of products, systems, processes and facilities. The design strategy employed in lean thinking is to incorporate the ability to undertake lean practices across the total life of a product or facility and also include flexibility to deal with unpredicted events. These issues are described more fully below.

6.2.5 Lean product design

Products can be designed with a number of lean attributes. These include:

● a reduction in the number of parts they contain and the materials from which they are made;

● features that aid assembly, such as asymmetrical parts that can be assembled in only one way;

● redundant features on common, core parts that allow variety to be achieved without complexity with the addition of peripheral parts;

● modular designs that allow parts to be upgraded over the product life.

6.2.6 Lean facility design

The facilities within which new products are developed and existing ones are made and delivered should be designed with lean attributes. Amongst these are:

● modular design of equipment to allow prompt repair and maintenance;

● modular design of layout to allow teams to be brought together with all the facilities they need, with the minimum of disruption, and then subsequently to be dispersed and reassembled elsewhere;

● small machines, ideally portable, which can be moved to match the demand for them;

● open systems architectures (both IT and physical ones) that allow equipment to fit together and work when it is moved and connected to other items.

6.2.7 Lean thinking summary

Lean thinking is based around the simple philosophy of waste minimisation. This concept can be applied to almost all business processes in almost any company. A simple method to help companies achieve this is for them to pursue the goal of single-piece flow, where the batch size passing through the processes of a company is a single item. Problems encountered during progress towards this goal reveal the areas that need to be resolved in order to become leaner.

To aid waste elimination, a number of practices have been developed. Key ones such as rapid changeover, presented here, provide standard solutions that should be generally applicable and help most companies to progress.

6.3 Vendor-managed inventory

Key issue: How can suppliers help to reduce waste in the customer's process?

Sections 6.3 and 6.4 continue the theme of just-in-time and lean thinking by considering how these principles have been applied to retailing supply chains in the form of *vendor-managed inventory* and *quick response* logistics (section 6.4). Vendor-managed inventory (VMI), is an approach to inventory and order fulfilment whereby the supplier, not the customer, is responsible for managing and replenishing inventory. This appears at first sight to counter the principle of pull scheduling, because the preceding process (the manufacturer) is deciding how many and when to send to the next process (the retailer). In practice, the basis on which decisions will be made is agreed with the retailer beforehand, and is based on the retailer's sales information. Under VMI, the supplier assumes responsibility for monitoring sales and inventory, and uses this information to trigger replenishment orders. In effect, suppliers take over the task of stock replenishment.

Automated VMI originated in the late 1980s with department stores in the USA as a solution to manage the difficulties in predicting demand for seasonal clothing. Prior to this *manual VMI* had been around for many years – particularly in the food industry. Under manual VMI, the manufacturer's salesman took a record of inventory levels and reordered product for delivery to the customer's store, where the manufacturer's representative would restock the shelves. As product variety has increased and life cycles have shortened, manual VMI has been replaced by automated VMI.

6.3.1 How VMI works

The supplier tracks product sales and inventory levels at their customers, sending goods only when stocks run low. The decision to supply is taken by the supplier, not the customer as is the case traditionally. The supplier takes this decision based on the ability of the current level of inventory to satisfy prevailing market demand, while factoring in the lead time to resupply.

The smooth running of VMI depends on a sound business system. It also requires effective teamwork between the retailer and the manufacturer. In order for both parties to gain full benefit from the system, appropriate performance measures need to be used. The top priority measure is that of product availability at the retailer. It is in both parties' interests to maximise product availability, avoiding lost sales in the short term and building customer-buying habits in the long term. By emphasising the supplier's responsibility for maximising product availability, VMI aims to achieve this with minimum inventories. In order to combine both of these apparently conflicting goals, it is necessary to have access to real-time demand at the customer.

The most widely used technology for broadcasting demand data from the customer is *electronic data interchange* (EDI). This provides the means for exchanging data from customer to suppliers in a standard format. Internet-based applications using EDI protocols are increasingly popular, providing the same facility at lower cost. Customer demand and inventory data are often processed through software packages to automate the application of decision rules and identify stock lines that need replenishment.

6.3.2 Potential benefits

The immediate benefit to a supplier engaged in VMI is access to data on:

● customer sales;
● inventory levels at the customer.

The assumption is that the supplier can use these data to provide better control of the supply chain and so deliver benefits for both the customer and themselves.

Having the supplier take the decision on replenishment aims to minimise the impact of *demand amplification*, which is discussed in Chapter 7. This critical problem erodes customer service, loses sales, and increases costs. The ability to dampen demand amplification caused by infrequent, large orders from customers is key to the success of VMI. The surplus capacity and excess finished goods held by suppliers to counteract such variation can then be reduced.

In the longer term, suppliers should integrate demand information into their organisation and develop the capability to drive production with it. This helps to replace the traditional push scheduling, based on forecasts and buffer stocks, with pull scheduling, based on meeting known demand instantaneously out of manufacturing.

Activity 6.1

There are a number of different ways in which the use of VMI can benefit the supplier and the customer. Make a list of those benefits you think exist under the headings of 'supplier benefits' and 'customer benefits'.

6.3.3 Potential problems in setting up a VMI system

Other than the practical difficulties of setting up a VMI system, a number of problems can prevent the attainment of the above benefits. Here are five of them:

Unwillingness to share data

Retailers may be unwilling to share their marketing plans and product range strategies with manufacturers. This is particularly true in the UK, where supermarkets have strong own brands that compete with those of the manufacturers.

Retailers continue to be the owners of information on actual demand passing through their tills. An inability to forward this information, whether due to reluctance or to procedural and technical problems, will prevent suppliers from responding effectively, leading to the need for buffer stocks and increasing the risk of stockouts.

Seasonal products

The benefits of VMI are quickly eroded in fashion and seasonal products, especially apparel. VMI in these cases can involve suppliers making to stock based on a pre-season forecast with little scope for manufacturing in season. Small quantities are delivered from this stock to the retailers over the season. Naturally the forecast is regularly at odds with actual demand, so products will be frequently understocked or overstocked. In effect all that has happened is that the burden of owning inventory and disposing of excesses has been moved onto the supplier.

Investment and restructuring costs

Adopting a VMI approach incurs a high investment by the customer and supplier. Setting up the processes and procedures for undertaking this new way of working takes time and effort. The customer will need to close their materials management function if they are to make cost savings, while the supplier will need to develop the capability to take over this task.

Retailer vulnerability

Having outsourced materials management to suppliers the customer becomes more dependent on them.

Lack of standard procedures

The practicalities of the processes and procedures that underpin VMI may not be transferable from one customer to another. Customers may ask for different tagging methods or bespoke labelling. With many industrial products there is no bar-code standard.

System maintenance

Errors creep into inventory records due to wrong counts, mislabelling, damage, loss and theft. These records need to be maintained through manual methods such as stock counts.

6.4 Quick response

Key issue: **How can capabilities across the supply chain be aligned to meet end customer demand?**

Another application of just-in-time and lean thinking is *quick response logistics*. Quick response (or QR for short) is an approach to meeting customer demand by supplying the right quantity, variety and quality at the right time to the right place at the right price. This concept originated in the US textile and apparel industry in response to the threat posed by overseas competitors. The concepts behind QR are based on taking a total supply chain view of an industry. From this perspective it is possible to understand overall performance and the causes of poor performance, and to identify opportunities for improvement.

Understanding overall performance involves mapping the processes needed to convert raw material into final product (see Chapter 5). The performance of the process is also assessed to determine its effectiveness. In the case of the apparel industry, mapping followed the process of converting raw material into fibre, then into fabric, then into apparel and finally delivery to the retailer. Key measures of the process were lead times, inventory levels and work in progress.

This investigation found that the total process of converting raw material into clothing took 66 weeks. A basic analysis of the process identified that 55 weeks were taken up with product sitting in various stores as inventory. The principal cause of the need for this inventory was identified as being lack of communication between the organisations in the supply network.

Such analysis is similar to that described in Chapter 5, with the process considered in this case being the whole supply chain from end to end. There are two main differences between QR and a time-based approach to improvement. First, there is an emphasis on using actual customer demand to pull products through the distribution and manufacturing system. Second, there is extensive use of information technology as the preferred way to achieve pull. These two issues are explored in more detail below.

6.4.1 JIT/QR relationship

Quick response has much in common with the principles behind just-in-time described in section 6.1. The same principle of making only to demand is applied to different parts of the supply network. QR applies the pull principle to the front-end process of distribution management between the retailer and the supplier. JIT applies this principle throughout the supply network. In the case of QR, items are supplied to the retailer in response to consumer demand. Deliveries are made just-in-time for them to be sold. Delivery to the retailer triggers the supplier to produce another item, so pulling further parts through the supply chain in a JIT manner.

This process is very different from the traditional approach of the apparel industry. It has been commonplace to make the whole of a season's forecasted demand in advance, and to deliver to store in line with the forecast. While a true 'make to demand' approach has not been achieved, applying QR has led the industry to make two important changes:

- Development lead times have been compressed. This allows designs to be released later, and thus more in line with the latest fashion trends.

- Production lead times are shorter. This allows smaller pre-season inventories to be built up. Instead, high-demand items are supplemented by production during the season. The effect is to maintain high availability of popular lines while minimising stocks of items which prove to be less popular and which would otherwise have to be discounted.

6.4.2 Role of enabling technologies

High variety in clothing markets – due to different sizes, styles and colours – and in grocery markets has led these industries to use information technologies as a means of enabling QR. These technologies are based around the use of uniform product codes and electronic data interchange (EDI). The process involves collecting merchandise information at the point of sale from the product bar code. Data are sent to the supplier via EDI, where they are compared with an inventory model for the store concerned. When appropriate, production is ordered for the specific items needed to restock the store to the requirements of the model. Once these items have been made, the cycle is completed when they are packed, shipped to the store and delivered to the shelf.

This process has enormous implications for links across the supply chain. With each retailer having a range of suppliers and each supplier servicing a number of retailers there is the need for common bar-code standards across the industry. The retailer needs to have a scanning and data capture system to identify the item being sold. It will need to have a reordering system that links the item to its manufacturer, and which places an order. Information needs to be exchanged between the parties in a common data format, which can be read by different IT systems. The high volume of transactions means that the systems handling the data exchange need to be robust and reliable. Having been informed of the sale, the supplier inputs this information to its manufacturing planning system in order to schedule production and the ordering of supplies.

It is hardly surprising that it is extremely difficult to achieve this integration across the whole of a supply network. There are significant implications for small businesses, which have difficulty justifying the cost of the IT system and the associated training. These set-up costs can deter new companies with innovative products from being able to supply. Recent developments in Internet-based applications are helping to resolve this situation because the implementation and data transfer costs are much lower.

Summary

What is JIT, and how does it apply to logistics?

- JIT is a broad-based philosophy of doing the simple things right and gradually doing them better. As applied to logistics, JIT can be conceived as a pyramid of key factors that centre on minimum delay and minimum inventory.

- 'How many?' and 'when?' to order are key questions that impact on delay and inventory. JIT contributes to the answers to these questions by cutting down the sources and causes of waste in logistics. Specific contributions include the reduction of changeover times and simple, paperless systems of material control.

- Long-standing approaches to material control, such as reorder point stock control (ROP), economic order quantities (EOQ) and material requirements planning (MRP), can be made far more responsive by the application of JIT principles. Examples are reducing batch sizes and reorder quantities, and reducing lead times. Synergies can be delivered, too: JIT pull scheduling works best for control, MRP for planning.

What is lean thinking, and how can it be applied to logistics?

- Lean thinking seeks perfection by gradually reducing waste from each of four areas: specifying value from the customer perspective; identifying the value stream (through time-based mapping); making the product flow through the supply network (by applying JIT principles); and letting the customer pull (through pull scheduling).

- Lean thinking focuses on how the seven wastes can be used to support lean principles. Lean thinking follows JIT principles via the concept of 'one piece flow'. Lean thinking extends these principles into product and facility design.

In what ways have JIT and lean thinking been applied to supply networks?

- Two of the ways in which JIT and lean thinking principles have been applied to logistics are covered in this chapter. Others follow in later chapters in this book.

- Under vendor-managed inventory (VMI), suppliers take responsibility for monitoring sales and inventory in the retailer's process. This information is used to trigger replenishment orders. VMI is facilitated by willingness to share data, the use of integrated systems, and standard procedures. It is made more difficult by such factors as long replenishment lead times, inaccurate data, and unwillingness by either party to invest in systems support.

- Quick response (QR) logistics take the lead from time-based mapping, and adopt a total supply chain view to following sales trends: for example, in the fashion industry. Instead of making a season's product in advance, QR aims to be responsive to market trends. This has had the effect of compressing development lead times and shortening production lead times to greatly improve the responsiveness of the supply network as a whole.

Discussion questions

1 Dealers have criticised the way auto assemblers use JIT as an excuse for buying parts from the inbound supply network 'so that their costs are kept down'. They then dump finished vehicles onto the dealer by matching '*their* perceptions of a marketplace demand with *their* constraints as a manufacturer, i.e. what they've produced' (adapted from Delbridge and Oliver, 1991). Referring to the Honda case in section 6.1, comment on the trade-offs implied in these comments from disgruntled dealers.

2 What matters more: value to the customer or value to the shareholder? Refer to section 3.4 of Chapter 3 in formulating your response. How does this question impact on the philosophy of lean thinking?

3 Explain the thinking behind quick response (QR) logistics. How can QR help a retailer to plan and control product lines for a new fashion season?

4 What is meant by the term *overproduction*? Why do you think this has been described as the biggest waste of all?

5. Explain the difference between pull scheduling and push scheduling. Under what circumstances might push scheduling be appropriate?

References

Chase, R.B. and Aquilano, N.J. (1992) *Production and Operations Management: A life cycle approach*, 2nd edn. Homewood, IL: Irwin.

Delbridge, R. and Oliver, N. (1991) Just-in-time or just the same? Developments in the auto industry: the retailers' views. *International Journal of Retail and Distribution Management*, **19**(2), 20–6.

Harrison, A. and Storey, J. (2000) Coping with World Class Manufacturing. *New Technology, Work and Employment*, **13**(3), 643–64.

Krafcik, J.F. and MacDuffie, J.P. (1989) *Explaining High Performance Manufacturing: The International Automotive Assembly Plant Study*. MIT: International Motor Vehicle Program.

Nakajima, S. (ed.) (1989) *TPM Development Program: Implementing total productive maintenance*. Cambridge, MA: Productivity Press.

Porter, M.E. (1985) *Competitive Advantage: Creating and sustaining superior performance*. New York: Free Press.

Schonberger, R.J. (1991) *Building a Chain of Customers: Linking business functions to build the world class company*. New York: Free Press.

Shingo, S. (1988) *Non-Stock Production*. Cambridge: Productivity Press.

Slack, N. (ed.) (1997) *Blackwell Encyclopedic Dictionary of Operations Management*. Oxford: Blackwell.

Vollman, T.E., Berry, W.L. and Whybark, D.C. (1997) *Manufacturing Planning and Control Systems*, 4th edn. Boston: Irwin.

Womack, J. and Jones, D. (1996) *Lean Thinking*. New York: Simon and Schuster.

Womack, J., Jones, D. and Roos, D. (1990) *The Machine that Changed the World*. New York: Rawson Associates.

Suggested further reading

Harrison, A.S. (1992) *Just in Time Manufacturing in Perspective*. Hemel Hempstead: Prentice Hall.

Vollman, T.E., Berry, W.L. and Whybark, D.C. (1997) *Manufacturing Planning and Control Systems*, 4th edn. Irwin.

Womack, J. and Jones, D. (1996) *Lean Thinking*. New York: Simon and Schuster.

The agile supply chain

The objectives of this chapter are to:

- explain the synergy between lean and agile mindsets and the relevance of this thinking to logistics strategy;
- explore the challenges and difficulties of coping with volatile demand situations;
- explain how capabilities can be developed and specifically targeted at thriving in conditions of market turbulence.

By the end of this chapter you should be able to:

- understand that different strategies are needed for different volume/variety conditions in the supply chain;
- understand the distinctions between lean and agile mindsets, and how the two can work together;
- understand the type of market conditions under which agile strategies are appropriate and how they can be operationalised.

In Chapter 9 we consider another key aspect of the agile supply chain – the virtual organisation.

Introduction

A key feature of present-day business is the idea that it is supply chains that compete, not companies (Christopher, 1998), and that the success or failure of supply chains is ultimately determined in the marketplace by the end consumer. Getting the right product, at the right price, at the right time to the end customer is not only the key to competitive success, but also the key to survival. Hence, satisfying the end customer and understanding the marketplace are crucial elements for consideration when attempting to establish logistics strategy. Only when the requirements and constraints of the marketplace are understood can an enterprise attempt to develop a strategy that will meet the needs of both the supply network and the end customer.

Supply chain performance improvement initiatives strive to match supply to demand, thereby driving down costs at the same time as improving customer satisfaction. This invariably requires that uncertainty within the supply network should be reduced as far as possible so as to facilitate a more predictable upstream demand (Mason-Jones *et al.*, 1999). Sometimes, however, uncertainty cannot be removed from the supply network because of product and market characteristics. For example, demand for a fashion product is usually hard to forecast. Hence, specific supply networks are faced with the situation where they have to accept *uncertainty*, but where they still need to develop a strategy that enables them to match supply and demand.

In Chapter 6 we looked at the concept of lean production, and the wider concept of the lean enterprise. The focus of the lean approach has essentially been on the elimination of waste or *muda*. A common view is that lean thinking works best where demand is relatively stable – and hence predictable – and where variety is low. But in situations where demand is volatile, and customer requirement for variety is high, the elimination of waste becomes a lower priority than responding rapidly to the turbulent marketplace. The capabilities needed to respond to such volatile conditions have been given a different and distinct term – the *agile supply chain*.

Agility is a supply chain-wide capability that aligns organisational structures, information systems, logistics processes and, in particular, mindsets. A key characteristic of an agile supply chain is flexibility. In that respect, the origins of agility as a business concept lie partially in *flexible manufacturing systems* (FMS). Initially it was thought that the route to manufacturing flexibility was through automation to enable rapid changeovers (i.e. reduced set-up times) and thus enable a greater responsiveness to changes in product mix or volume. Later this idea of manufacturing flexibility was extended into the wider business context (Nagel and Dove, 1991).

A useful distinction between lean and agile mindsets (Naylor *et al.*, 1999) is as follows:

● *Agility* means using market knowledge and a responsive supply network to exploit profitable opportunities in a volatile marketplace.

● *Leanness* means developing a value stream to eliminate all waste, including time, and to enable a level schedule.

The overall aim of this chapter is to explain the various ways in which these concepts may be combined to enable highly competitive supply chains that are adapted to perform well in volatile yet cost-conscious environments. In doing so we shall highlight important differences between the two paradigms, as well as showing how one may benefit from the other. There is a need in all change management programmes to consider the intellectual as well as the operational needs of the supply chain (Warnecke and Huser, 1995). Our integrated model seeks to describe the agile supply chain based on the concept of a seamless alignment of logistics processes.

Key issues   *This chapter addresses two key issues:*

1 **Market winners and qualifiers:** different ways to compete in the marketplace; combining lean and agile approaches.

2 **Agile practices**: benefiting from market turbulence, rapid response logistics, and managing low-volume products.

7.1 Market winners and qualifiers

Key issue: **How can lean and agile approaches be harnessed to competitive advantage?**

In Chapter 1 we considered the issue of competing through logistics. The relative importance of the five competitive factors (quality, speed, dependability, flexibility and cost) can be assessed with the help of order winners and order qualifiers. *Order qualifiers* comprise the entry-level factors that are needed to gain entry into a given market. To actually win orders demands that one or more factors must be better than those of the competition. These are called *order winners*. The definition of order qualifiers and order winners helps in the development of a suitable logistics strategy. We can use these important ideas to develop the wider, supply-chain-oriented concept of *market qualifiers* and *market winners*.

The connection between the concepts of 'qualifiers' and 'winners', and 'lean' and 'agile', is critical. At its simplest the lean paradigm is most powerful when the winning criteria are cost and quality. However, when service and customer value enhancement are the main order winners, then the likelihood is that agility will become the critical dimension. Figure 7.1 illustrates the key differences in focus between the lean and agile mindsets in relation to market qualifiers and market winners (Mason-Jones *et al.*, 1999).

It is in the dynamic nature of competition that last year's market winner will be replaced this year by a former market qualifier (Johansson *et al.*, 1993). This can be illustrated in the case of lean and agile mindsets by studying the transition

	Market qualifiers	Market winners
Agile supply	1 Quality 2 Cost 3 Lead time	1 Service level 2 Customer value
Lean supply	1 Lead time 2 Service level	1 Cost 2 Quality

Figure 7.1 Market winners – market qualifiers matrix for agile versus lean supply
(Source: After Mason-Jones *et al.*, 1999)

Table 7.1 **Summary of the transition in the personal computer supply chain from product-driven to customer-driven operations**

Supply chain evolution phase	I	II	III	IV
Supply chain time marker	Early 1980s	Late 1980s	Early 1990s	Late 1990s
Supply chain philosophy	Product driven	Market orientated	Market driven	Customer driven
Supply chain type	Lean functional silos	Lean supply chain	Leagile supply chain	Customised leagile supply chain
Market winner	Quality	Cost	Availability	Lead time
Market qualifiers	(a) Cost (b) Availability (c) Lead time	(a) Availability (b) Lead time (c) Quality	(a) Lead time (b) Quality (c) Cost	(a) Quality (b) Cost (c) Availability
Performance metrics	(a) Stock turns (b) Production cost	(a) Throughput time (b) Physical cost	(a) Market Share (b) Total cost	(a) Customer satisfaction (b) Value added

(Source: Christopher and Towill, 2000)

of the operation of the personal computer supply chain. Table 7.I describes the transition over a 15–20-year period from product driven through market oriented to market driven, and finally through to individual customer-driven enterprise (Christopher and Towill, 2000). During that change the market winner has rotated between quality, cost, availability and lead time. But at any one time the other competitive factors continue to be market qualifiers, which cannot be ignored if business is not to be lost.

7.1.1 Attributes of lean and agile supply

Whereas quality, service level, and leadtime are market qualifiers for lean supply, with the market winner then being cost, the latter benchmark is merely an important qualifier in agile supply (Christopher and Towill, 2000). Where the risk of obsolescence and/or the cost of a stockout are high relative to the cost of production and distribution, then a different supply chain solution is required (Fisher, 1997). This leads to the conclusion that the total costs for the *product delivery process* (PDP) are:

Supply chain total PDP costs = Physical PDP costs + Marketability costs

Where *physical costs* include all production, distribution, and storage costs; *marketability costs* include all obsolescence and stock-out costs.

The first cost source (PDP) dominates lean supply, whereas the second cost source (marketability costs) dominates agile supply. Note that lost sales are gone forever in the agile supply chain model, whether due to stockouts or to obsolescence. This is because the marketplace is extremely harsh and competitive, with little brand loyalty. As we shall see later, the requirement is that the product should be both affordable and available. Next, we make a detailed comparison of lean and agile supply by looking at specific attributes of each in relation to business strategy.

Both agile and lean mindsets demand high levels of product quality. They also require that total lead times (defined as the time taken from a customer's raising a request for a product or service until it is delivered) should be minimised. Total lead time has to be minimised to enable agility, as demand is highly volatile and thus difficult to forecast. If a supply chain has long end-to-end lead times in relation to the competition, then it will not be capable of responding quickly enough to market demand. Furthermore, *effective* reduction of lead times *always* leads to significant bottom line improvements in manufacturing costs and productivity (Towill, 1996).

Lead time needs to be reduced in lean manufacturing as, by definition, excess time is waste and leanness calls for the elimination of all waste. The essence of the difference between leanness and agility in terms of the total value provided to the customer is that service level (availability) is the critical factor calling for agility, whereas cost, and hence the sales price, is clearly linked to leanness. Although lead-time reduction may be a sufficient condition for achieving lean production, it is only *one* of the necessary conditions for enabling agile supply.

Table 7.2 illustrates the comparison of attributes between lean and agile supply. In the volatile unpredictable marketplace for 'fashion' goods, both stockout and obsolescence costs are punitive. Consequently the purchasing priorities change from:

- *placing orders upstream* for products that move in a regular flow to
- *assigning capacity* so that products can be made rapidly to meet demand that is difficult to forecast

Table 7.2 Comparison of lean supply with agile supply: the distinguishing attributes

Distinguishing attributes	Lean supply	Agile supply
Typical products	Commodities	Fashion goods
Marketplace demand	Predictable	Volatile
Product variety	Low	High
Product life cycle	Long	Short
Customer drivers	Cost	Availability
Profit margin	Low	High
Dominant costs	Physical costs	Marketability costs
Stockout penalties	Long-term contractual	Immediate and volatile
Purchasing policy	Buy materials	Assign capacity
Information enrichment	Highly desirable	Obligatory
Forecasting mechanism	Algorithmic	Consultative

(Source: Mason-Jones *et al.*, 1999)

The 'assign capacity' option requires that demand should be understood using *intelligent consultation*, maximising inputs from rich' marketplace insider sources (Fisher et al., 1994). Instead of placing detailed orders in advance of demand, this option reserves capacity at suppliers. Orders are placed on suppliers as late as possible, often on a day-to-day basis. And intelligent consultation takes a broad-based yet detailed view of demand trends from informed sources such as retail stores, consumers and fashion trends.

7.1.2 Practical ways to combine lean and agile mindsets

As we have indicated, there are a number of common elements between lean and agile mindsets. Provided the whole concept is fully thought through and properly managed, lean and agile businesses can coexist, even when on the same site and with some limited rotation of personnel (Aitken, 2000). Here are three ways in which the two mindsets have been brought together to provide available and affordable products for the end customer.

The Pareto curve approach

Many companies manufacturing or distributing a range of products will find that the Pareto rule applies, and can be exploited to determine supply strategy. Typically, 80% of total volume will be generated from just 20% of the total product line. The way in which this 20% is managed should probably be quite different from the way the remaining 80% are managed. For example, it could be argued that demand for the top 20% of products by volume is likely to be more predictable, and hence they lend themselves to lean principles of manufacturing and distribution. Demand for the relatively slow-moving 80%, on the other hand, will typically be less easy to predict, and will require a more agile mode of management. Figure 7.2 suggests one generic way in which supply chain strategies may be devised for the predictable 20% and the more volatile 80% of products.

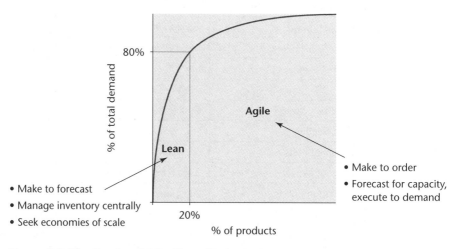

Figure 7.2 The Pareto distribution affects strategy

The decoupling point approach

A further combination of lean and agile mindsets can be achieved through the creation of a *decoupling point,* using what may be termed strategic inventory. Here the idea is to hold inventory in some generic or modular form and only to complete the final assembly or configuration when the precise customer requirement is known. This concept of *postponement* is now increasingly employed by organisations in a range of industries (van Hoek, 1998). As shown in Figure 7.3, organisations can use lean methods up to the decoupling point and agile methods beyond it. Companies such as Hewlett-Packard have successfully employed such strategies to enable products to be customised much closer in time to actual demand. Thus the 'basic' printer can be made in generic form using lean methods in North America, and customised according to known demand in the European market in which it is to be sold (Feitzinger and Lee, 1997).

A parallel concept to the 'material' decoupling point described above is that of the *information decoupling point* (Mason-Jones *et al.*, 1999). This represents the furthest point upstream to which supply is based on 'real' demand flows. Beyond the decoupling point, information is distorted by inventory policies such as reorder points and reorder quantities (see Chapter 6). The agile mindset requires that the information decoupling point should be positioned as far upstream as possible. In other words, as much of the supply chain as possible should operate using real-time demand information.

Separation of base and surge demands

Other hybrid strategies that have been employed with success are based upon separating demand patterns into *base* and *surge* aspects. Figure 7.4 highlights the differences. One possible level scheduling solution is shown, where capacity requirements are smoothed by intelligent switching of base production. Base demand can be forecast on the basis of past history, but surge demand typically cannot. Base demand can be met through lean methods to achieve economies of scale, whereas surge demand is met using more flexible (and probably higher cost) processes. Strategies such as these are increasingly being employed in the fashion industry, where the base demand is sourced to low-cost countries such as China, and surge demand is 'topped up' close to the market. Even though the

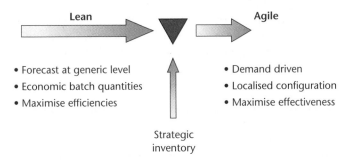

Figure 7.3 **The decoupling point**

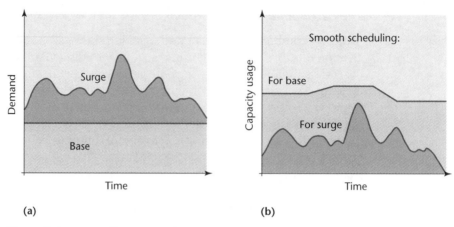

(a)   (b)

Figure 7.4 Responding to combinations of 'base' and 'surge' demands: (a) Total time phased demand; (b) level scheduling solution

unit cost of manufacture in local markets will be higher than that of sourcing from low-cost locations, the supply chain advantage in terms of product availability can be considerable.

Alternatively, arrangements can be made for dealing with both base and surge demands using one of two approaches:

- *separation in space*: using separate production lines or factories;
- *separation in time*: using slack periods to produce future base demand, which will always be needed.

Under lean production, the schedule is often fixed for a period in advance in order to permit *heijunka* (synchronised parts movements) in the inbound chain. The fixed period can often be extensive, as described in the Honda case in Chapter 6 (case study 6.2).

It is particularly important to relate the strategy throughout the whole supply network to the needs of the end customer in terms of both affordability and availability.

While these three strategies are complementary rather than mutually exclusive, it is likely that each may work better in certain conditions. A proposed set of conditions for applying the three hybrid strategies is shown in Table 7.3.

The three lean/agile hybrid strategies described above propose that the focus of supply chain re-engineering should be to seek ways in which the best combination of lean and agile strategies can be achieved. Our proposed integrated model described below provides the essential infrastructure.

7.1.3 An integrated approach to supply chain design

We start with the view that lean methods can be a powerful contributor to the creation of agile enterprises. In particular, where product ranges can be separated according to either or both:

Table 7.3 A contingency approach to supply chain strategy choice

Hybrid strategies	Appropriate market conditions and operating environment
Pareto curve: use lean methods for volume lines, and agile methods for the slow movers.	High levels of variety; demand is non-proportionate across the range.
Decoupling point: the aim is to be lean up to the decoupling point and agile beyond it.	Possibility of modular production or intermediate inventory; delayed final configuration or distribution.
Surge/base demand separation: manage the forecastable element of demand using lean principles, and use agile principles for the most volatile aspects of demand.	Where base level of demand can confidently be predicted from past experience and where local manufacturing, small batch capacity is available.

- *variety* (in terms of number of finished products) and *uncertainty* (in terms of demand)
- applicability of the *decoupling concept*

a real opportunity exists for employing hybrid lean/agile strategies. There is also one important sense in which lean precedes agile. Effective change requires the mapping and understanding of all the relevant business processes (see Chapter 5). The lean knowledge base is the basic starting point for developing capabilities: it can then be exploited in order to enable further performance improvements, including building in agility.

Figure 7.5 sets out our view of the agile supply chain (Harrison *et al.*, 1999). Firstly, the agile supply chain is *market sensitive*. By market sensitive we mean that the supply chain is capable of reading and responding to real demand. Most organisations are forecast-driven rather than demand-driven. In other words because they have little direct feed-forward from the marketplace by way of data on actual customer requirements they are forced to make forecasts based upon past sales or shipments and convert these forecasts into inventory. The break-throughs of the last decade in the form of efficient consumer response (ECR – see section 8.2) and the use of information technology to capture data on demand direct from the point-of-sale or point-of-use are now transforming the organisation's ability to hear the voice of the market and to respond directly to it.

The use of information technology to share data between buyers and suppliers is, in effect, creating a *virtual* supply chain (see section 10.2). Virtual supply chains are information based rather than inventory based.

Conventional logistics systems are based upon a paradigm that seeks to ident-ify the optimal quantities of inventory and its spatial location. Complex formu-lae and algorithms exist to support this inventory-based business model. Paradoxically, what we are now learning is that once we have visibility of demand through shared information, the premise upon which these formulae are based no longer holds electronic data interchange (EDI) and now the Internet have enabled partners in the supply chain to act upon the same data, i.e. real demand, rather than be dependent upon the distorted and noisy picture that

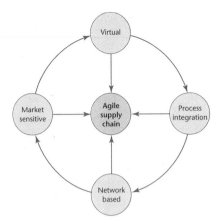

Figure 7.5 The agile supply chain

emerges when orders are transmitted from one step to another in an extended chain.

Shared information between supply chain partners can only be fully leveraged through *process integration*. By process integration is meant collaborative working between buyers and suppliers, joint product development, common systems and shared information. This form of cooperation in the supply chain is becoming ever more prevalent as companies focus on managing their core competencies and outsource all other activities. In this new world a greater reliance on suppliers and alliance partners becomes inevitable and, hence, a new style of relationship is essential. In the 'extended enterprise' as it is often called, there can be no boundaries and an ethos of trust and commitment must prevail. Along with process integration comes joint strategy determination, buyer–supplier teams, transparency of information and even open-book accounting.

This idea of the supply chain as a confederation of partners linked together as a *network* provides the fourth ingredient of agility. There is a growing recognition that individual businesses no longer compete as stand-alone entities but rather as supply chains. We are now entering the era of 'network competition' where the prizes will go to those organisations who can better structure, co-ordinate and manage the relationships with their partners in a network committed to better, closer and more agile relationships with their final customers. It can be argued that in today's challenging global markets, the route to sustainable advantage lies in being able to leverage the respective strengths and competencies of network partners to achieve greater responsiveness to market needs.

As suggested in Figure 7.5, enabling the agile supply chain requires many significant changes. Supply chain managers today need also to be change managers – not just managing change within the organisation, but managing change in the way that relationships between organisations are coordinated. One way to achieve this coordination is to make use of a 'pipeline integrator' or, as they have sometimes been termed, a *fourth-party logistics* service provider (4PL). These organisations make use of their expertise and knowledge of managing global supply chains to ensure that even in complex networks a more agile response can be achieved. An example of one company that is taking up this role on behalf of global clients is the Hong Kong based company Li and Fung (Magretta, 1998). Li and Fung was originally a trading company sourcing and distributing products on behalf of their principals. Over the years it has developed specific expertise and skills that enable it to manage and coordinate supply chains. For example, Li and Fung, on behalf of the US retailers, the Limited, will order undyed yarn from the yarn supplier, book weaving and dying capacity at fabric manufacturers' facilities and manufacturing capacity at the garment factories, all in advance of the actual requirement being known. As the Limited gets a clearer view of what the requirement is for actual styles, colours and sizes, then Li and Fung will issue precise orders and manage the entire supply chain. In the words of the Chairman, Victor Fung:

> It would be easier to let the factories worry about securing their own fabric and trim. But then the order would take three months, not five weeks. So to shrink the delivery cycle, I go upstream to organise production. And the shorter production time lets the retailer hold off before having to commit to fashion trend. It's all about flexibility, response time, small production runs, small minimum order quantities, and the ability to shift direction as the trends move (Magretta, 1995).

7.2 Agile practices

Key issue: How can we use agile practices to benefit from turbulence in the marketplace?

In this section we propose further actions that support the migration towards greater levels of agility in supply chains. Three characteristics of supply chain operations can be earmarked as directly related to becoming agile:

- mastering and benefiting from variance;
- rapid responsiveness;
- unique or small volume responsiveness.

Each of these characteristics is difficult to achieve under the traditional ways of organising because they obstruct stability, lead to smaller batches, and reduce the ability to plan in advance. This section will present progressive levels of practices within each of these three characteristics. All three are seen as opportunities by agile-oriented companies, because they use the characteristics to create competitive advantage over organisations that continue to focus on reducing demand variation, increasing time windows and raising volumes.

7.2.1 Benefiting from variance

Amplification of demand changes has been called the *bullwhip effect*. This principle recognises that changes in demand get amplified from one tier to the next in the supply chain. For example, the retailer may order only in full truck loads from its suppliers. Instead of understanding the actual end customer demand, the suppliers see huge swings in orders that are essentially due to the retailer's desire to minimise transport costs. This has the unfortunate impact of increasing manufacturing costs at the suppliers, because they are asked to make large quantities at irregular time intervals. What may originally have been stable demand through the till becomes heavily distorted.

Figure 7.6 shows an example of the bullwhip effect. Demand through the till is relatively stable, but orders on the supplier are anything but stable! The original range of variation has been amplified into something much worse. The only way in which the supplier can respond is to hold stocks – and even those vary enormously from one week to the next. Uncertainty about customer demand leads to large up-and-down swings in the need for capacity and in inventory levels. This effect ripples through the supply chain. Batching rules at the supplier make things even worse for tier 2 and 3 suppliers upstream.

Information exchange and postponement have been suggested as solutions to the wastes and uncertainties that are created. Delaying actions until orders have been received and sharing demand information are important ways to lower uncertainties. Better coordination of the supply chain helps to get rid of the bullwhip effect. But the question then remains: how do we cope with the remaining uncertainty in demand?

Three sources of demand uncertainty can be identified:

- *Seasonality*: some products sell more during summer than winter.

- *Product life cycles*: parts volumes for original equipment such as cars are much higher than volumes for spare parts after the model has been changed.

- *End customer demand*: a residual uncertainty always exists. For example, we go to the supermarket at different times from week to week to suit ourselves.

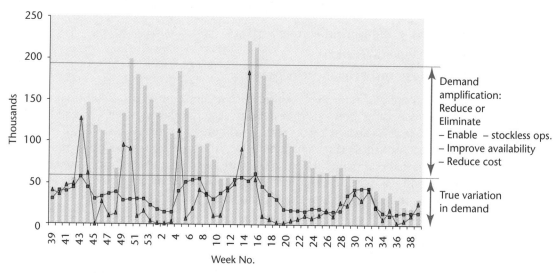

Figure 7.6 **The bullwhip effect at work**

Table 7.4 **The impact of seasonality**

Number of seasons	Example business	Level of postponement	Supply chain scope impact
1 (summer)	Garden furniture	–	One peak for which inventory is built up in advance
2 (summer and Christmas)	Ice cream	Semi-packaging	Limited; two peaks for which inventory is built up, while final packaging (label etc.) can be done once ordered
4 (2 mains and 2 shorts)	Fashion	Semi-manufacturing	Wide; take in orders from collection then plan, make and deliver before season starts

There are various levels at which seasonality of demand can impact on the supply chain. Examples are provided in Table 7.4. These differ in terms of number and length of seasons, businesses involved, relevant level of postponement, and scope of impact on the supply chain. Semi-postponement (that is, postponement to retailer order, not end consumer order) is used to cope with the uncertainty resulting from seasonality. 'Finalisation' or manufacturing is based on retail orders. These are used in addition to the main practice – that of *seasonality swapping*. The common two-season pattern is displayed in Figure 7.7(a). The peaks in the seasons are demanding in terms of the ability to meet demand from capacity and within competitive service windows. In order to ensure delivery, manufacturing can be swapped across the season in order to ensure a safety stock (for example based upon information exchange regarding pre-season demand expectations from the retailer, or based upon historical demand analysis), which will lower the impact of variance on the operations. This is displayed in Figure 7.7(b).

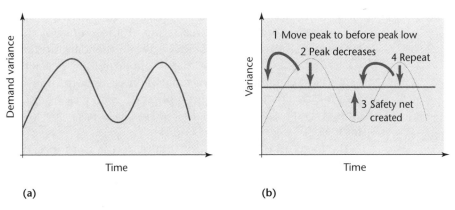

Figure 7.7 **Seasonality swapping: (a) two-season pattern; (b) two-season after swapping**

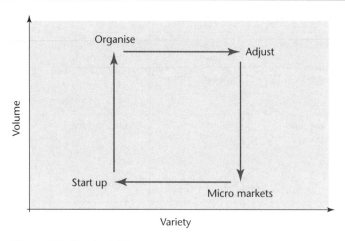

Figure 7.8 Product life

A second and less predictable type of variance is that driven by product life cycles. Here information exchange and (semi-)postponement is relevant but far from sufficient. The traditional four-stage life cycle passes through several quadrants of variance, as displayed in Figure 7.8. During the introduction or start-up phase little volume and variety is in place. Volume increases in the growth phase, and the supply chain has to get organised, formalised and structured to cope with the market. In the maturity phase variety increases as a response to decreasing market growth in the main product lines, and the supply chain has to be adjusted accordingly. In the decline stage variety continues to increase as market segments scatter into micro markets while overall market size declines.

What this pattern implies is that agile entrepreneurial responsiveness is mostly needed in the first and last stages of the cycle. It is in these two stages that market opportunities are most readily captured. In the other two stages, particularly the second, lean efficiency and structured standardisation are more important to cope with growth and high volume in a relatively stable product/service proposition. Figure 7.9 displays this pattern of *reversed life-cycling.*

Agile practices have much to offer to this pattern of operational challenges. Such practices facilitate the mastering of uncertainty by managing product lifecycles as a loop. The 'loop' works between the identification of a market opportunity in phase 1, letting those opportunities develop, and than rapidly exploring the market for additional and new opportunities at an increasing pace. This means a particular focus on phases 1, 3 and 4 – from identification through constant adjustment to micro markets as a basis for identifying new opportunities.

The focus on these stages contributes to the third level of uncertainty, that of demand fluctuations. If micro markets and unique market opportunities become the main fluctuations, then shifts of demand can propel uncertainty sky-high. Simple swapping or reversing of the life cycle focus are then no longer sufficient. The product life cycle focus can be transformed to a consumer lifetime value approach. Ultimately, a market opportunity in micro markets boils down to indi-

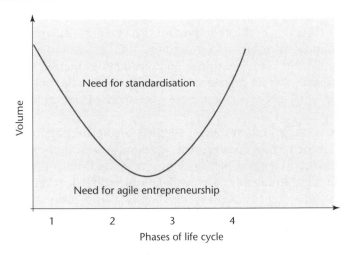

Figure 7.9 Reversed life cycling

vidual consumers. A solution to the uncertainty they create, as well as an opportunity to exploit it, is the concept of *prosuming*, the opposite of *consuming*. This means involving consumers proactively in supply chain design and in developing the product/service proposition. It involves asking consumers to specify their demand by selecting from options and constructing the most relevant response together. Information exchange and postponement are taken to higher levels. The consumer determines how sets of information will flow through the supply chain. Postponement becomes real consumer-driven postponement, potentially throughout the entire supply chain.

7.2.2 Benefiting from short time windows

With ever-decreasing time windows for product/service fulfilment, delivery reliability achieved through the mastering of uncertainty becomes another major concern. This can be experienced at three levels, each requiring different levels of agility:

- speed of replenishment;
- upstream time sensitivity;
- information dissemination and alignment.

The need for *speed* traditionally starts at the end of the supply chain, driven by end consumer demand. In Chapter 5 we referred to speed of response to customer demand as *D-time*. In a recent survey of distribution patterns it was found that the time sensitivity of shipments in outbound flows is nearly twice as great as it is for inbound flows. Time sensitivity at the end of the chain can be attributed to the urgent need of customers, which can sometimes be contributed to mall-planning of supplies. The solution to this can be helped by supplier-involved replenishment programmes such as vendor-managed inventory (Chapter 6). More important, however, is the urgent need for delivery given narrow windows of opportunity. Where customer demand is invisible upstream, rapid response to the end customer is limited to what can be done downstream. Vendor-managed inventory (VMI) and quick response are two examples – described in Chapter 6 – of such partial attempts at supply chain integration.

Cross-docking and in-transit merging are related approaches within distribution. When cross-docking, the warehouse is still in place in the delivery pipeline; the inventory just does not get stored, but only passes by and goes through rapid unloading, deconsolidation/reconsolidation and reloading. With in-transit merging the delivery pipeline is still in place as well, but individual shipments are grouped on the way to the point of delivery. An example of both types of approach is provided by the core depot operation of Marks and Spencer for boxed goods at Coventry in the UK, operated by Exel as third-party logistics provider. Suppliers are instructed daily to make up loads for each of the retail stores. Each box is labelled by bar code with product specification and store destination. Loads from each supplier are collected daily on a 'milk round' system and merged with those of other suppliers in the round. At the core depot in Coventry the boxes are unloaded from the trailers in two inbound bays, and are automatically routed to the correct outbound trailers. The outbound trailers are arranged in 24 outbound bays for destinations around the UK and (currently!) mainland Europe. The whole sortation process (the process of sorting products by destination) takes place with bar code readers and sortation equipment like baggage-handling equipment at an airport. Coventry is a *living warehouse* operation: no goods are stored between supplier and local distribution centre.

There are various reasons for extending rapid response upstream. For example, JIT and *kanban* approaches aim to align supply with production and ultimately with demand (see Chapter 6). These can be useful in case of resource scarcity or turbulent supply markets. Consider mobile telephones: both Ericsson and Philips have recently indicated that a drop in sales was caused by a shortage of parts, particularly microprocessors. Both companies were unable to supply sufficient products because of parts shortages. Capacity at SE Thompson, a microprocessor manufacturer, is booked for the next five years. Furthermore, rapid price fluctuations in parts pushed electronics manufacturers into delayed purchasing and local sourcing. Such actions help to avoid the necessity of shipping finished products through a lengthy pipeline while prices fluctuate rapidly.

These examples indicate how there can be separate reasons for upstream time sensitivity. Over-focus on ensuring supply, however, should not lead to an under-focus on the end consumer. And in more advanced upstream time-based approaches the customer order really works its way further upstream. Semi-postponement is no longer sufficient in these situations, and JIT is no more than semi-postponement. Fewer intermediate hold-ups and less consolidation/cross-docking and reconsolidation increase speed. Let us next consider the three-week fulfilment cycle in the Smart car supply chain.

The Smart car

Micro Compact Car AG (MCC), a Mercedes-Benz company, introduced a new vehicle concept, named Smart. The car is a so-called two-seater mini car (smaller than the Fiat 500), developed mainly for in-city use. Both the car itself and the processes needed for producing and distributing the car to the final customer are focused on increasing the responsiveness to customer demands as much as possible. In general, three stages in the supply chain are involved in actually achieving customisation.

First, the generic car is assembled in the plant at Hambach in Elzas-Lothringen, France (referred to as Smart Ville). The car is based on an integral body-frame (called Tridion) to which modules are attached/assembled. The car consists of five main modules: the platform, the powertrain, the doors and roof, the electronics, and the cockpit, containing submodules and components. The modules are supplied, in sequence for final assembly, by a small number of first-tier suppliers of which seven suppliers are fully integrated in the final assembly plant. These seven companies are located at the same site as MCC and supply 'supermodules' based on a postponed purchasing approach. Modules are bought by the OEM only when they are needed in the final assembly process (postponed purchasing). For example, a complete rear, including wheels, suspension and engine, is preassembled by one supplier which maintains the module in its possession until it is needed on the assembly line. The same is true for the doors and for the dashboard system. Together these seven suppliers deliver 50% of the total value of the purchased goods.

In order to maintain a smooth flow of goods within the plant, the car is moved along the work stations of the assembly line, which is laid out in the form of a cross (Figure 7.10). In this way, the integrated suppliers are able to supply their finished products directly to the final assembly line from their workshop in the factory. The effect of this enlarged role for the supermodule suppliers is that MCC is able to assemble the car in 4.5 hours. Apart from short lead times the benefit of the product design and flexible manufacturing system is that, at a module level parts can be combined into a wide variety of products.

Also, other activities traditionally considered to be core activities of manufacturers, such as the pressing of body-parts, the painting process, and even the coordination of internal logistics, are no longer performed by MCC. Not only is there a close participation of the suppliers in the final assembly of the car, but the suppliers are also strongly involved in the development, planning and launching of the product. What can be said about the outsourcing of components and modules manufacturing is also true for supporting services such as transportation, and it applies to ownership of the production buildings and site management.

As a second stage of the supply chain the distribution system is geared totally towards responding quickly to ever-changing customer needs. The car is sold at lifestyle centres located in shopping centres and other highly frequented places in urbanised areas. These franchise organisations use multimedia systems to enable clients to 'build' their car in the showroom, and to forward the order for the car to the distribution centres. The customer can thus be involved in the design process, and sales can become more consultative, based on a direct dialogue with individual customers. Within an order-to-delivery lead time of less than one day, five interregional distribution centres in Europe supply the dealer with the requested car. Some of the final assembly tasks, such as

▶

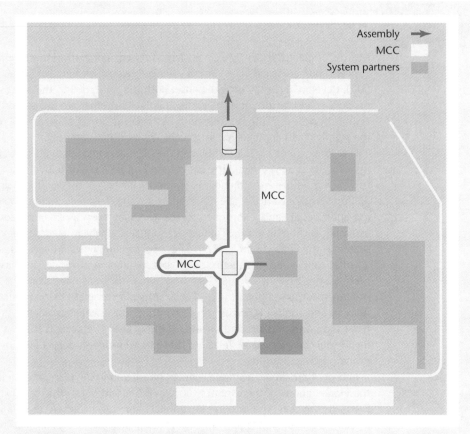

Figure 7.10 **Factory layout at Smart**

adding special features or light final assembly, are performed at these distribution centres. This is an example of postponed manufacturing. In order to perform final finishing, the distribution centre stores cars and changeable modules.

Finally, the modular concept of the car enables the customer to renew and upgrade the product completely during its lifetime, based on adding product-features and rapidly replacing body parts. As a result the car is more of a consumption product than a fixed capital good, and customers can be kept for life.

Question

How has SMART speeded up the process from customer order to customer receipt of the ordered vehicle?

A further impact of time sensitivity is that it not only works its way upstream, requiring channel adjustments, but also calls for dissemination and alignment of information flow through information decoupling. Time sensitivity does not just mean speed of information flow. It also means that the flow should take place accurately, and that fluctuations in response times required to link end consumers with the rest of the chain should be understood by all concerned. The dissemination takes place through information exchange throughout the supply chain, in which the information decoupling point actually penetrates deeper and wider into the supply chain. For example, information exchange formats can be shared – as can customer profiles and market intelligence. A free flow of information can to some extent be expected to harm competitive positions in supply chains. However, because the players in the chain are dependent on each other there is a further reason. The actual creation of market intelligence and information alignment is a competence in itself, whatever information is shared. A timely and accurate response to customer demand is developed in advance through superior information exchange. These approaches are in addition to the transactional information exchange that is often also practised in rapid replenishment approaches, where point of sale information triggers delivery (see for example vendor-managed inventory in Chapter 6).

7.2.3 Benefiting from small volumes

Small volumes are a result of micro markets, customisation and rapid responsiveness. They represent a threat under the traditional model, structured as it is around large batches, full container loads, standardisation and frozen production runs. There are three areas in which small volumes can be used within the dynamic contingency approach, which is leveraged to benefit from agile capabilities. These are: change over flexibility, modularity at the network level, and service- and information-based solutions.

Starting with the first area (changeover flexibility), techniques such as single-minute exchange of dies (SMED – see Chapter 6), flexible automation and milk run deliveries (where a supplier makes multiple deliveries from a single load) are among the well-known answers to a need for smaller volume outputs and fulfilment. They have proved their value from the JIT era and before, although it is still common among manufacturers to challenge their value in terms of economics of output. In reality this discussion is one between different mindsets. If the market value of small volumes is not important, tools such as these tend to have a lower priority

In the second area (modularity), smaller volumes approach the level of craft/one-piece production, requiring greater agility and mass customisation at the supply chain level. This requires modularity applied at the product and process level to be extended the supply chain level, as suggested in previous chapters. Even when it is difficult to modularise products or processes, supply chains can still be organised into distinct functional, geographical and organisational zones. The supply network coordinator can cherry-pick from such zones when needed from an end-consumer point of view. While elements or individual players in the network can achieve scale and standardisation by participating in multiple supply networks, the output of the individual supply network can be specifically tuned to a given micro market. Organising for supply networks involves:

- stipulating interfaces between elements;
- creating a shared coordination and information exchange infrastructure;

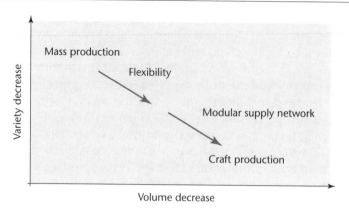

Figure 7.11 **Towards smaller volumes**

- building the portfolio of elements in response to market opportunities
- developing network relations with those market opportunities that are temporal and partial rather than exclusive, rigid and volume based.

On these grounds it is possible to avoid the trap of complete craft production without the sophistication and economics of modern supply chains (see Figure 7.11).

The third area, characterised by even lower volumes, demands attention to information flow as well as to material flow. The Batman case study 2.2 in Chapter 2 show how the service and information content of a product can be increasingly customised while the physical content remains unchanged. Services are customised around *mini projects*, each designed around a specific customer requirement. This can further increase the value proposition for small-volume products. Regarding information and knowledge content, it is well known that the average user of a word-processor uses only about 5% of its built-in features regularly. This means that the end consumer can benefit from many unique features, whereas the next end consumer can do so as well. They both apply the product for their specific requirements, even though the product is the same.

Figure 7.12 integrates the practices in one framework for moving forward with agility.

7.2.4 Conclusion

It is becoming increasingly apparent that competitive advantage derives from the combined capabilities of the network of linked organisations that we now know as the supply chain. This is a fundamental shift in the traditionally held view of a business model based upon a single firm. It has also become apparent that markets today are increasingly volatile and hence less predictable, and so the need for a more agile response is increasing. Putting these two ideas together leads us to the conclusion that a prerequisite for success in such markets will be the agile supply chain.

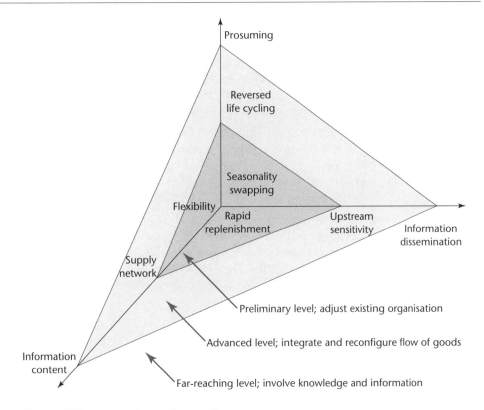

Figure 7.12 **Progressive agile practices**

What we have proposed in this chapter is a framework for agility that is contingent upon the context in which the business operates. Thus we have sought to bring together lean and agile mindsets, not just to highlight the differences but also to show how they might be combined for enhanced competitiveness. Increasingly, managers need to understand how market conditions and the wider operating environment will demand not a single off-the-shelf solution, but hybrid strategies that are context specific. In Chapter 9, we consider another key aspect of the agile supply chain – the virtual organisation.

Summary

What is agility, and how does it contribute to competitiveness of the supply network?

- Agility is a supply-chain-wide capability that aligns organisational structures, information systems, logistics processes and, in particular, mindsets. It means using market knowledge and a responsive supply chain to exploit profitable opportunities in a volatile marketplace. Agile supply is concerned with developing capabilities proactively to position a supply chain to benefit from marketplaces in which product life cycles are shrinking, product variety is increasing, and the ability to forecast demand is reducing.

- Lean thinking (Chapter 6) is concerned primarily with the elimination of waste. The order winners that are supported by this mindset are cost and quality. Agility is concerned primarily with supporting order winners of service levels and customer value. Time compression is a fundamental requirement for leanness, but only one of the enablers of agility.

- A key difference in supply strategy is that lean thinking is concerned with placing orders upstream for products that move in a regular flow. Agile strategy is concerned with assigning capacity so that products can be made rapidly to meet demand that is difficult to forecast.

- Three ways of merging lean and agile mindsets to improve overall competitiveness are the *Pareto* curve approach (to differentiate high-volume, low-variety products from low-volume, high-variety products); the decoupling point approach (to distinguish generic intermediates from customised final products), and the separation of base and surge demands (to focus supply chain processes accordingly).

- The integrated model for enabling the agile supply chain envisages a combination of postponed fulfilment and rapid replenishment at level 1 supported by level 2 programmes such as quick response and agile supply, and level 3 actions such as process management and cross-functional teams. Supply chain managers need to be change managers in order to handle the massive implications for management of change.

What are the agile practices that help to underpin the agile supply chain?

- First, to understand the sources and causes of uncertainty in demand, and to take steps to position the supply chain to benefit from this uncertainty. The easy option is high-volume, low-variety, low-demand uncertainty. The tough option is the opposite of all three. Agility seeks not only to eliminate the bullwhip effect (amplification of demand uncertainty upstream), but also to create capabilities for dealing with seasonality, stages in the product life cycle, and end customer demand uncertainty.

- Second, to develop capabilities for dealing with shrinking time windows for customer demand fulfilment. Speed of replenishment is usually much better downstream than upstream. Developing upstream time sensitivity is therefore a major enabler. And information dissemination and alignment bring capabilities of dealing with rapid and accurate response using supply-chain-wide dissemination and exchange.

- Third, to facilitate servicing the 'market segment of one' by investing in flexible processes, modularity at the product and process level, and capabilities to support the information and knowledge content of products and services.

Discussion questions

1 Suggest market-winning and market-qualifying criteria for the following product environments:

   a reprocessing nuclear fuel

   b upstream petroleum refining

   c downstream manufacture of petroleum products

   d high-value automotive products such as Land Rover Defender or BMW 5 series

   To what extent would lean and agile mindsets contribute to the support of such products in the marketplace?

2 Figure 7.13 shows a demand series for a high-volume grocery product with a comparatively stable demand. The vertical lines mark the end of each trading week, which is Sunday midnight.

   Suggest key features of this trading pattern. The retailer now wishes to implement two stock-replenishment 'waves' each day from the supplier: one in the morning (75% of volume) and the other in the afternoon (25% of volume). Previously, only one replenishment delivery was made per day. What are the potential benefits to the retailer, and what are the likely risks to the supplier?

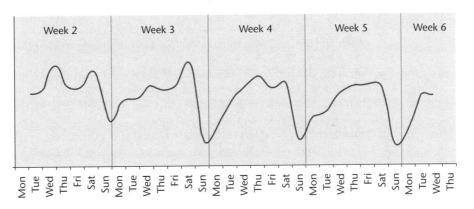

Figure 7.13 Demand series for a high-volume grocery product

3 Explain the difference between surge and base demands. Multi Electronique SA (ME) produces a range of electrical connectors for the automotive industry. Currently, the six production lines at its factory in Toulouse are fully loaded, operating a three-shift system for 5 days per week. One of ME's major customers wants to place an order that would add loading equivalent to a seventh production line, but only for the summer months (May to September). Sales are keen to accept the new order, but it would need to be taken at prices that are no higher than for current business. Suggest options for how ME might manage this order if they accepted it.

4 Refer back to Figure 2.2 in Chapter 2: it shows a Pareto curve for the sales per sku of a book stockist. A small number of 'hot sellers' constitute most of the sales, while there is a lengthy tail of slow-selling lines and new introductions. The operations people are pressing for the 'tail' to be chopped in half, arguing that it adds cost, not value, to the business. They argue that each order is taken at fixed cost, regardless of size. Sales order

processing and pick and dispatch from the warehouse are examples of such fixed costs. 'Instead, we should focus on the core of the business: 90% of our business comes from just 10% of the titles,' the operations director argues. 'We could chop our costs in half and only lose 5–7% of the business. Think of the effect on margin!' Sales, on the other hand, are reluctant to give up any of the titles, arguing that it is customer choice that drives the business. 'We have built up this business on the strength of our product range', the sales director argues. 'Retailers come to us because we are a one-stop shop. If we haven't got it in stock, we get it.' Explain the above in terms of a lean versus agile debate, using the concepts of market winners and qualifiers and benefiting from small volumes.

References

Aitken, J. (2000) Agility and leanness: a successful and complementary partnership in the lighting industry. *Proceedings LRN 2000 Conference*, pp. 1–7.

Christopher, M. (1998) *Logistics and Supply Chain Management: Strategies for reducing cost and improving service*, 2nd edn. London: Financial Times Pitman.

Christopher, M. and Towill, D.R. (2000) Supply chain migration from lean and functional to agile and customised. *International Journal of Supply Chain Management*, **5**(4), 206–13.

Feitzinger, E. and Lee, H.K. (1997) Mass customisation at Hewlett-Packard: the power of postponement. *Harvard Business Review*, Jan/Feb, 116–21.

Fisher, M. (1997) What is the right supply chain for your product? *Harvard Business Review*, March/April, 105–16.

Fisher, M., Obermeyer, W., Hammond, J. and Raman, A. (1994) Accurate response: the key to profiting from quick response. *Bobbin*, February, 48–63.

Harrison, A., Christopher, M. and van Hoek, R. (1999) *Creating the Agile Supply Chain*, Corby: Institute of Transport and Logistics.

Johansson, H.J., McHugh, P., Pendlebury, A.J. and Wheeler, W.A. (1993) *Business Process Reengineering: Breakpoint strategies for market dominance*. Chichester: John Wiley.

Kotzab, H. (2000) Managing the fast moving goods supply chain: does efficient customer response matter? *Proceedings of the Logistics Research Network Conference, Cardiff University*, pp. 336–42.

Magretta, J. (1998) Fast global and entrepreneurial: supply chain management Hong Kong style. *Harvard Business Review*, Sept/Oct, 102–14.

Mason-Jones, R., Naylor, B. and Towill, D.R. (1999) Agile, or leagile: matching your supply chain to the marketplace. In *Proceedings 15th International Conference on Production Research, Limerick*, pp. 593–6.

Nagel, R. and Dove, R. (1991) *21st Century Manufacturing Enterprise Strategy*. Lehigh University: Iacocca Institute.

Naylor, J.B., Naim, M.M. and Berry, D. (1999) Leagility: interfacing the lean and agile manufacturing paradigm in the total supply chain. *International Journal of Production Economics*, **62**, 107–18.

Towill, D.R. (1996) Time compression and supply chain management: a guided tour. *Supply Chain Management*, **1**(1), 15–27.

van Hoek, R. (1998) Reconfiguring the supply chain to implement postponed manufacturing. *International Journal of Logistics Management*, **9**(1), 95–110.

Warnecke, H.J. and Huser, M. (1995) Lean production. *International Journal of Production Economics*, **41**, 37–43.

Suggested further reading

Cusumano, M. and Nobeoka, K. (1998) *Thinking Beyond Lean*. New York: Free Press.
Goldman, S., Nagel, R. and Preiss, K. (1995) *Agile Competitors and Virtual Organisations*. New York: Van Nostrand Reinhold.

Part Three

SUPPLIER INTERFACES

In a supply network, no organisation stands on its own. While Part Two focused on the central logistics task of ensuring responsiveness to customer demand, most organisations cannot achieve this without the support of their suppliers. Complete vertical integration of industries has become a largely obsolete logistics strategy. Functional specialisation of suppliers on those parts of the value proposition in which they excel, coupled with integration into the supply network, is common wisdom nowadays.

This is becoming especially relevant as some manufacturing organisations, for example in the electronics and automotive industries, nowadays add only 10–20% of total added value internally. The rest is created in the supply base – by commodity suppliers, by co-designers and co-manufacturers, by main suppliers, and by partners. Chapter 8 offers approaches to collaboration and interaction in the supply chain, and Chapter 9 offers specific approaches to managing different types of relations and the supply base.

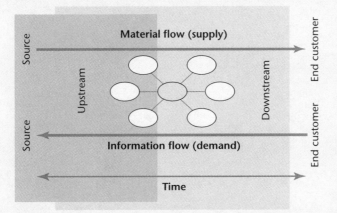

Managing the supply chain

The objectives of this chapter are to:

- explain the need for aligning processes and collaborating between organisations within supply chains;
- show how the management of supply chains can be leveraged by improving new product introductions, promotions, product ranges and replenishment;
- identify methods for implementing collaborative planning between supply chain members;
- develop a framework for managing the supply chain.

By the end of this chapter, you should be able to:

- understand the benefits of collaboration within supply chains;
- understand ways to improve responsiveness to the end customer;
- understand key aspects of managing the supply chain.

Introduction

Chapters 6, on lean thinking, and Chapter 7 on creating the agile supply chain, dealt with two ways of managing the supply chain. They show how supply chain processes can be prepared for better performance by eliminating the sources of waste. Cutting out waste in this way offers the opportunity to produce and deliver goods cheaper, faster, and with better quality. This chapter draws on these ideas and suggests a vision of *flow-through* logistics, whereby only the end customer is free to place an order whenever he or she wants. After that, the system takes over. Flow-through logistics offers the customer:

immediate availability of products at the point of sale

or

rapid configuration and delivery of customer-specified products.

The overall aim of this chapter is to show how the supply chain can be managed to maximise the opportunities of streamlined, waste-free processes to achieve superior customer service.

This chapter addresses five key issues:

1 **Collaboration in the supply chain:** the benefits of the internal collaboration and external collaboration.

2 **Efficient consumer response:** the total supply chain working together with an objective to fulfil the demands of the end consumer.

3 **Collaboration planning, forecasting and replenishment:** an approach to effective supply chain and organisational strategy.

4 **Managing supply chain relationships:** the objective of deeper, closer relationships in the supply chain and the factors for achieving them.

5 **A framework for managing the supply chain:** six building blocks to help managers to overcome obstacles and position organisations for supply chain success.

8.1 Collaboration in the supply chain

Key issue: **How can we collaborate internally, externally and electronically?**

What drives collaboration in the supply chain? It is the conviction that working together to meet end-customer demand beats arm's length relationships by a long way. As an illustration, the following are four principles of Procter & Gamble's supply chain strategy:

● Produce every product that needs to be produced every day through short cycle production

● Communicate with suppliers in real time – suppliers with whom we have built long term relationships

● Draw demand data from the point nearest to the customer – in this case, the retail cash register

● Let innovation and new technologies drive the implementation

The first three principles are about collaboration – both internal and external. The fourth principle is about using IT developments to enable even closer collaboration.

8.1.1 Internal collaboration: function to function

A recent survey of over 300 organisations in the United States revealed some interesting findings in terms of the collaboration between marketing and logistics functions within a firm (Stank, Daugherty and Ellington, 1999). More frequent collaborative behaviour between marketing and logistics resulted in better performance and better interdepartmental effectiveness. This may seem obvious, but the improvements in performance included cycle time reduction, better in-stock performance, increased product availability levels, and improvements in order-to-delivery lead times.

Firms with higher collaborative integration demonstrated higher relative logistics performance compared with less integrated firms. There was no difference between 'high' and 'low' integration firms on basic service: that is, consistent delivery on request data and advance notification of delays and shortages. However, on the 'higher value' service elements, such as delivery reliability, there was a significant difference. High-integration firms had greater performance in terms of meeting customer needs, accommodating special customer requests, and new product introductions. This resulted in an enhanced customer perception of the organisations.

The implications of this research are that organisations should continue to work at improving internal integration. For example, functional barriers between purchasing, manufacturing and distribution may lead to the following scenario:

- Purchasing buys castings on the basis of low price, but the supplier has a poor record for delivery reliability and quality. Manufacturing is faced with uncertain deliveries and high reject rates.

- Manufacturing aims to keep machine and labour productivity high, so batch sizes are kept high. Distribution is faced with poor availability, especially of class B and C parts.

- Distribution wants to maintain a fast throughput warehousing operation, so resists carrying out any post-manufacturing operations. Manufacturing is faced with the additional complexity of customising products.

Activity 8.1

1 Taking your business (or one well known to you) as example, how well do the internal functions collaborate?
2 Consider the purchasing–manufacturing–distribution example above and develop a scenario for the company, using the company's names for the functions concerned. What impact does your scenario have on material flow?

8.1.2 Intercompany collaboration: a manual approach

If significant improvements can be achieved by internal collaboration and integration, the potential for the benefits of external collaboration are potentially even higher. This was demonstrated by the Bose Corporation (a US-based manufacturer of hi-fi equipment) in the early 1990s when they developed the *JIT2* concept. Bose recognised that, if the traditional buyer–supplier relationship were to be made more effective, more people would be required in their organisation. However, budget constraints meant that no additional people could be employed in this role. This acted as a driver to develop the JIT2 concept.

A logical extension of the just-in-time concept described in Chapter 6 is to place customer and supplier processes closer together. The JIT2 approach goes a stage further by eliminating the buyer and the salesman from the customer–supplier relationship, thus fostering increased communication between the parties. The principle is simple: a supplier employee who resides full time in the customer's purchasing office replaces the buyer and supplier. This *supplier-in-plant* is empowered to use the customer's scheduling system to place orders with their own company. The supplier-in-plant also does the material planning for the materials supplied by his company.

The 'in-plant' is also part of the production planning process, so production is planned concurrently with the supplier organisation. This form of collaboration streamlines the supply process by removing the multi-level planner–buyer––salesman–supplier's plant process by making this the responsibility of one individual. This dramatically reduces the demand uncertainty experienced by the supplier organisations. The benefits of this streamlining have also resulted in major business improvements for Bose. These include:

- 50% improvement in terms of on-time deliveries, damage and shortages;
- 6% reduction in material costs;
- 26% improvement in equipment utilisation;
- major reductions in inventory holdings.

The Bose supplier-in-plant concept demonstrates how collaboration and integration can benefit the supply chain. The supplier-in-plant can, to a large degree, be superseded by today's electronic collaboration techniques.

Activity 8.2

1 What are the opportunities for the JIT2 supplier-in-plant principle in your chosen company?
2 Could the principle help to improve collaboration, either by a company representative working in the customer's organisation, or by representatives from major suppliers working in your chosen company?

8.1.3 Electronic collaboration

Much of the pioneering work for electronic collaboration has been in the fast-moving consumer goods (FMCG) business. Therefore, most of the leading examples have been developed by retailer–manufacturer collaboration. Trading partners can collaborate electronically in three ways: transactional, information sharing and collaborative planning.

Transactional: the electronic execution of transactions

This is usually found in business to business (B2B) e-commerce, with the trading partners focusing on the automation of business transactions such as purchase orders, invoices, order and advanced shipment notices, load tendering and acknowledgements, and freight invoices and payments. These transactions involve the electronic transmission of a fixed-format document with predefined data and information fields.

Information sharing: *the electronic sharing or exchange of information*

This occurs where trading partners are given access to a system that has shared information on it. Often, however, one partner transmits shared information to the other partner. The information is sent on a 'for your information' basis; the recipient uses the data as it stands, and no feedback is given. Shared information may include product descriptions and pricing, promotional calendars, inventory levels, shipment tracking and tracing. This type of arrangement only supports independent planning done by each partner. Uncertainty is reduced by each partner's becoming aware of the other partner's activities. However, trading partners do not have the opportunity to comment on or change the plan in any way.

Collaborative planning: *strategic, tactical and operational exchange*

Collaborative planning embraces electronic collaboration at all levels: strategic, tactical and operational. This is the most sophisticated form of electronic collaboration. It enables trading partners to work together to understand future demand better and to put plans in place to satisfy such demand profitably. The trading partners collaborate on new product planning, demand forecasting and replenishment planning, and work closely to align their organisations' plans.

The discussion on collaborative planning is developed later in section 8.3. Here, the concept of information sharing is developed by means of a case study in *quick response* (QR). Quick response logistics is a pioneering approach to using developments in IT to replenish demand quickly from the manufacturer. Using electronic point of sale (EPOS) data to track customer demand through the till, QR shares data from retailer to supplier. The aim is for the supplier to replace quickly what has been sold today, so that stock availability on the shelf is maintained at the retailer. Case study 8.1 gives an example.

CASE STUDY 8.1   ## Quick response at Cott

The easy way to achieve quick response logistics is for the supplier to set up buffer stocks between itself and the retailer, so that demand can be met out of stock. A much more challenging way is to supply out of manufacturing. Here, the advantages are that only the current demand is made: thus, the prize is greater freshness and less obsolescence (stock write-off due to expiry of shelf life), more accurate demand fulfilment (fewer lost sales due to out-of-stock situations), and lower inventories.

Cott, the Canadian-owned maker of many own-brand cola-based soft drinks, set out to achieve at least a partial solution to the 'supply out of manufacturing' challenge. Figure 8.1 shows how. At the far left, the consumer purchases cans of cola at the customer's retail store, and creates a total EPOS demand for day 1 for each Cott stock-keeping unit (sku). The customer (Asda in this case) makes the day 1 demand available to Cott on the Internet, and Cott downloads these data at the start of day 2. If more production is needed to meet this demand (and there should be unless demand has   ▶

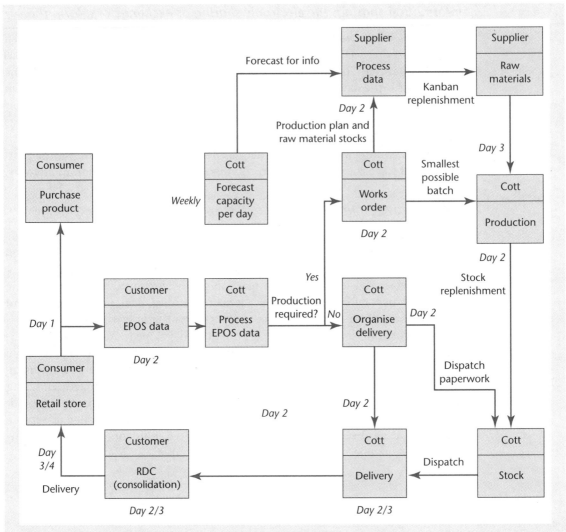

Figure 8.1 Integrating the supply chain
(Source: Steve Walker, Cott)

recently plummeted), a fresh works order is raised by Cott. This is one of the innovations that was introduced: the works order specifies only the minimum batch quantity needed to meet demand. Instead of fixed batch quantities Cott is prepared to accept batch quantities that are not 'economic' in manufacturing terms. This means more changeovers and greater manufacturing costs. Cott's packaging and raw material suppliers are scheduled on a weekly forecasting system using the more up-to-date EPOS demand data.

By the end of day 2 the new works order has been produced and packed. It is dispatched from Cott and transported to Asda's regional distribution centre (RDC). A further day or so is needed for the new production to make its way through the RDC and into the store.

Modelling the effect of the new system helped to justify the additional costs needed

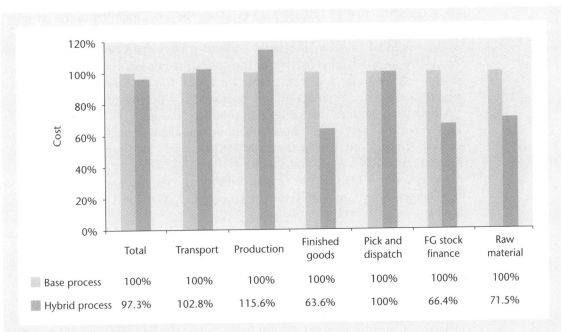

Figure 8.2 The effect on costs

in some areas of the supply chain. Figure 8.2 compares 'before' (light blue columns, 100% of former values) with 'after' (dark blue columns). While transport and manufacturing costs have increased, stocks of finished goods and raw materials have reduced, leading to an overall cost saving. Further, product availability in Asda stores has improved from below 90% to around 98%.

Questions

1 List the strengths and weaknesses of the Cott quick response system according to the above account.

2 Cott reduced the number of sku's by more than 30% prior to introducing the above system. Why do you think they did this, and what are the implications for marketing strategy? What could Cott do in future to re-extend the range?

8.2 Efficient consumer response

Key issue: **How can collaboration be extended across the supply chain to focus on meeting consumer demand?**

Established as a grocery industry initiative, *efficient consumer response* (ECR) is designed to integrate and rationalise product assortment, promotion, new product development and replenishment across the supply chain. It aims to fulfil the changing demands and requirements of the end customer through effective collaboration across all supply chain members, in order to enhance the effectiveness of merchandising efforts, inventory flow and supply chain administration.

The origin of ECR can be traced back to work carried out by Kurt Salmon Associates (in the United States) for the apparel sector (Salmon, 1993) and, later, the grocery sector (Fernie, 1998). Since then, ECR has increased industrial awareness of the growing problem of non-value-added supply chain costs.

Originating within the consumer products industry, ECR emerged partly because of the increased competition from new retail formats entering the traditional grocery industry in the early 1990s, as well as through the joint initiatives between Wal-Mart and Procter & Gamble. In Europe, ECR programmes commenced in 1993 with the commissioning of a series of projects, for example the Coopers & Lybrand survey of the grocery supply chain (Coopers & Lybrand, 1996).

The focus of ECR is to integrate supply chain management with demand management. This requires supplier–retailer collaboration – but in spite of the apparent emphasis on the end consumer, a lot of the early ECR studies focused on the supply side. Subsequent increased focus on demand and category management, however, has led to the adoption of a more holistic view of the supply chain when discussing ECR initiatives. In addition, ECR has also stimulated collaborative efforts that have increased companies' emphasis on key areas such as EDI, cross-docking (see Chapter 7 section 7.2) and continuous replenishment.

Other examples of studies of ECR initiatives include the Coca-Cola survey evaluating supply chain collaboration within 127 European companies; PE International's 1997 survey, and IGD's 1997 report (Boitoult, 1997). Generally, ECR initiatives aim to promote greater collaboration between manufacturers and retailers. Effective logistics strategies as well as administrative and information technology are essential for its successful implementation. These required techniques are available within most organisations, but the main problem facing most organisations is ensuring that people use these existing tools differently in order to secure or achieve their maximum potential.

The main focus areas addressed under ECR initiatives are category management, product replenishment and enabling technologies. These can be broken down into 14 areas where individual as well as well-integrated improvements can be made in order to enhance efficiency (see Figure 8.3).

8.2.1 Category management

As demand management principles have become more important to supply chain initiatives, the category management process has increased in popularity. With an objective of preventing stockout situations and improving supplier–retailer relations, category management aims to balance retailers' product volume and variety objectives. Activities included in the category management process include the capture and utilisation of knowledge of the drivers behind consumer attitudes and choices.

By focusing on category management and measuring promotional efficiency, ECR enables organisations to utilise their joint resources to reduce supply chain

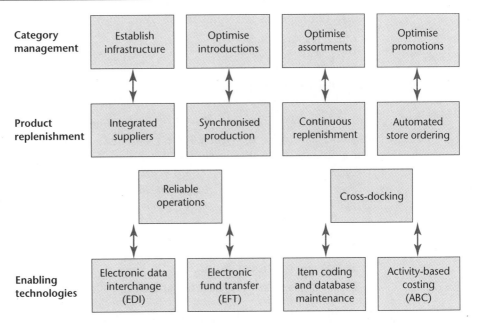

Figure 8.3 ECR improvement categories
(Source: Fernie, 1998: 30)

inventory levels, streamline product flows, and utilise cross-dock options where appropriate. Thus category management represents a focus on the development of at least some of the following capabilities:

● account management;
● demand management;
● multifunctional selling teams;
● price list restructuring;
● effective and customised promotions.

8.2.2 Product replenishment

Continuous product replenishment offers both retailers and their suppliers the opportunity to manage their inventory in a more efficient manner (Mitchell, 1997; PE International, 1997). Each of the six stages that make up the product replenishment process (illustrated in Figure 8.3) represents a link that integrates the supply chain from product suppliers right through to end consumers. In addition, effective replenishment strategies require the development of the following capabilities:

● joint inventory management;
● cross-dock operations;
● continuous replenishment;

- effective logistics strategies and product flows;
- quick response.

8.2.3 Enabling technologies

These drive ECR and make it work. They include scanning data, data warehousing and data mining, which have facilitated our understanding of customer requirements. Examples include EDI, which is increasingly about synchronising trading data among supply chain partners in advance of doing business as it allows the transmission of forecasting data back up through the supply chain. Other capabilities required by organisations in order to implement an effective ECR initiative include:

- effective information sharing;
- automated order generation;
- bar coding and the use of other scanning technology.

In addition, the data to be shared and communicated at various stages in the supply chain depend on what will provide the most overall benefit. These data should include:

- demand/consumption/sales information;
- cash flow;
- stocks of finished goods/work in progress;
- delivery and output status.

However, many of the problems in sharing and using these data and implementing EDI networks are related to difficulties in achieving a critical mass of companies sufficient to generate substantial benefits.

CASE STUDY 8.2

ECR in the UK

Dutchman Paul Polman did a stint as General Manager of Procter & Gamble UK and Eire from 1995 to 1999. While admiring the UK's advanced retailing systems, he saw opportunities for all four of the 'pillars of ECR' – range, new items, promotions and replenishment. The following is extracted from the text of a speech he made to the Institute of Grocery Distribution.

Range

The average store now holds 17 000 sku's – that's 35% more than 5 years ago, yet a typical consumer buys just 18 on a trip. A quarter of these sku's sell less than 6 units a week! The number of sku's offered by manufacturers and stores has become too large and complex. My company is equally guilty in this area. No question, we make too many sku's. I can assure you we are working on it. Actually, our overall sku count in laundry is already down 20% compared to this time last year. What's more, business is up. Clearly, we have an opportunity to rationalise our ranges. As long as we do this in an ECR way – focusing on what consumers want – we will all win. The consumer will see a clearer range. Retailers and manufacturers will carry less inventory and less complexity. The result will be cost savings across the whole supply chain and stronger margins.

New items

There were 16 000 new sku's last year. Yet 80% lasted less than a year. You don't need to be an accountant to imagine the costs associated with this kind of activity. And look how this has changed. Since 1975, the number of new sku introductions has increased eightfold. Yet their life expectancy has shrunk from around 5 years in 1975 to about 9 months now. We can hardly call this progress.

Promotions

In promotions it's the same story. Take laundry detergents. This is a fairly stable market. Yet we're spending 50% more on promotions than 2 years ago, with consumers buying nearly 30% more of their volume on promotions. This not only creates an inefficient supply chain, or in some cases poor in-store availability, but, more importantly, has reduced the value of the category and likely the retailers' profit. We're all aware of the inefficiencies promotions cause in the system, such as problems in production, inventory and in-store availability. They all create extra costs, which ultimately have to be recouped in price. But there's a higher cost. As promotions are increasing, they are *decreasing* customer loyalty to both stores and brands by 16% during the period of the promotion. We commissioned a report by Professor Barwise of the London Business School. He called it *Taming the Multi-buy Dragon*. The report shows us that over 70% of Laundry promotional investment goes on multi-buys. The level of investment on multi-buys has increased by 60% over the last 3 years. There's been a 50% increase behind brands and a doubling of investment behind own labels. Contrary to what we thought, most of this volume is not going to a broad base of households. It is going to a small minority. 71% of all multi-buy volume is bought by just 14% of households. Just 2% of multi-buy volume goes to 55% of households. We really are focusing our spending on influencing and rewarding a very small minority of people indeed.

Replenishment

Based on the escalating activity I've just [referred to], costs are unnecessarily high. There are huge cost savings also here, up to 6%, by removing the non-value-added sku's and inefficient new brand and promotional activity

Questions

1 Cutting down on range, new items and promotions is presumably going to lead to 'everyday low prices'. Is this lean thinking by another name?

2 Procter & Gamble's major laundry brand in the US is Tide. This is marketed in some 60 pack presentations, some of which have less than 0.1% share. The proliferation of these pack presentations is considered to have been instrumental in increasing Tide's market share from 20% to 40% of the US market in the last 5 years. Clearly, this is a major issue within P&G. What are the logistics pros and cons of sku proliferation?

8.3 Collaborative planning, forecasting and replenishment

Key issue: How can collaboration be extended to strategic as to well as operational levels?

Collaborative planning, forecasting and replenishment (CPFR) is aimed at improving collaboration between buyer and supplier so that customer service is improved while inventory management is made more efficient. The trade-off between customer service and inventory is thereby altered.

The CPFR movement originated in 1995. It was the initiative of five companies: Wal-Mart, Warner-Lambert, Benchmarking Partners, and two software companies, SAP and Manugistics. The goal was to develop a business model to collaboratively forecast and replenish inventory. An initial pilot was tested between Wal-Mart and Warner Lambert using the Listerine mouthwash product and focusing on stocks kept in the retail outlets. The concept and process was tested initially by exchanging pieces of paper. This generated clear visibility of the process required and the requirements for the IT specification. The two companies later demonstrated in a computer laboratory that the Internet could be used as a channel for this information exchange.

In 1998 the Voluntary Inter-industry Commerce Standards Committee (VICS) became involved in the movement, which enabled it to make major strides forward. VICS was formed in 1986 to develop bar code and electronic data interchange standards for the retail industry. The involvement of VICS meant that other organisations could participate in the validation and testing of the CPFR concept. With VICS support, organisations including Procter & Gamble, Kmart and Kimberly Clark undertook pilots to test the idea of sharing information to improve inventory handling. One of the early pilots is described in case study 8.3.

CASE STUDY 8.3	CPFR development at Wegman's and Nabisco

Wegman's Food markets and the US Food Group division of Nabisco launched a 13-week CPFR pilot in July 1998. Before the trial, the supply chain was characterised by poor communication and poor customer service.

The pilot began (see Figure 8.4) with the formation of teams to create a joint business plan for a snack category, and the business processes to share forecasts, sales and promotional data. The two companies shared quarterly forecast data on 22 items. The sales force at Nabisco would develop a forecast for these items; this was then compared electronically with Wegman's own forecasts for its stores. If a major variance occurred between these two forecasts, the software used would send an e-mail to alert both parties, who would then discuss the issue and rectify the problem. The parties also monitored execution against plan. The trial resulted in sales growth in the pilot category of

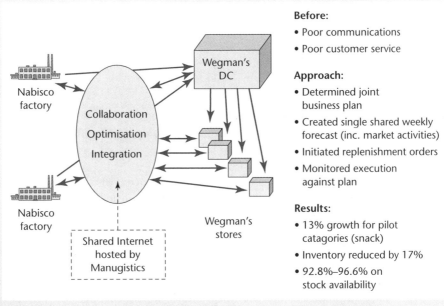

Before:
- Poor communications
- Poor customer service

Approach:
- Determined joint business plan
- Created single shared weekly forecast (inc. market activities)
- Initiated replenishment orders
- Monitored execution against plan

Results:
- 13% growth for pilot catagories (snack)
- Inventory reduced by 17%
- 92.8%–96.6% on stock availability

Figure 8.4 Nabisco and Wegman CPFR pilot

47%, improved warehouse service levels, and a reduction of inventory of 17% within the supply chain. The trial also revealed that enhancements in the software application were needed to improve the reliability of the data exchange over the Internet. The correction of these problems is today nearing completion.

(Source: Adapted from Doherty, 1998)

In Autumn 1999 VICS published a tutorial for CPFR implementation. This is available in hardcopy, or can be accessed on its web site at www.cpfr.org. This 'road map' offers organisations a structured approach to CPFR implementation based on the experiences of the companies involved in the CPFR pilots.

Having shown that the CPFR concept can have bottom-line impact on their businesses, companies are looking to expand the programmes from the handful of items involved in the pilots to the hundreds or thousands of items covered in most trading relationships. This has been a challenge for all organisations, including the software providers, for whom a major focus has been to ensure that software is scaleable: that is, that there are no barriers to the number of organisations and products involved in the CPFR network.

When implementing CPFR, a significant amount of time and effort is required up front to negotiate specific items such as goals and objectives, frequency of updates to plan, exception criteria and key performance measures. The result is a published document defining the relevant issues for each organisation that has been jointly developed and agreed.

A nine-step business model has been developed that provides an insight into the effort required by both supplier and customer. The model is as follows:

1 Develop front-end agreement.

2 Create joint business plans.

3 Create individual sales forecasts.

4 Identify exceptions to sales forecasts.

5 Resolve/collaborate on exception items.

6 Create order forecast.

7 Identify exceptions to order forecast.

8 Resolve/collaborate on exception items.

9 Generate orders.

In summary, CPFR focuses on the process of forecasting supply and demand by bringing various plans and projections from both the supplier and the customer into synchronisation. CPFR requires extensive support in the form of Internet-based products, which can result in major changes to the key business processes. An academic survey of the success of CPFR (Oliviera and Barratt, 2001) found a significant correlation between companies with high information systems capabilities and the success of CPFR projects. The firms with high levels of CPFR implementation use information systems capable of providing timely, accurate, user-friendly and inter-functional information in real time.

8.3.1 Benefits of electronic collaboration

Nestlé UK states that the benefits of collaborative systems are significant, and lists the following benefits:

- There is improved availability of product to the consumer, and hence more sales.

- Total service is improved, total costs are reduced (including inventory, waste and resources), and capacities can be reduced owing the reductions in uncertainty achieved.

- Processes that span two or more companies become far more integrated and hence simple, standard, speedy and certain.

- Information is communicated quickly, in a more structured way, and is transparent across the supply chain to all authorised users. All users know where to find up-to-date information.

- An audit trail can be provided to say when information was amended.

- E-mail prompts can update users of variance and progress, and can confirm authorisations.

- The data that are in the system can be used for monitoring and evaluation purposes.

- The process can be completed in a quick timescale, at a lower total cost.

- All trading partners become more committed to the shared plans and objectives. Changes are made with more care, and are immediately visible to all.

Many of these benefits are being experience by those implementing the CPFR philosophy. Wal-Mart and Sara Lee experienced sales increases of 45% and a decline in weeks-on-hand inventory of 23%. The benefits experienced by Procter & Gamble and its retail partners include a reduction in replenishment cycle time of 20%. The increased visibility of the supply chain resulted in a reduction of in-store availability from 99% to 88% being detected with sufficient lead time to respond. This saved 3 to 4 days of stockouts for the retailer. Forecast accuracy improvements of 20% have also been experienced.

8.4 Managing supply chain relationships

Key issue: How can broader-based relationships be formed between trading partners in the supply chain?

8.4.1 Creating closer relationships

The traditional supplier–customer relationship has been limited to contact primarily between the customer's buyer and the supplier's salesperson. Other functions, such as information systems, are kept very much at arm's length. Indeed, the customer's buyer argues that dealings with the supplier should only go through him or her: in that way, they ensure that sensitive communications such as those affecting price, are limited to a single channel.

This traditional style of relationship ('bow tie') is contrasted with the multiple-contact model ('diamond') proposed in Figure 8.5. Here, contacts between different functions are positively encouraged, and the arm's length relationship is replaced of active relationship management and supplier development processes. This is exemplified by the remarkable changes in the supplier portfolio at the UK High Street retailer BhS. In the early 1990s BhS had over 1000 suppliers. Now it has just 50. But the nature of the relationship with the 50 is quite different. There

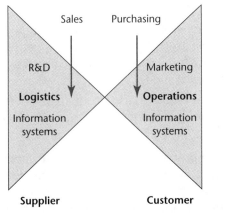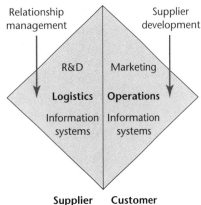

Figure 8.5 Creating closer relationships

are now multilevel connections between the supply chain players, and a high level of electronic collaboration. There is also a much greater involvement by the remaining 50 suppliers in high-level strategy development at BhS.

However attractive such processes of bonding may appear, in practice the organisational boundaries and vested interests inhibit the rate at which relationships deepen. These have been described as a series of factors as a result of research in the auto industry.

8.4.2 Factors in forming supply chain relationships

Lamming (1993) proposed nine factors for analysing customer–supplier relationships, which have been modified and extended below:

- *What the market winners are*: For example, price, product range, technology advantage, superior product quality.

- *How sourcing decisions are made*: Is it, for example, competitive tender, auctions, supplier accreditation, and sole source?

- *The nature of electronic collaboration*: Is it transactional, information sharing or collaborative?

- *The attitude to capacity planning*: Is this seen as the supplier's problem, as a problem for the buyer (tactical make/buy/additional sources), or as a shared strategic issue?

- *Call-off requirements*: Does the customer (for example) alter schedules with no notice, require JIT delivery against specified time windows, or require synchronised deliveries of major subassemblies to the point of use?

- *Price negotiations*: Are price reductions imposed by the buyer subject to game playing by both parties, the result of joint continuous improvement projects, etc.?

- *Managing product quality*: Does the customer help the supplier to improve process capability? Are aggressive targets (e.g. 50 ppm defects) set by the customer? Is the supplier responsible for quality of incoming goods and warranty of the parts in service?

- *Managing research and development*: Does the customer impose new designs and have the supplier follow instructions? Does the supplier become involved in new product development? Is the supplier expected to design and develop the complete product for the next model?

- *The level of pressure*: How far does the customer place pressure for improvement on the supplier to avoid complacency (e.g. 30% price reduction in the next 2 years)?

Within the European auto industry at present, the most significant factor seems to be the last. Over-capacity among the assemblers has created massive pressures for cost reduction. The supply chain accounts for 70–80% of an assembler's costs, so this is the primary target. While long-term mutually beneficial relationships are often talked about, the reality can be very different!

Select an industry of your choice and, within this, review the nine factors listed in section 8.4.2. How would you classify the state of supply chain relationships in this industry?

8.5 A framework for managing the supply chain

Key issue: **What are the management implications of logistic supply chain strategies?**

The supply chain is the conduit for getting products from source to ultimate customer. As a result, it is affected by almost every function within the organisations that it comprises. If managed effectively, the supply chain provides one of the greatest opportunities for improving customer satisfaction, and a major source of competitive advantage.

If we examine the above statement further, it is obvious that we need to manage the supply chain more strategically and holistically than ever before. The management of the supply chain requires an approach that is driven by the organisation's objectives, and combines strategy, people, processes and systems. To further develop our understanding of how to manage the supply chain more effectively, and to realise the opportunities that effective supply chain management can offer, here are six key building blocks (see Figure 8.6) that help in understanding how supply chains can be managed.

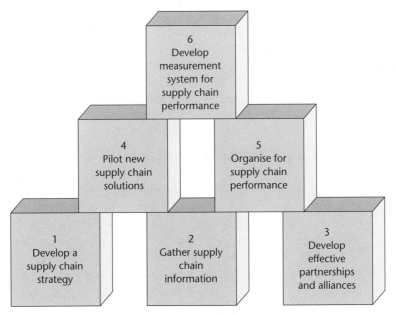

Figure 8.6 Six building blocks for effective SCM
(Source: Adapted from Derocher and Kilpatrick, 2000)

8.5.1 Develop a supply chain strategy

The development of a formal supply chain strategy is a critical step to undertake for every organisation. Failure to do so will mean that the significant resources committed (capital, time and people) will be wasted, and the potential benefits of supply chain management will never be realised.

Not only is a supply chain strategy critical for success, it also provides a framework for defining and prioritising initiative for business process redesign, systems enhancements and organisational restructuring. Many organisations deploy numerous projects aimed at becoming more customer focused and efficient, but in most cases without fully understanding their customers' service expectations. The outcome of this is that the projects simply become cost-cutting exercises that rarely deliver the expected benefits.

What constitutes a comprehensive supply chain strategy? The following elements must be incorporated:

● customer service requirements;

● plant and distribution centre network design;

● inventory management;

● outsourcing and third-party logistics relationships;

● business processes;

● organisational design and training requirements;

● performance metrics and goals.

If the supply chain strategy is to be effective, then it must be linked with the overall business strategy, effectively aligning the supply chain to fulfil the vision for delivering value to the customer.

Having developed the supply chain strategy, the next step is to translate this into a tactical plan, which can be used to traverse the gap between the existing supply chain capabilities and those capabilities required to support the business's future direction. This tactical plan identifies and prioritises the business and system initiatives needed to serve the customer more effectively.

8.5.2 Gather supply chain information

If the organisation is to make effective supply chain decisions, then it needs to ensure that there is an accurate, timely flow of information across the supply chain as a whole. If companies are to achieve this, they need to ensure that they have a set of systems that are capable of viewing the entire supply chain process. This would include everything from supplier inventory positioning through levels of true customer demand to delivery modes.

Organisations have counted on *enterprise resource planning* (ERP) systems to facilitate the flow of information across their organisation. Many organisations have gone through considerable 'implementation pain' with their ERP systems, which has generated significant cynicism and disaffection with systems in general. To make the broader-based decisions demanded by SCM, organisations require a capability that extends far beyond the scope of ERP systems alone.

Some organisations have already made this leap of faith and are implementing claimed 'supply-chain-wide solutions', such as those offered by software vendors such as Manugistics and i2. These pioneers are reporting significant early benefits, but as the scope of the solutions spreads across the entire supply chain these benefits are likely to grow further still.

8.5.3 Develop effective partnerships and alliances

There is a growing recognition that organisations on their own cannot maintain all the necessary capabilities required to succeed in the highly competitive environments in which they compete. It has become recognised that it is supply chains that compete, rather than individual companies. To do this effectively the organisation must be able to develop alliances, partnerships and joint ventures with its suppliers and customers, and possibly even with some of its competitors. It is by this extension of the supply chain that better decisions are made possible, in terms of procurement, production, inventory and fulfilment.

When organisations seek to manage the extended supply chain, they run into an initial problem. Despite all the readily apparent benefits of partnering, suppliers and customers are not always ready to collaborate. This reluctance arises from the fact that some organisations are unable to establish relationships that serve the business objectives of both parties. Another problem is that such relationships take a considerable amount of time to develop and nurture.

A further major barrier to such a collaborative approach is that, while organisations readily seek improved business performance, they shy away from sharing information and risk. Such an attitude will simply prevent those organisations from ever becoming the leading companies in their chosen markets. For every link in the supply chain, the relationships between the two organisations that form that link must be as strong as possible. Processes must be aligned and systems integrated to allow the fast and accurate flow of products and information.

Relationships may probably not be formed with all suppliers and customers. Only key suppliers and customers will be chosen for this approach. It would not be possible to develop close relationships with all suppliers and customers, owing to the time and resources required. With the advent of the Internet as a means of sharing information across the supply chain quickly and cheaply, the appropriate levels of relationships must be in place.

8.5.4 Pilot new supply chain solutions

Most organisations tend to be bastions of conservatism when it comes to supply chain innovation: they perceive a significant risk attached to being seen as leading edge or first movers into a new market. The risk of possible mishaps and potential harm to existing relationships is enough for most short-term-thinking managers not to get involved with new projects. Organisations need to recognise the importance of pilot projects within the change management process. Piloting initiatives on a small scale reduces risk, and can encourage buy-in from others within the organisation or supply chain.

Real breakthroughs in supply chain management have come about only when organisations are prepared to question the status quo and participate in a number of projects that appear on the surface to be leaps of faith.

The smart companies will be the ones that implement a number of small, relatively risk-free (if not at least greatly reduced in terms of risk) pilot projects, to test their ideas prior to a broader roll-out if successful. The projects that do fail will be seen as learning experiences, so that similar mistakes are not repeated. Another reason for the pilot projects is that in today's highly competitive environment supply chains that do not function properly will not survive long. Pilot projects help in the fine tuning of supply chain solutions before they are rolled out. New processes are perfect candidates for pilot projects, so as to avoid damaging customer relationships while new processes are implemented on a broad scale.

Successful supply chain improvements may arise from including all the following elements in any such pilot projects:

- Involvement of key stakeholders, suppliers, customers and employees.
- Selection of scope and environment: which site, business, group of items, or customers should be host to the pilot? This activity should focus on avoiding risk whilst ensuring exposure to a wide range of business scenarios.
- Identification of the key questions that the pilot must answer: what are the critical success factors?

It becomes critical to measure the results of pilot projects carefully. This should ensure that the expected benefits are achieved and any adjustments are made before rolling out the project more broadly across the organisation.

8.5.5 Organise for supply chain performance

If we look at most organisational structures we shall see that a clear majority of the organisations have one thing in common: functionally based structures that run counter to the seamless efficiency demanded of today's supply chain. These organisational structures lack cross-functional objectives, and do not support teamwork. Each of the functional areas (such as procurement, production planning and accounts payable) can undermine overall supply chain effectiveness, as each seeks and is motivated to focus on its own success. This is a critical weakness of the functional structure, as one decision may be right for a functional area, but detrimental to the supply chain as a whole. Along with the myriad of corporate initiatives ongoing in most if not all organisations, the implementation of business process changes becomes extremely difficult if not sometimes impossible.

A skill shortage in terms of being able to manage the flow of materials, information and funds across the supply chain is another major weakness common in most organisations. Many supply chain managers lack strategic planning skills and financial literacy. The outcome of this is that most supply chain initiative are purely cost focused. Few organisations adopt a value-based perspective, one in which the impact of the initiative on revenues, costs, investments, and cash flows – the drivers of shareholder value – is considered. If supply chain performance is to improve, then organisational change seems to be the obvious answer.

8.5.6 Develop measurement systems for supply chain performance

The complexity of supply chains has increased significantly in recent years. At the same time technology has created a change in the ways in which companies can plan, synchronise and execute their supply chain plans. However, many companies have not adapted their performance measurement regimes to align them on supply chain performance. Traditional performance measurements within the organisation have a number of significant deficiencies. They are often function focused, tracking individual activities: this can promote the optimisation of the function rather than of the complete supply chain system.

A survey of supply chain measures by the management consultants Arthur D. Little found that 64% of companies were focused on procurement measures, 27% on order fulfilment measures, and only 9% on systems that spanned the complete breadth of the supply chain.

There is a clear need for cross-supply chain measures. As a general rule, effective measures should have the following characteristics.

- simple to understand;
- no more than 10 in total number;
- representative of a significant causal relationship;
- have an associated target;
- capable of being shared across the supply chain.

Relatively few measures are needed to cover the supply chain. The following have been found to be useful in most situations, and can be adapted to focus on issues experienced in specific industries:

- *on time in full, outbound*: a measure of customer orders fulfilled, complete and on time, conforming to specification;
- *on time in full, inbound*: a measure of supplier deliveries received, complete and on time, conforming to specification;
- *internal defect rates*: a measure of process conformance and control (rather than inspection);
- *new product introduction rate*: a measure of supply chain product responsiveness;
- *cost reduction*: a measure of sustainable product and process development;
- *stock turns*: a measure of supply chain goods flow (this measure is useful only when applied to specific products and their supply chains);

- *order to delivery lead time*: a measure of supply chain process responsiveness;
- *fiscal flexibility*: a measure of how easy it is to structure the supply chain for financial advantage (with international supply chains, channelling operations through low-tax locations for purposes of gaining supply chain cost benefits should be considered).

The main benefits of these measures are that they are applicable to all levels in the supply chain, and they can increase visibility and control for all players.

Activity 8.4

1 Using the six building blocks identified for effective supply chain performance, undertake an audit for any organisation of your choice.
2 How does your selected organisation address each building block?
3 Describe activities that can be undertaken to improve the way the organisation undertakes the six building blocks.

Summary

What are the benefits of collaboration in the supply chain?

- Collaboration within the organisation leads to improved results according to a recent US survey. More frequent collaboration between marketing and logistics results in better performance in areas such as cycle times, inventories, product availability, and order-to-delivery lead times.
- Benefits of electronic collaboration listed by Nestlé UK include improved availability of product to the consumer, and hence more sales. The total service is improved, total costs are reduced (including inventory, waste and resources), and capacities can be reduced owing to the reductions in uncertainty achieved. In addition, processes that span two or more companies become far more integrated and hence simple, standard, speedy and certain. Trading partners become more committed to the shared plans and objectives.
- Replacement of the single point of contact (bow-tie relationship) by the multiple-contact model (diamond relationship) suggests an arm's length process being replaced by a broad-based, cross-functional process. In spite of such ideals, research in the auto industry indicates that massive downward cost pressures on suppliers limit the progress at which relationships deepen.

How can collaboration be put into practice?

- JIT2 aims to achieve inter-company collaboration manually by placing customer and supplier together as supplier-in-plant.
- Electronic collaboration can be undertaken in three ways: transactional (the transmission of fixed-format documents with predefined data and information fields); information sharing (a one-way process of providing access to infor-

mation such as product description and pricing, sales information, inventory and promotional calendars); and collaborative planning (electronic collaboration at strategic, operational and tactical levels).

- Efficient consumer response (ECR) aims to integrate and rationalise product range, new product introductions, promotions, and replenishment across the supply chain. It is an industry-wide initiative that has many followers in retailing and manufacturing of fast-moving consumer goods across Europe and the US. ECR seek to operationalise its aims by means of category management, product replenishment and enabling technologies.

- Collaborative planning, forecasting and replenishment (CPFR) is aimed at 'making inventory management more efficient and cost-effective, while improving customer service and leveraging technology to significantly improve profitability'. CPFR focuses on the process of forecasting supply and demand by synchronising the plans and projections of both the supplier and customer. Replenishment of needed products is then more accurate and timely.

Discussion questions

1 What is the purpose of collaboration in the supply chain, and why should it lead to value added from the customer perspective?

2 In both the Cott and Procter & Gamble case studies, the advice is to cut down on the number of sku's on offer in order to improve replenishment. Is this collaboration or defeatism?

3 Compare and contrast the aims of ECR and CPFR. Is CPFR a more advanced set of logistics concepts?

4 'You can talk collaboration as much as you like: at the end of the day, it's a raw struggle for power, and the retailers are winning hands down.' Discuss the relative merits of the factors in forming supply chain relationships (section 8.4) from both the suppliers' (manufacturers) and retailers' viewpoints.

5 Discuss critically the six building blocks of supply chain management in section 8.5.

6 Compare the proposals for key performance incursions in block 6 of the framework for managing supply chains (section 8.5.6) with the principles of the performance prism (Chapter 3, section 3.4).

References

Boitoult, L. (1997) *Building the Foundations: An introduction to total supply chain management.* Watford: Institute of Grocery Distribution.

Coopers & Lybrand (1996) *European Value Chain Analysis Study: Final report.* Utrecht: ECR Europe.

Derocher, R. and Kilpatrick, J. (2000) Six supply chain lessons for the new millennium. *Supply Chain Management Review*, **3**(4), 34–40.

Doherty, K. (1998) Wegman's Nabisco pilot deemed a success. *Food Logistics*, Nov/Dec, 14.

Fernie, J. (1998) Relationships in the supply chain. In Fernie, J. and Sparks, L. (eds), *Logistics and Retail Management: Insights into current practice and trends from leading experts*, pp. 23–46. London: Kogan Page.

Lamming, R. (1993) *Beyond Partnership: Strategies for innovation and lean supply*. New York: Prentice Hall.

Mitchell, A. (1997) *Efficient Consumer Response: A new paradigm for the European FMCG sector*. London: FT/Pearson Professional.

Oliveira, A. and Barratt, M. (2001) Exploring the experience of collaborative planning initiatives. *International Journal of Physical Distribution and Logistics Management*, **31**(4), 266–89.

PE International (1997) *Efficient Consumer Response: Supply chain management of the new millennium*. Corby: Institute of Logistics.

Salmon, K. (1993) *Efficient Consumer Response: Enhancing consumer value in the supply chain*, Washington, DC: Kurt Salmon.

Stank, T.P., Daughtery, P.J. and Ellington, A.E. (1999) Marketing/Logistics Integration and Firm Performance, *The International Journall of Logistics Management*, **10**(1), 11–24.

Suggested further reading

Christopher, M. (1998) *Logistics and Supply Chain Management: Strategies for reducing cost and improving service*, 2nd edn, pp. 213–54. London: Financial Times Prentice Hall.

Gattorna, J.L. and Walters, D.W. (1996) *Managing the Supply Chain: A strategic perspective*. Aldershot: Macmillan.

GEA Consultia (1994) *Supplier–Retailer Collaboration in Supply Chain Management*. London: Coca-Cola Retailing Research Group Europe.

Lamming, R. (1993) *Beyond Partnership: Strategies for innovation and lean supply*. New York: Prentice Hall.

McGrath, M. (1997) *A Guide to Category Management*. Watford: IGD.

O'Sullivan, D. (1997) ECR: will it end in tears? *Logistics Focus*, **5**(7), 2–5.

Sharp, D. and Hill, R. (1998) ECR: from harmful competition to winning collaboration. In Gattorna, J.L. (ed.), *Strategic Supply Chain Alignment*, pp. 104–22. Aldershot: Gower.

CHAPTER 9

Partnerships in the supply chain

Objectives

The objectives of this chapter are to:

- introduce a range of types of intercompany relationships;
- describe the nature of partnerships;
- describe the implications for suppliers of entering into partnerships.

By the end of this chapter, you should be able to:

- understand the range of different intercompany relationships;
- understand the benefits and difficulties of operating supply chain partnerships;
- understand ways of approaching implementation issues.

Introduction

A number of new supply chain structures are emerging, based upon networks and interfirm collaboration. Optimising the supply chain process inevitably leads to a growing interdependence amongst the parties in the supply chain. With this interdependence has come a realisation that cooperation and partnership are necessary to achieve long-term mutual benefit. The implications for competitive strategy of this growth of collaborative supply chains are considerable – in particular the need to develop those skills that enable a company to transform established buyer–supplier relationships and successfully manage them on a day-to-day basis.

The overall aim of this chapter is to introduce the concept of partnerships and to present the context in which they can be beneficial.

Key issues

This chapter addresses six key issues:

1 **Choosing the right relationship:** which relationship is appropriate in different circumstances – bottleneck items, strategic items, non-critical items and leverage items.

2 **Partnerships in the supply chain:** cooperative, coordinated and collaborative relationships; their advantages and their disadvantages.

3 **Supply base rationalisation:** Dealing with a smaller number of suppliers to enable high-intensity relationship to develop.

4 **Supplier networks:** the development of supplies associations, and the Japanese equivalent, *keiretsu.*

5 **Supplier development:** managing upstream suppliers through intergrated processes and synchronous production.

6 **Implementing partnerships:** the potential pitfalls in moving from open market negotiations to collaborative relationships.

9.1 Choosing the right relationships

Key issues: **What types of relationships can be observed in supply chains? How can each type of relationship be tailored to different types of product?**

There are many types and forms of relationship in the supply chain. These form a continuum ranging from *arm's length*, where the relationship is conducted through the marketplace with price as its foundation, to full *vertical integration*, where the relationship is cemented through common ownership of the two organisations. This continuum is shown in Figure 9.1. Each of these relationship styles has motivating factors that drive development, and which govern the operating environment. The duration, breadth, strength and closeness of the relationship vary from case to case and over time.

An organisation will not have the same type of relationship with all of its customers and suppliers. Instead it will have a large range, spanning the entire spectrum of relationships. Choosing which type of relationship to establish is an important starting point.

Companies tend to deal with a large number of suppliers, even after the supply base has been rationalised. Treating them all in the same way fails to recognise that some are more important than others. Differentiating the role of suppliers and applying appropriate practices towards them allows a firm to target purchasing and supply chain management resources to better effect.

A popular view is that Japanese companies consider all of their tier 1 suppliers as partners. This is not the case. Even with Japanese automotive manufacturers, not all suppliers are equal. In fact amongst the typical 100–200 tier 1 suppliers to an OEM only about a dozen will enjoy partnership status with their customer. Typically, these elite few tend to be big suppliers.

A number of approaches exist to the segmentation of suppliers into categories.

| Arm's-length relationship style | Typical small account relationship | National account selling | Strategic alliances | Joint ventures | Full vertical integration |

Figure 9.1 Relationship style continuum
(Source: Cooper and Gardner, 1993)

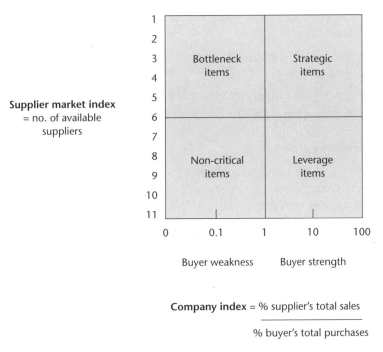

Figure 9.2 Purchase portfolio matrix
(Source: Syson, 1992)

The *purchase portfolio matrix* presented in Figure 9.2 is based on the notion that a customer will seek to maximise purchasing power when it can. This approach assumes that the key factors that affect the relationship are the strength of the buying company in the buyer–supplier relationship, and the number of suppliers able and willing to supply a product in the short term.

Strategic items

Strategic items are those for which the buyer has strength but there are few available suppliers. In this situation, purchasing should use its strength carefully to draw suppliers into a relationship that ensures supply in the long term.

Bottleneck items

Where the buyer has little power and there are few alternatives then these items are termed *bottlenecks*. The aim of purchasing in this situation is to reduce dependence on these items through diversification to find additional suppliers, seek substitute products and work with design teams to ensure that the bottleneck items are avoided in new products where possible.

Non-critical items

With a good choice of suppliers, possibly through following a strategy of using standardised parts, the traditional buying mechanism of competitive tendering is most valid for non-critical items. Such items are the ones with the following characteristics:

- not jointly developed;
- unbranded;
- do not affect performance and safety in particular;
- have required low investment in specific tools and equipment.

Leverage items

Where there are a large number of available suppliers and the buyer has high spending power then they will be able to leverage this to reduce prices and demand preferential treatment. Naturally, care should be taken not to antagonise suppliers just in case these favourable market conditions change.

This approach is heavily weighted towards the buyer's viewpoint. It is also a little unfashionable because it uses the term 'power' in supplier relationships, and assumes that traditional market-based negotiations will be used for some product groups. However, it applies to many firms today, and reflects the tough approach taken by the purchasing teams in some of their customers. Accepting that these sorts of circumstances are likely to prevail, it is clear that suppliers must become strategically important to the customer to have a chance of participating fully in any partnership.

Research in the automotive industry has predicted the emergence of two types of supplier (Lamming, 1993):

- *Type 1*: local companies that are flexible and responsive;
- *Type 2*: companies that would supply to customers on a global basis, possibly through establishing a local presence next to each customer site. These multinational companies would typically have a high level of value adding, possess technological expertise, and undertake their own R&D.

Both of these company types align themselves closely to customer needs and reduce the number of alternative suppliers they compete against. As a result, each has a high company index with its customer's individual sites. Plotting these factors on the grid in Figure 9.2, both of these types of firm are likely to be in a position to form partnerships with their customers. These are the companies that will survive as tier 1 suppliers.

This leads to the development of a third type of supplier in addition to those world class product/service companies. This is the group of firms demoted to the second tier of supply, where they will have to compete against global players on price, delivery and flexibility.

Activity 9.1

1 Selecting an organisation of your choice, use a copy of the purchase portfolio matrix (Figure 9.2) and plot on it the names of its top 10 customers and top 10 suppliers.
2 Which position would your chosen company prefer to be in? Suggest actions that would make the situation better.

Automotive supply chains: a range of inbound logistics solutions

Automotive assemblers and their inbound supply chains have developed many solutions to orchestrate the manufacturing and delivery of the thousands of parts that go to make up a given product line. The many potential logistics solutions are summarised in Figure 9.3.

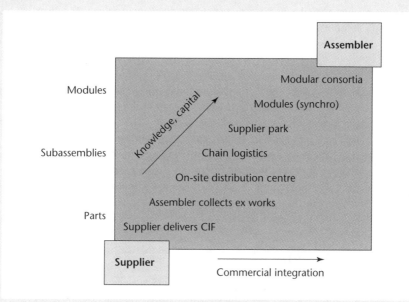

Figure 9.3 Evolving inbound relationships

These changes are of increasing value to the assemblers. The complexity of the logistics operation has been greatly downsized by slashing the number of tier 1 suppliers by broadening their responsibilities. Yet the ability of the assemblers to customise their finished products has increased. Quality consistency increases towards 50 ppm, while tough price reduction targets are demanded.

Supplier delivers CIF (carriage, insurance and freight)

The supplier delivers the ordered parts to the assembler's factory, and includes the distribution costs in the piece part price.

Assembler collects ex-works

The assembler subcontracts the process of parts collection from a number of suppliers, who are visited at a predetermined frequency (e.g. daily). The parts are taken to a consolidation centre, where they are decanted into trailers destined for different assembly plants. An example of this is the Ford operation that is run by Exel at Birmingham in the UK. Parts collections are made from the Midlands region of the UK, and dispatched to 22 Ford plants around Europe.

▶

On-site distribution centre

Instead of delivering parts directly into the assembler's plant, the logistics partner may instead deliver into a distribution centre positioned close to the assembler's plant. The advantages are much more controlled inbound parts movements into the plant. The assembler is able to call up loads of parts that are needed for a relatively short time period, and thus greatly improve material flow into the plant and reduce vehicle congestion. Additional value-adding activities may also be carried out in the DC. Thus, for example suppliers carry out some final assembly and sequencing tasks in the new Integrated Logistics Centre at BMW, Cowley.

Chain logistics

Here the objective is to increase the overall velocity of the inbound supply chain. If not planned and managed, drivers' hours regulations across Europe can lead to waste as the supply chain stops to allow for rests. The higher the velocity, the lower the stock that needs to be held at the plant. A useful further advantage is that the higher the velocity, the less packaging and containers are needed in the supply chain. An example of chain logistics is the ALUK operation that supports the Toyota plant at Burnaston in the UK. Parts movements from a supplier in southern Spain are planned in four-hour stages, where the full trailer is swapped for an empty one in a similar fashion to the Pony Express in the days of the Wild West!

Supplier park

Major tier 1 subassembly manufacturers are positioned on a supplier park close to the assembly hall. Major subassemblies are then sequenced into the assembly hall in response to a 'drumbeat' (based on the master schedule – see Chapter 6), which identifies the precise specification of the next body to be dropped onto the trim and final assembly track. Suppliers then have a finite amount of time to complete assembly and deliver to the point of use on the track. An example here is the Exel operation at the VW–Seat plant at Martorell near Barcelona, where material movements on the supplier park are specified and orchestrated by means of Exel's IT systems.

Modules

The VW–Seat plant at Martorell demonstrates a further advance in logistics thinking. Instead of delivering a large number of subassemblies, why not get the tier 1 suppliers to coordinate all the parts needed to produce a complete module that can then be simply bolted onto the car? Product variety can be increased by customisation of the modules. The advantages are shown in Figure 9.4.

Modular designs offer less WIP and a considerably downsized process for the assembler, and greater variety for the customer. Downsizing of the assembly process means that it is shorter, and can be positioned closer to customer demand. Complexity can then be added later in the pipeline between customer order and delivery of the specified car into the customer's hands – a concept called *postponed variety*. The term *synchro supply* has been used to describe the delivery of modules not just at the correct

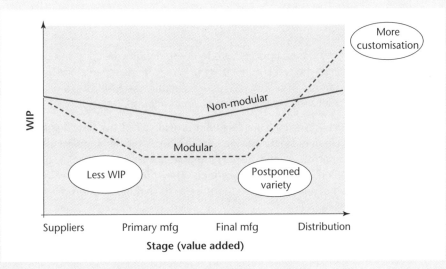

Figure 9.4 Modularisation: doing more with less
(Source: van Hoek and Weken, 1998)

quality and correct time, but on a real-time basis with the assembler and with the added challenge of zero safety stock.

Modular consortia

The VW bus and truck plant in Brazil is an experiment in the further development of the modular concept. The truck assembly operation has been divided into seven modules, with a supplier responsible for each. All the direct workers are on the supplier's payroll, and the supplier not only assembles the module, but also performs final assembly of the vehicle. The assembler's task has been downsized to engineering, design, supervision and administration. The Mercedes plant at Hambach in France, which produces the micro compact Smart car (see case study in Chapter 7), divides the vehicle into five main modules. Seven suppliers are fully integrated into the final assembly plant, while 16 non-integrated suppliers deliver submodules and parts. The whole information system – which supports manufacturing, logistics and distribution – is outsourced to Accenture.

Implications for suppliers

The demands on tier 1 suppliers increase in proportion to the various logistics solutions described earlier. A clear trend towards supplier parks and modularisation can be seen in the logistics strategies of automotive assemblers. Increasingly, tier 1 suppliers are being expected to control subsequent tiers in the supply chain, while ensuring delivery and quality to the assembler. At the same time, challenging cost reduction targets are being set, while the whole process is facilitated by tier 1 outbound defect levels that are less than 50 ppm. Many suppliers question whether the draconian demands for 'cost down' targets are compatible with such defect levels.

Three distinct stages can be seen in the development of capabilities by tier 1 suppliers:

● *Tier 1 basic*: suppliers with in-house design capability and project management capability who can ensure timely delivery and reasonable quality reliability (<50 ppm). An example would be a tyre manufacturer who holds 4–5 days' stock and who delivers to set time windows: that is, limited logistics capability.

● *Tier 1 synchro*: suppliers who provide all of the basic capabilities, but with virtually no safety stock. Additional capabilities for the supplier are synchro logistics and IT expertise which is closely integrated with the assembler, greater flexibility and more secure emergency procedures. They operate through 'clone' plants that are situated on supplier parks no more than 10 minutes' travel time from the assembler's production line.

● *Tier 0.5*: full service providers, who integrate component manufacturing through supply chain management to achieve the optimum design of a given module. They carry out pre-emptive market research and develop innovative designs through *shelf engineering* (designs that are prepared proactively in advance of need and placed 'on the shelf', thus saving time in the event that the need does arise). They are partners in major cost reduction projects at each model change, and in continuous improvement projects in between.

There is a substantial passing of risk from the assembler to the tier 1 supplier at each stage. Increasingly, the supplier takes responsibility for designing and developing new products of increasing complexity in advance of new model programmes. And there is no guarantee that the supplier will get the work, because competitive tenders are issued for each new model. This forces suppliers to keep primary manufacturing and core business at a 'home' location, and to construct low-cost, late-configuration 'postponement' plants near the OEM's assembly hall to enable synchro deliveries. The decision by BMW / Rover to switch R50 (Mini) assembly from Longbridge to Cowley left a number of suppliers with £2m synchro assembly units in the wrong place.

The strategic dilemma for tier 1 suppliers who currently supply the assemblers directly is whether to expand into system integrators ('tier 0.5'), or to become indirect suppliers to such organisations. Siegfried Wolf of Magna International described the tier 0.5 transition as follows:

> **To become part of this new tier, companies will require a worldwide presence, global sourcing, programme management, technology, JIT and JIS know-how and specialist production knowledge. They will also require a high level of R&D spend.**

(JIS = just in sequence: the capability to supply a module in accordance with the drumbeat requirements of an assembler.) So, after tier 0.5, where do the competitive challenges lie? Tier 2 suppliers will still be largely low-overhead, product-based companies who have limited service capability. Price pressure will continue to be severe, and return on sales often little above break-even. Tier 2 suppliers often cannot afford expensive inspection and test resources, so defect levels will continue to be relatively high, often in the range 1000–2000 ppm (i.e. 1–2%). This will present major challenges for tier 0.5 suppliers, who must also guarantee delivery reliability to the assembly track, and a module that fits perfectly at all times. Chrysler sees the challenge as one of 'integrating the operations of our suppliers with those of our assembly plants'. In one example, four suppliers shipped parts separately to the minivan plant in Windsor, Ontario – at different times, by different carriers, and in different containers. Three of those plants now ship to the fourth, which sequences them for just-in-time delivery. The parts are now received at Windsor in frequent, small-lot deliveries, using one carrier and one standard container design.

(Source: Harrison, 2000)

Question
Summarise the advantages and risks to suppliers who want to achieve 'tier 0.5' status.

9.2 Partnerships in the supply chain

Key issues: What are partnerships, and what are their advantages and disadvantages?

Generally, cooperative relationships or 'partnerships' have been characterised as being based upon:

● the sharing of information;
● trust and openness;
● coordination and planning;
● mutual benefits and sharing of risks;
● a recognition of mutual interdependence;
● shared goals;
● compatibility of corporate philosophies.

Amongst these, perhaps the key characteristic is that concerning the sharing of information. This should include demand and supply information. Chapter 8 showed how collaborative planning is being used to share information between retailers and manufacturers.

Contained within the term 'partnership' are a number of types of partnership 'style' relationships. Figure 9.5 shows three such types of partnership in the context of a range of relationships. These types of partnership have the characteristics, described in Table 9.1.

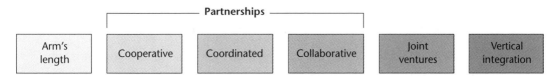

Figure 9.5 **Types of relationship**

Table 9.1   Characteristics of partnership types

Partnership type	Activities	Time horizon	Scope of activities
Cooperation	Fewer suppliers Longer-term contracts	Short-term	Single functional area
Coordination	Information linkages WIP linkages EDI exchange	Long-term	Multiple functional areas
Collaboration	Supply chain integration Joint planning Technology sharing	Long-term with no fixed date	Firms see each other as extensions of their own firm

9.2.1   Economic justification for partnerships

Entering into a partnership with a company, to whatever extent, implies a transition away from the rules of the open marketplace and towards alternatives. These different structures must demonstrate benefits otherwise they will not deliver competitive advantage.

Open market relationships are typified by short-term contracts, arm's length relations, little joint development, and many suppliers per part. Observing that Japanese practice and consequently the lean model of supply differs significantly from this indicates that other, non-market mechanisms must be operating.

The Japanese tend to infuse their transactions with the non-economic qualities of commitment and trust. These characteristics are important in successful partnerships. While this may increase transaction costs and risks, it appears that these are offset by securing other economic and strategic advantages that cannot be achieved though the market system.

9.2.2   Advantages of partnerships

Within partnerships, savings come in the form of reduced negotiations and drawing up of separate contracts, reduced monitoring of supplier soundness, including supply quality, and increased productivity. These are accompanied by strategic advantages of shortened lead times and product cycles, and conditions amenable to longer-term investment.

These advantages, however, need to be set against the problems that can be associated with the introduction of commitment and trust.

9.2.3   Disadvantages of partnerships

Some of the examples of potential disadvantages of partnerships include the following:

● the inability to price accurately qualitative matters such as design work;
● the need for organisations to gather substantial information about potential partners on which to base decisions;

- the risk of divulging competitively sensitive information to competitors;
- potential opportunism by suppliers.

In the long term, additional factors occur when companies enter into partnerships. With the outsourcing of the R&D of components and subsystems, buyers benefit from the decreased investment they have to make. Working with suppliers who fund their own R&D leads to their earlier involvement in new product development where buyers benefit from suppliers' ability to cut costs and develop better-performing products. This scenario leads to greater buyer risk owing to dependence on a smaller number of suppliers for designs, and also the potential for opportunism through the smaller number of other companies able to compete with the incumbent suppliers for their work.

Activity 9.2

Consider the reasons why a company would wish to enter into a partnership with a customer or supplier. List the advantages and disadvantages you can think of.

9.3 Supply base rationalisation

Key issue: **What are the drivers for reducing the numbers of direct suppliers?**

True supply chain integration requires that a company's processes align with those of its upstream, as well as its downstream, partners. Clearly it is not practical to contemplate inter-organisational process integration between the firm and a large number of suppliers. Instead, high-intensity relationships can be managed only with a limited supplier base. Clearly one of the key concerns for logistics management has to be the criteria by which lead suppliers are chosen.

9.3.1 Supplier management

Supplier management is the aspect of supply chain management that seeks to organise the sourcing of materials and components from a suitable set of suppliers. The emphasis in this area is on the 'suitable set of suppliers'. The automotive case study above explains some of the considerations in this process, as does the Global Lighting case in Chapter 2 (case study 2.3).

Generally, companies are seeking to reduce the numbers of suppliers they deal with by focusing on those with the right set of capabilities. The extent to which companies have undertaken this and have tiered their supply chains is exceptional. Even in the early 1990s, two-thirds of companies were reported to be reducing their supplier base. Anecdotal accounts of the reductions abound. For example, Sun Microsystems was reported to have consolidated the top 85% of its purchasing spend from across 100 suppliers in 1990 to just 20 a few years later.

1 Consider an organisation of your choice: have its major customers consolidated their supply base over the past five years? If so, by how much?
2 What criteria did these customers use to decide which companies to keep and which to 'demote' to a lower tier?

9.3.2 Lead suppliers

While true single-sourcing strategies are the exception rather than the rule, the concept of the *lead supplier* is now widely accepted. Over the past 10 years many large companies have consolidated their supplier base. In some cases this has seen the number of suppliers reduce from around a 1000 to 2000 or so. However, many of the original suppliers still contribute to the OEM's products, but they now do so from lower tiers. The responsibility for managing them now lies with the suppliers left at the first tier. In some cases this responsibility is new and has had to be learnt.

Has the position of your selected organisation changed in the supply chain? If it has risen up the supply chain, or remained at the same tier whilst others were 'demoted', what new capabilities had to be developed? If it was demoted, why did this happen? Was it a good thing or a bad thing to happen?

9.4 Supplier networks

Key issues: What are supplier associations, and the Japanese *keiretsu*?

Supplier networks can be formal or informal groups of companies whose common interest is that they all supply a particular customer, usually an assembler or tier 1 supplier. Two such networks are considered here:

● supplier associations;
● Japanese *keiretsu*.

9.4.1 Supplier associations

Aitken (1998) defines a supplier association as

the network of a company's important suppliers brought together for the purpose of coordination and development. Through the supplier association forum this company provides training and resource for production and logistics process improvements. The association also provides the opportunity for its members to improve the quality and frequency of communications, a critical factor for improving operational performance.

Supplier associations may be traced back to the late 1930s with the oldest known group being one linked to Japanese automotive manufacturer Toyota. This early group consisted of 18 suppliers producing basic commodity items such as screws, nuts and bolts. These suppliers formed the group for the benefit of themselves. The Toyota organisation itself did not perform an active role in the beginning of the association. However, the distant role of Toyota was to change, as raw materials became scarce during the Second World War. As part of wartime control

Table 9.2 Primary objectives for establishing and developing supplier associations

Objective	Rationale
Provide manufacturing tools and techniques such as JIT, *kanban* and TQM	Improve knowledge and application of best-practice tools and techniques within the supply base
Produce a uniform supply system	Remove *muda* (waste) from the system, then standardise process management in all parts of the supply chain
Facilitate flow of information and strategy formulation	The assembler assists the suppliers in formulating an improvement strategy by providing best-practice information
Increase trust between buyer and supplier	The result of gaining improvements in the first three objectives is an improvement in trust
Keep suppliers and customers in touch with market need	Assemblers aid their suppliers in understanding the needs of the customer through sharing market intelligence, sales plans and development opportunities
Enhance reputation of assembler within supply base	Assemblers attempt to prove to their suppliers that they are worth dealing with
Aid smaller suppliers	Some supplier associations are established to aid smaller associations, who could not support the development or improvement programmes necessary to achieve world-class manufacturing standards from their own internal resources
Increase length of trading relationship	Through supporting suppliers in the development of their operations the assembler needs to invest resource. Through committing resource the assembler increases the asset specificity of the supplier, and it is therefore important that the relationship is maintained
Share development benefits	The association forum supports not only supplier–assembler improvements but, also supplier–supplier knowledge sharing
Provide examples to suppliers of how to develop their own supply base	The performance of the entire supply chain is improved by cascading supply chain management techniques into it

by the Japanese government, small and medium-sized firms were directed to supply larger firms, which were being utilised as distributors of raw material by the government. Prescribing the flow of materials forced the movement of scarce raw materials to key manufacturers. Through this direct interventionist approach the government tried to force assemblers and the subcontractors to work together to increase the efficiency of the supply chain.

The policy employed by the government therefore encouraged assemblers to establish links with suppliers to ensure component supplies. The carrot and stick approach of the government assisted the foundation of several associations. The institutionalist approach by government succeeded in determining the future structure of the supply chain for Japanese automotive companies. Japanese car assemblers changed their modus operandi to align with the prevailing governmental coercive isomorphic forces, thereby obtaining social legitimacy. However, it was not until the early 1940s that assemblers began to recognise the potential benefits of becoming active members of the associations. In 1943 Toyota became interested in the management of the association. Through the provision of management support Toyota started to develop and improve confidence and trust between members and itself.

There can be many improvement objectives of a supplier association, and these will vary between associations and industry sectors. Research has identified 10 primary objectives for establishing and developing an association, as shown in Table 9.2.

CASE STUDY 9.2

Supplier association

A major supplier of digital telecommunications systems, which we shall call 'Cymru', had established a successful manufacturing plant in Wales. The European region had been restructured into five customer-facing divisions, which would provide major customers with a single point of contact for integrated solutions. This would in turn focus operations by key account, and boost Cymru's commitment to quality and customer satisfaction. Cymru's major customer was TELE, a national telecomms service provider. Following deregulation of markets in Europe, TELE started to buy telephone handsets in the global market at prices that were well below those of Cymru. A two-year contract was replaced by a four-month contract, and call-off quantities became much more uncertain for Cymru and its suppliers.

In order to compete, Cymru decided that it would have to improve customer service in terms of availability, speed of new product introduction and cost. A new logistics programme was conceived whereby Cymru bypassed TELE's internal distribution structure and delivered direct to TELE's customers. This meant that TELE carried no inventories and that Cymru took over the distribution task with superior service levels. TELE signed a five-year deal with Cymru, and both parties enjoyed better margins.

In order to support the better service levels, it was essential that Cymru's supply base was integrated into the new logistics programme. This meant that the relationship style (Figure 9.1) would need to be moved from arm's length to strategic. As the procurement manager commented:

'I quickly realised that the old way of communicating on a one-to-one basis would no longer work. I'd never get round the suppliers quickly enough to get them all in a mindset of what had to change and when.'

Suppliers had previously been informed of future plans on a 'need to know' basis through their organisational 'gatekeepers' in the purchasing department at Cymru. New work was put out to tender, and the lowest-price bid secured the business.

Setting up a supplier association was viewed as the best way to address the needs and timescales for changing the supply chain. Suppliers could be involved simultaneously in reducing lead times from 2 weeks to 2 days (receipt of order from TELE to delivery at end user's site). This would be achieved through improved responsiveness, both inbound and outbound. Far Eastern competitors would be unable to match such service levels and total logistics costs.

In setting up the supplier association, priority was given to suppliers who supplied parts for final assembly of the telephone, especially those who supplied colour-related and mechanical parts which would have maximum impact on lead-time reduction. Seven tier 1 suppliers and one tier 2 supplier agreed to take part, and the network is shown in Figure 9.6.

The Cymru supplier association was therefore formed from a wide variety of companies, in terms of both size and industry sector. In a marked break with the past, Cymru kicked off the association with an inaugural meeting that presented confidential product development and market information. The aim of the association was 'to promote best practice, improve overall supply chain performance and support product development'. This was to be achieved by self-help teams committed to sharing knowledge and experience in an open and cooperative manner. Many suppliers were concerned that the association was being formed 'as a disguise for margin reduction', and were reassured when Cymru insisted that the main task was cost reduction. More open communications and an emphasis on mutual cost reduction were seen by suppliers as essential foundations for the new association.

The initial activity was to benchmark all members to 'gain an understanding of the strengths and weaknesses of current processes and practices relative to a best practice model'. Areas for benchmarking were those that Cymru had itself established already as competitive priorities. They were:

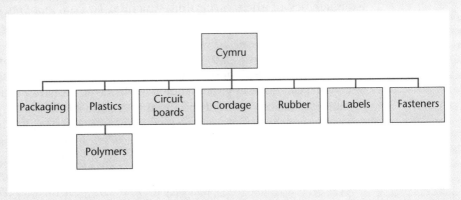

Figure 9.6 Cymru supplier association

- *Quality*: ppm of components received, goods produced and goods shipped;
- *Productivity*: value added per employee, throughput and operation times;
- *Delivery*: percentage of deliveries on time to customer and from suppliers;
- *Stock turns*: stock turn ratio;
- *Continuous improvement*: improvement plans, team activities and employee development programmes.

The results of the benchmarking process stimulated much interest among the suppliers. The account manager of one of them commented:

> 'Benchmarking is very important. We need to know from the customer what he thinks of us. How do we rate against other suppliers in the association? I want to know because it could be I've got something to learn from another supplier.'

Following the benchmarking phase, suppliers met every quarter to formulate strategy, share market and product development information, and share plans for implementing best practice. The new plans were then deployed within individual supplier companies by training workshops. In turn, these plans spawned improvement projects aimed at achieving the competitive priorities.

(Source: Aitken, 1998)

Question

The supplier association described above eventually collapsed. What causes do you think might have led to this collapse?

9.4.2 Japanese *keiretsu*

One of the Japanese business structures that have received interest from Western business is the *keiretsu*. *Keiretsu* is a term used to describe Japanese business consortia based on cooperation, coordination, joint ownership and control.

The *keiretsu* possesses the particular characteristic of having ownership and control based on equity exchanges between supply chain members. Despite the complexities of their ownership structure, *keiretsu* represents a supply chain model that helps to explain the organisation of most companies in the automotive and electronics sectors in Japan.

The supply chain *keiretsu* is a network in which activities are organised by a lead firm. The typical supplier networks of large automobile and electronics firms are managed and led by the major assemblers, as shown in Figure 9.7.

The formation of *keiretsus* occurred as a result of the strategy in the 1960s of assemblers outsourcing subassemblies to increase capacity, leading de facto to the emergence of a tiered structure. The *keiretsu* became instrumental in developing the pyramidal structure of the supply base with its tiered arrangement to ensure that the assembler only works directly with a reduced number of suppliers. These suppliers in turn take responsibility for managing the next level down, and so on. The tiered *keiretsu* style of arrangement has now become the favourite supply structure in the automotive industry worldwide.

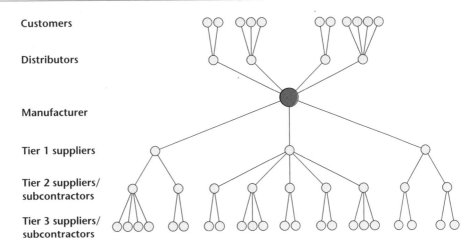

Customers

Distributors

Manufacturer

Tier 1 suppliers

Tier 2 suppliers/
subcontractors

Tier 3 suppliers/
subcontractors

Figure 9.7 Japanese *keiretsu* structure
(Source: Aitken, 1998)

Brazilian-born Carlos Ghosn was despatched to Nissan after Renault took a 36.8% stake in the Japanese car maker in 1999. What he has done in turning round Nissan's €15bn of debt and chronic losses has sent shock waves through Japanese business thinking. One of his main targets for change has been the *keiretsu* system, which he described as a 'gross waste of capital'. Ghosn has broken up Nissan's *keiretsu* system, and is reducing the number of suppliers from 1200 to 600. Masaaki Kanno, head of economic research at JP Morgan's Asian office, is quoted as saying: 'While many people in Japan realised this system should be changed, it has taken a foreigner to change it. I am not exaggerating when I say Ghosn is a hero in Japan now. People believe that he has saved Nissan from death.'

The system that has acted as a model for Western auto inbound logistics is being dismantled by Nissan. Is this anomalous?

9.5 Supplier development

Key issue: How can upstream supplier processes be integrated to improve material flow?

One of the keys to increased responsiveness in the supply chain is a high level of integration with upstream suppliers. Analysis of the supply chain often uncovers that the lead time of products flowing through it is usually measured in weeks rather than days. This is caused by significant inventories of raw materials, packaging materials, intermediate products and so forth are being carried upstream of the final point of manufacture. Not only does this represent a significant cost burden, it also adversely affects the responsiveness of the supply chain.

Where suppliers appear unable to make improvements, or fail to do so at a sufficient rate, customers who feel their own performance is being hampered – yet remain committed to the relationship with the supplier – often seek ways to remedy the situation. Many buying firms actively facilitate supplier performance and capability through supplier development. This typically results in activities aimed at developing and improving the overall capabilities and performance of the supplier towards the goal of meeting and serving the needs of the customer.

Supplier development consists of any effort of a buying firm with a supplier to increase its performance or capabilities and meet the buying firm's short-term or long-term supply needs. Unfortunately the temptation for buyers to gain short-term advantage still exists in supplier development to the detriment of long-term partnerships. Also, meeting the needs of buying firms is not necessarily linked to development that would enhance overall supply chain competitiveness. Therefore care must be taken not to lose sight of end-customer needs in the transactions between specific pairs of companies.

Various trends are observable as leading-edge companies seek to improve their management of the upstream supply chain, including:

- integrated processes;
- synchronous production.

9.5.1 Integrated processes

A key focus of supplier development should be the alignment of critical processes: that is, new product development, material replenishment and payment. These ideas should be founded upon a platform of collaborative planning and strategy development.

It is perhaps this concept of joint strategy determination that distinguishes truly integrated supply chains from mere 'marriages of convenience'. While the customer will always be pre-eminent in the determination of their strategic goals, the involvement of key suppliers in that process can only be to the benefit of both parties.

Process integration can be enhanced through the creation of *supplier development teams*. The purpose of these teams is to work with suppliers to explore ways in which process alignment can be achieved: for example, seeking to establish a common 'information highway' between the vendor and the customer, or working to establish common product identification codes. Nissan in the UK reports that supplier development teams have been a significant element in its success in creating a more responsive supply chain.

9.5.2 Synchronous production

Linking upstream production schedules with downstream demand helps to improve material flow. The creation of a 'seamless' network of processes aims to dramatically reduce inventories while greatly enhancing responsiveness. The Japanese concept of *heijunka* seeks coordination of material movements between different processes in the supply network (see the Honda case study (6.2) in Chapter 6). Transparency of information upstream and downstream is essential for synchronisation to work. For example, the supplier must be able to access the customer's forward production schedules, and the customer must be able to see into the supplier's 'stockroom'. The *virtual supply chain* envisages partners in the chain being linked together by a common information system, so that information replaces the need for inventories.

Another approach that seeks to improve synchronous supply chain processes is that of *vendor-managed inventory* (VMI). Here, the supplier takes responsibility for the management of the customer's inventory (see section 6.3, Chapter 6). The advantage is that a large element of uncertainty in the supply chain is removed through shared information. The need for safety stock can thereby be dramatically reduced.

9.6 Implementing partnerships

Key issue: **What are the barriers to achieving partnerships in the supply chain?**

The goal of 'partnership' often proves to be elusive to customer–supplier links within supply networks. Despite a recognition of the need for partnership, there are many obstacles to overcome if the concept of process alignment is to realise its full potential within a given network. It is therefore helpful to understand the inherent difficulties in order to gauge how the goal of 'partnership' might be achieved.

A transition route from open market negotiation to collaboration, along which relationships evolve, is shown in Figure 9.8. Before seeking to develop a partnership it is necessary to determine where the most appropriate point along this path is for your relationship with another company. There is no point in pursuing a partnership just because this is further along the scale. In some cases, as described earlier, open market negotiations will be most appropriate.

The transition from multiple sourcing and arm's length negotiation of short-term, purchase-price-allocated contracts to one based on cooperation, collaboration, trust and commitment requires a supply chain process to be put in place which needs designing, developing, optimising and managing. A key step in achieving this is to ensure that supplier development and purchasing teams are fully involved in the change.

Failure to do this often leads to purchasing executives undertaking behaviour incompatible with fostering successful supply chain partnerships. While many are familiar with – and voice support for – partnerships, in practice their approach and practices are not supportive. Barriers that have been identified include the following:

Figure 9.8 The transition from open market negotiations to collaboration

- There is an inappropriate use of *power* over the supply chain partner.
- Buyers focus on their own company's *self-interest.*
- There is a focus on the *negative implications* of entering into partnership.
- While buyers value trust, commitment and reliability, they continue to be *opportunistic* and seek gains at their partner's expense.
- *Price* is viewed as the key attribute in evaluations of suppliers.

These barriers, which are explained below, show that the decision criteria used by buyers retain a legacy of the traditional approach where the choice of lowest price remains the most defining characteristic. Unless such behaviour is changed, it prevents supply chain relationships from developing beyond a crude application of commercial power, where the free market is used to instil discipline and promote a supply base in which it is assumed that the fit survive. An explanation of the above barriers is as follows.

Power

The ability of one member in the supply chain to control another member at a different level can be detrimental to the overall supply network, and can provide a source of conflict. Conflict is clearly associated with power, arising when one organisation impedes the achievement of the goals of another. For example, in retailing, shelf space is a key resource that has potentially conflicting implications for the retailer and for its suppliers. The retailer looks for maximum return on space and contribution to its image, while the supplier seeks maximum shelf space, trial for new products, and preference over competitors.

Focus on negative implications of partnership

Buyers consider the benefits gained through heightened dependence on a smaller number of suppliers less favourably, and tend to highlight the risks. Buyers also consistently view the cost-saving aspects of supply chain management as more important than the revenue-enhancing benefits.

Opportunism

A key issue that prevents partnerships from enduring appears to be the gap between the strategic requirements of long-term partnerships and tactical-level manoeuvring – in particular, opportunism. It is a problem to resolve this, given that the dimensions that characterise close working relationships also provide both opportunity and increased incentive for opportunistic behaviour. This is caused when partners cannot easily obtain similar benefits outside the relationship and when specialised investments have been made. Buyers often assume that suppliers will take advantage if they become too important, and as such act to prevent this. The consequences for the partnership relationship come second in their considerations.

Self-interest

Companies face difficulties in establishing and maintaining supply chain partnerships. Even in the automotive industry, often considered the supply chain exemplar, companies keen to implement single sourcing still continue to multi-source, particularly for non-critical items and commodity items. They rarely enter into collaboration even when the customer is dependent on the supplier – that is, when the product is strategically important and alternatives are limited – and instead set their self-interest higher than the need to act according to common best interest.

Focus on price

The focus on price may be due in some part to buyers having trouble valuing matters such as know-how, technological capability, a particular style of production or a spirit of innovation, and therefore being unable to price them accurately. Their concern that suppliers may act opportunistically tends to lead them to avoid entering into areas where these factors prevail. Significantly, one of the key areas that feature these traits is that of design and development. It seems that, in this area, buyers find it extremely difficult to measure designer performance or the amount of productive time spent during design, and therefore feel the need to guard against high bids from suppliers.

Summary

What are the different types of relationship in the supply chain?

- Supply chain relationships can vary from arm's length at one extreme (characterised by a focus on price, and by few points of contact between the organisations concerned), to vertical integration at the other (characterised by integration of processes, and by contacts at all levels).

- The choice of the appropriate relationship is helped by recognising that some suppliers are more important than others. One way to segment the supplier base is to use the purchase portfolio index, and to divide suppliers according to strategic, bottleneck, non-critical and leverage characteristics.

- The role of partnership in the supply chain has been described using seven factors: the sharing of information, trust and openness, coordination and planning, mutual benefits and sharing of risks, a recognition of mutual interdependence, shared goals, and compatibility of corporate philosophies.

- Three stages of the development of partnerships have been defined: cooperation, coordination and collaboration. The move towards collaborative partnerships is characterised by increases in the time horizon and the scope of activities involved.

How can closer supply chain relationships be implemented?

- Supply base rationalisation seeks to reduce the suppliers with whom an organisation deals directly to a smaller number of strategic suppliers. Rationalisation involves re-tiering the supply chain so that other suppliers are placed under a lead supplier, or 'tier 1' supplier.

● Supplier associations bring suppliers to an OEM or tier 1 supplier together for the purpose of coordination and development. They also aim to improve the quality and frequency of communications between members. In practice, association companies benchmark each other, and formulate improvement projects aimed at increasing the competitiveness of the overall network.

● *Keiretsu* is the term used to describe the supplier association in Japan. Here, the additional characteristics are that ownership and control of the network are based on equity exchanges between members. *Keiretsu* structures have attracted much recent criticism owing to their relative inflexibility and high cost.

● Improved responsiveness from supply chains is facilitated by integrated processes (including joint strategy determination) and synchronisation (coordinated flow facilitated by transparency of information upstream and downstream).

● Barriers to implementation include the inappropriate use of power, self-interest, a focus on negative implications, opportunism, and a pre-occupation with price.

Discussion questions

1 Consider the use of partnerships with customers to improve competitiveness. Discuss this within a group scenario using the following guidelines:

a Make a list of companies in your chosen company's industry known to undertake supplier development. This should include all its customers and other companies that are potential customers.

b Make a list of all the types of development and improvement that your chosen company would like help with.

c Assemble these lists along the two sides of a grid, following the example shown in Figure 9.9. Mark on the grid where each of the companies is able to provide the necessary help.

d Examine the grid you have constructed and identify the following:
  ● issues that require help that current customers provide;
  ● issues that require help that only potential customers provide;
  ● issues that require help that no one provides;
  ● customers (current or potential) that provide a great deal of help;
  ● customers (current or potential) that provide little or no help.

e Use these five criteria as the basis for identifying companies that should be valuable in ensuring your company's long-term success. These companies are the ones that should be considered as likely partners.

f Having identified the likely partners, identify the difficulties in establishing partnerships and the problems in maintaining them.

g Conclude with the actions that you would undertake to overcome the problems associated with partnerships in order to achieve their advantages.

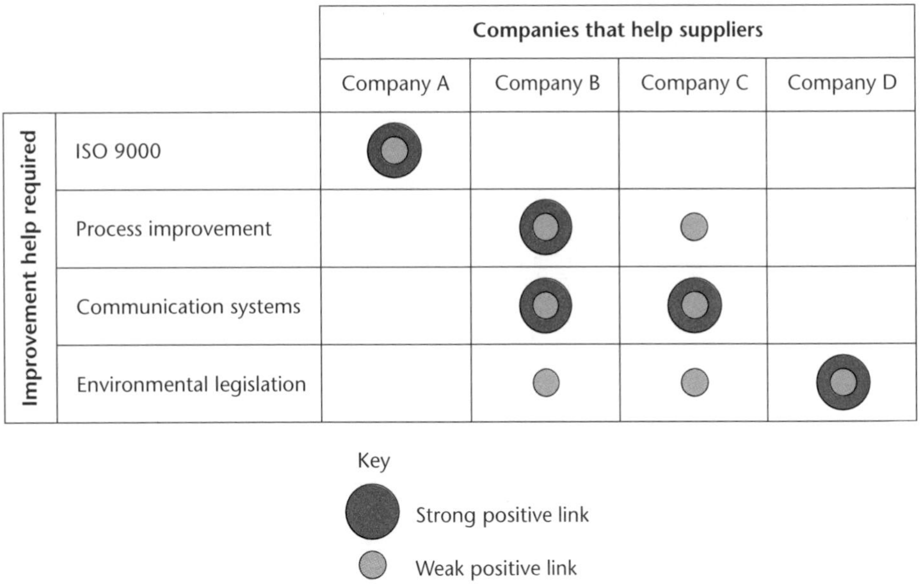

		Companies that help suppliers			
		Company A	Company B	Company C	Company D
Improvement help required	ISO 9000	⊚			
	Process improvement		⊚	◯	
	Communication systems		⊚	⊚	
	Environmental legislation		◯	◯	⊚

Key

⬤ Strong positive link

◯ Weak positive link

Figure 9.9 A supplier development grid

2 'Supply chain relationships don't mean anything. At the end of the day, it depends entirely on who has the most power. It's the big boys in the supply chain who decide just how much of a relationship there's going to be.'

Discuss the implications of this statement.

References

Aitken, J. (1998) *Integration of the Supply Chain: The Effect of Inter-Organisational Interactions between Purchasing-Sales-Logistics*. PhD thesis, Cranfield School of Management.

Cooper, M. and Gardner, J. (1993) Building good business relationships – more than just partnering or strategic alliances? *International Journal of Physical Distribution and Logistics Management*, **23**(6), 14–26.

Harrison A.S. (2000) Perestroika in automotive inbound. *Supply Chain Practice*, **2**(3), 28–39.

Lamming, R. (1993) *Beyond Partnership*. Hemel Hempstead: Prentice Hall.

Syson, R. (1992) *Improving Purchase Performance*. London, Pitman.

Van Hoek, R. and Weken, H.A.M. (1998) The Impact of Modular Production on the Dynamics of Supply Chains. *International Journal of Logistics Management*, **9**(2), 25–50.

Suggested further reading

Das T.K. and Teng, B.S. (1998) Between trust and control: developing confidence in partner co-operation in alliances. *Academy of Management Review*, **23**, 491–513.

Scarborough, H. (2000) The HR implications of supply chain relationships. *Human Resource Management Journal*, **10**, 5–17.

Storey, J. (ed) (1994) *New Wave Manufacturing Strategies: Organisational and human resource management dimensions*. London: Paul Chapman Publishing.

Part Four

CHANGING THE FUTURE

The final part of this book takes a somewhat different approach. It takes the lessons learned in the previous nine chapters and considers how progress can be expected based upon those combined with current leading-edge thinking on logistics. Chapter 10 assesses current approaches to the supply network, and their impact on logistics in several areas such as postponement, modern planning tools and the Internet. The chapter ends with a section on managing change, which is 'where the rubber meets the road'. The management of change is also where many ambitious visions founder, and where every logistics manager should have at least a basic understanding. Finally, a set of diagnostic questions is offered in the Appendix for reflection upon further improvement opportunities in practical environments and logistics thinking. We hope that this will provide input to the process of taking the lessons learned in this book off the page and putting them into practice.

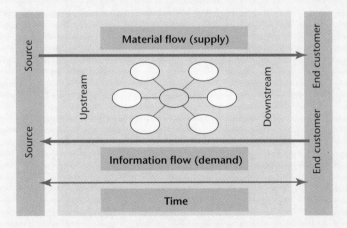

CHAPTER 10

Logistics future challenge

Objectives

The objectives of this chapter are to:

- collect together the major changes that are impacting on supply chain strategies;
- identify how management of the supply chains of the future will be affected by the advance of new structures and reconfiguration of material and information flow;
- explain the role of the Internet in evolving new supply chain strategies;
- list key issues in managing the transition process towards future state supply chains.

By the end of this chapter, you should be able to:

- understand key issues that will affect the way supply chains of the future will be structured;
- understand the different ways in which supply chains may compete in the marketplace;
- understand ways of approaching implementation issues.

Introduction

Having reviewed the principles and practices of management and strategy for logistics in the supply chain, this final chapter concludes by considering logistics developments that will challenge our thinking in the years to come. While these developments have an impact now, their significance extends beyond our current capabilities. As a result this chapter has a more forward-looking and exploratory outlook.

The chapter begins by listing key principles of the supply network of the future. These are not entirely new; they are principles that have been developed in previous chapters. But together as a new way of working they form a formidable challenge. Overall, they have the potential to change the way that supply chains and logistics operations are structured, and place new challenges on the management task.

The overall aim of this chapter is to inform you of advances in thinking that are shaping management and strategy for logistics in the supply chain.

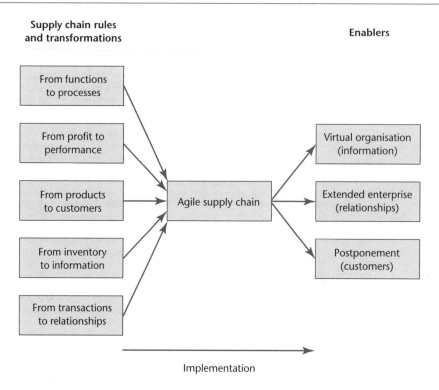

Figure 10.1 **Framework for this chapter**

Figure 10.1 illustrates the structure of the chapter. The transformations in the supply chain environment are compared with market challenges leading towards the creation of the agile supply chain. The transition process from left to right is driven by a set of forces that are explained in section 10.4 of this chapter.

Key issues   *This chapter addresses four key issues:*

1 **The new supply chain environment:** three developments that are transforming the flow of materials and information in supply chains.

2 **Managing the supply chain of the future:** changes in supply chain structure and product configuration that are offering new opportunities.

3 **The role of the Internet in supply chains:** revisiting the electronic collaboration issues raised in Chapter 8 to project the future role of the Internet.

4 **Implementation issues:** the forces at work in managing the transition process.

10.1   The new supply chain environment

Key issues: **How can we characterise the new logistics environment? How can we work towards this new environment?**

Key drivers of change in developing the supply network of the future will be consumer demand for greater choice and improved value. In parallel, competition between supply chains and the organisations participating in them will increase. Product and technology life cycles are likely to continue to shorten, while demand will be increasingly difficult to forecast. For most product service propositions, the marketplace will be increasingly turbulent, placing greater pressure on supply chains to respond in an agile manner.

Consumer demand for new products will lead organisations to introduce new products – and to promote existing ones – more frequently in order to maintain or to increase sales. Consumers are also likely to demand the delivery of goods and services through innovative channels alongside the traditional ones.

Competition amongst organisations will increase as a result of a combination of factors, notably:

- *globalisation of supply chains*: while localisation of service, products and distribution remains important;
- *convergence of low-cost computing and low-cost communications*: making information integration in the supply chain a more feasible proposition and the achievement of it more a management challenge, and less of technology, challenge;
- *increased capability to extend product variety and reduce product life cycles*: while remaining cost competitive.

These competitive factors are changing the means by which organisations compete. Organisations such as Dell have developed a competitive agenda that does not need sizeable physical assets and inventories.

These changes in the competitive environment are likely to have a number of consequences. Based on previous chapters, a set of supply chain principles can be put forward as a basis for the future organisational landscape:

- *Principle 1*. The supply chain exists to serve the end customer, not the other way round. Therefore responsiveness across functional, organisational and geographic boundaries, and speed of flow of goods and information, are key capabilities.
- *Principle 2*. The output of supply chain management is not just a physical product, but a combination of time, place, form and function of a product/service proposition.
- *Principle 3*. Moving beyond the strategic vision established by the top team is a key challenge for logistics management. Implementing and operationalising the vision are just as important as the vision itself.
- *Principle 4*. A linear view of the supply chain is too simple because it relies on an outdated, internal concept of 'our organisation' and its immediate neighbours. It fails to engage with the integrated needs of today's market environment.

- *Principle 5.* Immediate customers in the supply chain have an essential role to play in communicating, translating and coordinating end customer demand. They must stop obscuring that demand by batching rules and the like that serve their own selfish ends.

- *Principle 6.* Supply network priorities are constantly changing, and lead to an ongoing need for coordinated, time-based responses.

- *Principle 7.* There is no universal 'solution' to supply chain challenges and opportunities.

This chapter will end with a set of diagnostic questions that can be used to position an organisation with respect to these principles.

We begin our review of how these principles will contribute to the logistics future challenge by looking at what is happening in retail supply chains. Figure 10.2 shows the traditional retail chain from manufacturer to consumer via either a retailer or a wholesaler. New channels to market are opening up, and they tend not to replace the old ones but to place increased pressure upon them and the relationships between the organisations concerned. The increase in routes to market when coupled with a proliferation of new products and marketing promotions makes the marketplace more turbulent.

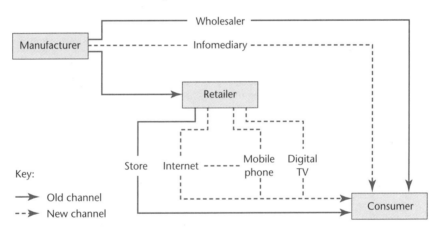

Figure 10.2 **Channels to market**

10.1.1 Five pressures on retail supply chains (Aldridge and Harrison, 2000)

- *Replenishment ordering*: this process matches purchase orders placed with suppliers to the rate of sale within the retail store. The business imperatives for such action are clear. On average, retailers are holding in the region of two to three weeks' inventory within their distribution systems. The potential to reduce this to two days or less will release corresponding capital employed and at the same time reduce the space and cost needed to run distribution warehouses. Half of the retailer's operating costs are attributable to in-store replenishment, leading to a call for simplified, 'one touch replenishment' systems.

- *7 Day-24 hour ordering and supply*: the larger supermarkets are already open 24 hours, with deliveries from the distribution centres taking place throughout the night. To smooth out product movement through the distribution centres it is only a matter of time before the suppliers are expected to also take orders and deliver throughout the night with order to delivery lead times of 24 hours or less.

- *Cross-docking*: developing the concept of stockless warehousing, with multi-product orders delivered to the receiving dock at the distribution centre. Orders have been coded by store by the supplier, and are then split into each store's requirement and loaded on to vehicles on the dispatch docks.

- *Product tracking*: as the volume of stock within the supply chain is reduced, it becomes critical to identify exactly where that stock is at any point in time. The need is to be able to distinguish the critical information from the mass that is available. Product tracking aims to achieve this ideal in a similar way to parcel tracking at UPS Global Logistics or Federal Express.

- *Improved vehicle utilisation and reduced vehicle movements*: over 50% of the goods vehicles travelling on Britain's roads are empty or less than fully loaded (McKinnon, 1996). Motorways are becoming increasingly congested, leading to increased journey times along with rising fuel prices. Such environmental pressures demand that vehicle utilisation is substantially improved.

Furthermore, in pursuit of the benefits of just-in-time operations, retailers will be demanding more frequent deliveries and smaller order sizes. For example, Seven Eleven Japan demands that many of its suppliers deliver in three 'waves' each day, so that stocks are topped up regularly in line with actual demand patterns.

10.1.2 Emerging techniques and technologies

Any manufacturer supplying the major grocery retailers is familiar with the use of electronic data interchange (EDI) as a means of communicating orders. Many retailers have extended the concept of e-commerce by providing sales and inventory data to their suppliers over the Internet (see case study 1.1). This provides consolidated information on stocks held in the distribution centres and retail sales; this sales data is available about four hours after the sale has taken place. The expectation is that this information will be used for joint demand and promotion planning. What new technologies are available to help maximise the opportunities and address the pressures being imposed on the supply chains? We propose that six developing concepts will be of particular interest in meeting the expectations and pressures described above.

- *The use of shared data via the Internet*: we have yet to see the true potential of this method of communication for business to business trade. But its use in collaborative planning is already encouraging a broader view of end-customer demand in the supply chain. The onus is on manufacturers to come up with new planning and scheduling systems that overcome the fixed batch size, fixed leadtime mindset.

- *The ECRate (returnable transit packaging)*: the ECRate is an ECR-Europe project that seeks to develop an industry standard plastic crate for transporting product throughout the retail supply chain. These crates, similar to those already in use for fresh vegetables, could be shared between all retailers and controlled through a central pool operator, in the same way as current pallet pools operate. The crate was launched to the trade in October 1998, although achieving acceptance is proving problematic.

- *RFID (radio frequency identification)*: small data storage and transmission devices that are capable of being attached to products or outer packaging, and that can be interrogated through a scanner. This technology is expected to complement the bar code in future, offering improved read rates without the 'line of sight' requirement of bar codes, together with improved security opportunities.

- *'Mr Tag'* – the combination of the ECRate and RFID to create intelligent crates: this innovation is in the process of being developed by an industry team made up of representatives of the major retailers and a number of their larger suppliers. These intelligent crates will be capable of storing information on their contents, product manufacturing details, expiry dates, together with a full history of all movements and any other required information.

- *Distribution warehouse sortation systems*: conveyor based systems that facilitate the automation of product movement from warehouse storage location to store order assembly point. In addition to this benefit these systems offer the possibility of stockless distribution centres operated on a true cross-docking principle.

- *Intermodal transport*: the combination of road and rail transport to reduce road traffic by using the rail network for long distance movements. this will help to reduce carbon dioxide emissions, road traffic congestion and indeed overall transport costs.

10.1.3 New alliances between trading partners

The combination of such pressures and the emerging new technologies will create a new dynamism in future logistics solutions. Figure 10.3 shows a temporary 'transaction chain' that has emerged from a stable platform of relationships. Such transaction chains are formed by selected partners who spot an opportunity to collaborate together. For example, several manufacturers may collaborate to share transport costs or even their DC facilities. They may develop new IT systems together. They may even collaborate across a whole industry: for example, pharmaceutical companies have collaborated to develop a B2B exchange (www.ghx.com). Such collaborations will most often be temporary, lasting only as long as they create value for the platform as a whole. We develop these points in the next section.

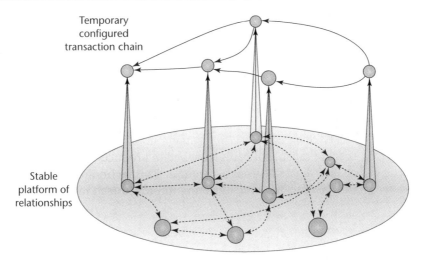

Figure 10.3 Supply network relationships
(Source: Schuh *et al.*, 1998)

10.2 Three key management challenges

Key issue: **What are the new structures that will facilitate customer responsiveness?**

Organisations in future are less likely to be vertically integrated by owning and maintaining substantial chunks of the assets of a given supply chain. Instead, new structures are evolving that provide better ways of organising resources so that the supply chain can respond more quickly to customer-led changes.

This section tracks three such trends, which support the creation of a more agile supply chain. The first is the *virtual organisation*, in which different organisations agree common terms on which they can cooperate and so behave as a much larger organisation. Second is the *extended enterprise*, characterised by retention of core competences in house and the delegation of non-core processes to inbound suppliers. Third is delaying customisation of a product until the latest possible time, a supply chain strategy called *postponement*.

10.2.1 Virtual organisation

Virtual organisations are characterised by groups of separate organisations that operate as a single entity. Customers of such an organisation are often unaware that they are dealing with a number of different companies. For this reason the virtual organisation should have its own identity, such as a brand, or common packaging. Companies that make up the virtual organisation should operate to a consistent set of procedures and standards, and have access to a common data source on customers and their orders. As a result, whenever customers come into contact with any of the parts of the virtual organisation they will be able to recognise it and experience a consistent level of service. An example of a virtual organisation is provided by Bearing Partners, a group of SMEs who decided to cooperate to compete. This is described in the case study below.

One advantage of a virtual organisation lies in its ability to reconfigure itself. When demand requires, new companies partner with the organisation to provide access to additional resources, while others leave when their resources become superfluous. In this way, skills and capacity can be matched to demand with the minimum of waste.

Bearing Partners

The origins of Bearing Partners can be traced back to 1991, when the leading manufacturer of roller bearings in Europe, SKF, formed a retailer committee in Germany in order to counter the economic recession. This committee was abandoned some years later, but the participating retailers had developed a close relationship with each other. They started to exchange products in situations where customer orders could not be satisfied from their own stocks. To develop this cooperation, six members of the former SKF retailer committee formed a partnership in 1997, formalised by a cooperation agreement and the establishment of GbR (Society of Civil Law) as a common legal entity. Bearing Partners' aims are to pool purchasing volumes from manufacturers, to increase product availability, and to reduce inventory at the same time. Today, Bearing Partners has eight member companies with 26 locations in Germany in order to ensure a country-wide service to its customers. The total sales of the partnership are about DM 320 million, of which DM 180 million is roller bearings. The partnership has a permanent available stock of around DM 50 million. The combined partnership employs about 600 people, and processes about 90 000 deliveries every month to 50 000 customers.

Bearing Partners is a horizontal cooperation of retailers that are geographically dispersed all over Germany, and therefore the partners are in direct competition in only a few overlapping areas. Figure 10.4 illustrates the horizontal cooperation between retailers.

The partnership is managed by a steering committee (multiple leadership). Bearing Partners has neither a head office nor permanent staff. The managing director of one of the partner companies has been appointed as the partnership spokesman. Besides the joint development of the Virtual Logistics Centre, described below, the partnership has set up special interest groups (SIGs), which deal with topics of general interest to member companies. Another important feature of the partnership is the regular face-to-face meetings. The managing directors of the partner companies meet four times a year, and organise face-to-face meetings for their key personnel. This is an important step in building up personal relationships and trust, which facilitates day-to-day relationships between partner companies. It also shows that technology (in the form of

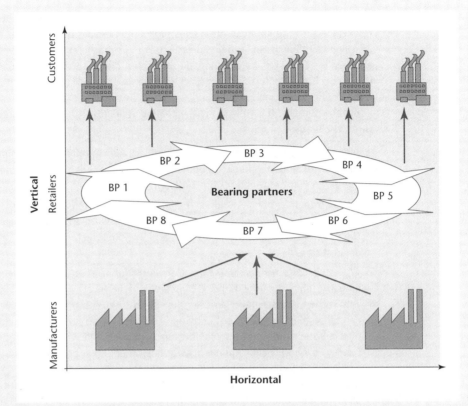

Figure 10.4 Horizontal cooperation at Bearing Partners
(Source: Franke and Jockel, 2000)

the Virtual Logistics Centre) is not the sole driver of virtualisation. Further, the partners do not pay a fixed membership contribution, and share all costs equally.

The competitive environment

The German roller bearing market is the biggest market of its kind in Europe. The main customers for roller bearings are OEMs, and manufacturers deliver 85% of their supply directly. The major European manufacturers (SKF, FAG, and INA) maintain a network of small and medium-sized appointed retailers in Germany. Although the network of appointed retailers has only 15% of the OEM market, this market counts for about half of their business. The other half of their business is the after-sales market.

At a European level, the market structure is different. There are three major English retailers (BRAMME, WYKO, and BSC), which operate differently from the German multi-brand retailers. Besides their traditionally strong position in the after-sales market, their market share in the OEM segment is much larger than that of the German retailers. Owing to the higher purchase volume these retailers have a stronger bargaining position, which leads to better purchase conditions.

The retailers' share of the OEM segment is likely to increase owing to the modular manufacturing strategies of industrial engineering companies. This has led to a wider geographical dispersion of OEM manufacturers, who are increasingly supplied by selected retailers. In the lucrative after-sales segment, German retailers have to face increasing competition from other European multi-brand retailers, particularly the UK companies. These have a traditionally strong hold in the after-sales market, and are not tied to exclusive dealerships, which enables them to purchase directly from most of the main bearing manufacturers.

At the moment, the German roller bearing market faces serious market and competition challenges:

- *Internationalisation*: Since the German roller bearing market is the biggest in Europe (owing to the large German engineering industry), it is very attractive for the larger European competitors to enter the German market.

- *Concentration processes within the industry*: The increasing competition on the German roller bearing market has led to takeovers of smaller retailers. This concentration process further increases the competition, which results in more mergers and acquisitions.

- *Changing customer requirements*: Concentration processes also affect the German industry. One the one hand OEMs are also involved in mergers and acquisitions within their industry, and on the other hand there is a trend for larger companies to centralise their procurement activities. In order to bid for contracts, retailers have to offer a wide product range (multi-brands) as well as a wider geographical coverage. Further, the logistical requirements of customers have been changing. Former large deliveries to central warehouses are now split into several smaller deliveries direct to manufacturing plants. This trend is in particular accelerated by outsourcing and modular manufacturing in the engineering industry. Both the direct OEM market and the after-sales market are influenced by these trends.

All these market and competition changes have led a group of roller bearing retailers to join forces and to establish Bearing Partners. The major benefits of the cooperation are the geographical coverage of whole Germany, access to a wider product range, and increased purchasing power. Altogether it improves the competitiveness of each individual member company because they are able to offer their customers better services and prices.

The Virtual Logistics Centre

The Virtual Logistics Centre (VLC) is the first major project of Bearing Partners aimed at improving competitiveness. The basic idea is to create a virtual stock, a common inventory of all eight partners from which each individual partner can obtain the items it needs to satisfy customer orders. The VLC is intended to manage geographically dispersed inventory from various organisational locations in real time.

A common business understanding of the partner companies has developed the idea for the VLC, for which Bearing Partners set the following objectives:

- to simplify communication amongst the partners and to reduce costs;
- to process stock orders to and from other partner companies electronically;
- to gain total visibility of common stock items to increase customer responsiveness;
- to reduce inventory at every warehouse location.

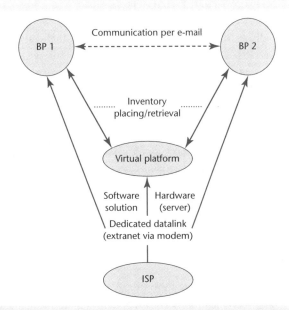

Figure 10.5 The role of Bearing Partners and the Internet service provider in the VLC

(Source: Franke and Jockel, 2000)

The main problem of programming a common inventory database was that, although four of the partners worked with a similar company software package, the other four partners used different software packages. Another problem was that of maintaining the confidentiality of sensitive data. Basically, Bearing Partners searched for a software house that would be able to establish a common inventory database, to program the interfaces to the database, to install firewalls, and to develop user-friendly Internet applications. They found this partner in Cybernet AG, Munich, a provider of business solutions for integrated communication and Internet services.

Figure 10.5 illustrates the VLC, a virtual platform to which each partner is linked via the Internet. The VLC features a central database holding the inventory information of all partners, such as products, item numbers, quantity, locations, and prices. This data-base is kept on a central server at Cybernet's premises, which can be accessed by each partner through a dial-in/dial-out interface that is firewall-protected. Furthermore, Cybernet provides the Internet access to Bearing Partners member companies, and acts as system administrator to the VLC database.

The VLC provides visibility and access to the common inventory of the 26 different warehouse locations of all partners, which represents the 'virtual stock' of Bearing Partners.

The virtual stock is updated every night through a batch download from the different Bearing Partners' warehouse management systems to the central database

(Source: Franke and Jockel, 2000)

Questions

From the account given above, explain the competitive advantage that Bearing Partners has developed over its larger, UK-based rivals.

10.2.2 The extended enterprise

A discernible trend that is set to continue is the increased contribution of suppliers to value-enhancing activities. This will extend beyond the outsourcing of basic services and subcontracting of production to include responsibility for inventory management, management of lower tiers of suppliers, and devolution of the design authority during product development. The retreat by OEMs and large tier 1 companies into their core competences of programme management and system integration will require suppliers to develop these new capabilities. In consequence, this move will provide the opportunity for suppliers to provide additional value-adding services to their customers, or be forced to supply via intermediaries who are able to do so. This move is likely to extend beyond component and system suppliers to include service suppliers.

CASE STUDY 10.2

UPS Logistics

This case study presents the experiences of UPS Worldwide Logistics in developing *fourth-party logistics service provider* (4PL) applications. IT capabilities have been used to progress the client's supply chain towards greater added value. The 4PL is a supply chain service provider that participates in supply chain coordination more than it does in supply chain operational services. It is highly information based, and coordinates asset-based players (for example), on behalf of its clients. This implies a great focus on using information and ICT to support supply chain competitiveness. Implementation required a major transition for UPS – which has its origins in express and physical logistics services – towards the creation of supply chains based on operational and strategic applications of information.

The business model of the 4PL, as it has developed with UPS Worldwide Logistics clients, is displayed in Figure 10.6. Traditionally, various transport and warehousing companies and third-party logistics service providers (3PLs) have provided logistics services to OEMs (phase A). Once a former 3PL develops a 4PL role, the supply chain structure changes to phase B, in which the 4PL takes over the management of material flow on behalf of the OEM. The company takes over logistics problems and starts managing the physical supply of logistics on behalf of the client. An intermediate layer is created coordinating logistics service operations and providing the client with a single point of contact. The company may occasionally extend its role by taking over employees with expertise in the product or in client–customer interactions in order to build up capability in supply chain processes focused on client-customer satisfaction and expectation management.

The 4PL relationship is typically information based, with few assets. Customer relations that have evolved from 3PL origins may have retained some physical assets (such as trucks and warehouses). But the critical factor is a change from an inward-looking mindset based on ownership of hard assets and asset utilisation to a broader focus on total supply chain effectiveness and process optimisation. The 3PL aspects of supply chain services are *outsourced* to asset-based providers. The role of UPS is then to source and coordinate operations on behalf of the client. The UPS business unit does not engage in day-to-day physical operations, but rather provides overall process man-

Phase A Traditional 3PL

Various 3PLs offer services

Phase B Establishment of 4PL coordination of 3PL

Various 3PLs offer services

Phase C Development of supply chain scope 4PL 1

Various 3PLs offer services

Phase D Development of supply chain

Various 3PLs offer services

Figure 10.6 Change process implementing 4PL with UPS Worldwide Logistics

agement of the logistics activities being executed by the 3PLs. UPS Worldwide Logistics may source services from within UPS itself, but will also source from other 3PLs depending upon which provider can offer best overall value (based on service level, quality, consistency and cost) for a given aspect of the client's virtual distribution network. The 3PL selection is sometimes partially based upon recommendations or stipulations from the client, but selection is then the responsibility of the client. If the 3PL performs poorly, then the client cannot hold UPS Worldwide Logistics accountable, until such time as the 3PL has been endorsed after a period of performance evaluation. Taking over the logistics problems of the clients does not involve taking over the logistics personnel of the client (which competitors are sometimes prepared to do). This would transfer bad habits: removal of bad habits is a primary objective in the step-change process.

In phase C the 4PL starts to develop a supply chain focus and to progress into a supply chain manager for the client. The 4PL starts to engage in supplier interfaces by calling off supplies. This can be based upon call-off rules (once inventory goes below a certain level, replenishments are ordered) or on modelling. Furthermore, the 4PL starts to engage in customer-facing processes. The 4PL can receive and handle first- or second-level calls from the client's customers ordering shipments, and order fulfilment activities.

Once the transition to supply chain management has been made, a further move (phase D) is to engage in coordinating manufacturing interfaces. Knowing customer orders and supply operations, the 4PL can coordinate manufacturing inputs, and end up in a position where the client has only a virtual or design and marketing organisation role. The 4PL integrates and runs the entire supply chain on its behalf. This could include implementation of supplementary services in the area of postponed manufacturing. Obviously, there may be battles between the 4PL and the manufacturers as to who should manage the supply chain. In the same way, there may be battles between 3PLs as to who is the best player to perform the 4PL role when progressing from phase A to B. In this battle, implementation and management capabilities in the change process are key differentiators among players.

Managing the change process

The process outlined in Figure 10.6 is one that reflects *unfreezing* and *re-freezing* change processes. Initially the supply chain is unfrozen (phases A–D) with suppliers and different layers separated from the client. Refreezing, at a greater level of sophistication, is then achieved around the 4PL. How should this transformation in the supply chain be managed?

UPS Worldwide Logistics does not participate in many 'traditional' tender processes any more. It generally consults to clients in supply chain design and re-engineering projects. The company enters into a co-design process, which moves the relation away from a sales and buying effort. UPS Worldwide Logistics will bring the logistical and supply chain experience to the table and co-develop the business model for a company that faces change or growth. A competitive market fee for consulting is charged because of the anticipated supply chain management business opportunity. But if at the end of the process UPS Worldwide Logistics is not commissioned as a 4PL there is an additional charge to compensate for the effort. This places UPS in a more neutral position. Its initial focus is not on selling but on assisting the client in developing a business model that makes use of existing and best-of-breed capacity in the marketplace. At the same time, UPS seeks to maintain a sense of reality on the motivation of the 3PLs, and how to effectively combine them into a 'seamless' collaborative supply chain.

Once the 4PL model is in place (phase B) UPS Worldwide Logistics begins to interact further with various functional areas of the client's organisation. Manufacturing and marketing units, for example, have to be convinced of the prospect of the 4PL model. In developing the 4PL model into phases C and D, UPS actually starts to implement supply chain management on their behalf. UPS functions as the flexible process 'glue' in the supply chain operation once it is up and running. The change of mindset within the former 3PL and, more importantly, within the client's organisation may be time-consuming and demanding. Benefits such as transparency and improved communication systems achieved in phase B are used as a link with other parts of the client's organisation. Cost savings are the traditional argument for the development of logistics services, and in convincing other parts of the client's organisation. When it progresses into supply chain services, however, service enhancement becomes more critical. Once the 4PL model has developed initially, moving up the scale becomes more important for sustainable improvements and longer-term relationships. In fact, client relations that do not progress into that area would quite likely terminate because of a longer-term mismatch in joint aspirations between the supply chain owner (client) and manager (4PL).

Question

What are the essential differences between 3PL and 4PL logistics providers, and what additional capabilities does the 4PL need to develop?

10.2.3 Postponement

The third trend that supports development of the agile supply chain is the supply chain strategy called *postponement*. Postponement is defined as

> **the delay of value-adding activities in the supply chain until customer orders are received. Orders are then executed with the intention of customising product/service requirements when they are on the way to the customer.**

Postponement can be applied at various levels in the supply chain. Based upon a large-scale survey of companies in Europe (van Hoek, 2000), Figure 10.7 presents

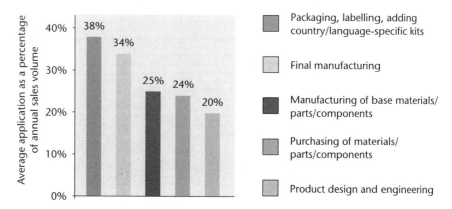

Figure 10.7 Postponement applications across supply chain operations

average application levels for postponement along given supply chain operations aggregated across various sectors, countries and supply chain positions. The overall pattern indicates that the application of postponement decreases when moving further upstream and away from the end customer. Downstream, postponement applications are ahead of those upstream, with over one third of predelivery packaging activities performed according to end customer specifications and needs. Obviously, these activities do not generate the greatest level of customisation, but in addition to delivery services (timetable etc.) they can tune the logistics link with the end customer. Further, over one third of final manufacturing activities, which lead to further customisation of form and function of products, are also postponed. The overall pattern as displayed confirms the cross-functional relevance of postponement, since it is practised across different functions, ranging from engineering, through supply and production to predelivery activities.

The applicability of postponement differs depending upon the operating environment, which differs by industry. Figure 10.8 presents the application of postponement across industry sectors from the same study. Respondents were divided into three groups: those who did not apply postponement, or who applied it to 10% or less of sales volume; those with medium-level postponement applications (defined as 11–50% of sales volume); and those with high-level postponement applications (defined as greater than 50% of sales volume). The scores used here are averages across all the postponement applications listed above.

Overall, postponement applications are highest in the automotive sector, followed by electronics, while food and other industries lag behind. This can be explained by the different operating circumstances in industries like food, which do not favour high levels of postponement across the supply chain. Food products can be packaged and adjusted to orders, but manufacturing, if involved, is more pressured for time and more difficult to organise around standardised discrete modules that can be assembled into customised finished products, as is possible in the other industries. It is more difficult to delay process steps in food

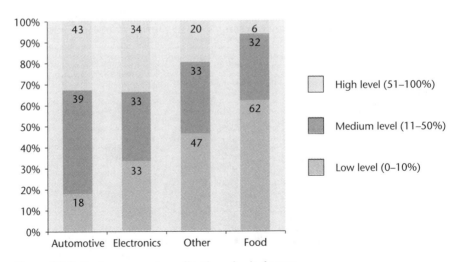

Figure 10.8 Postponement applications by industry

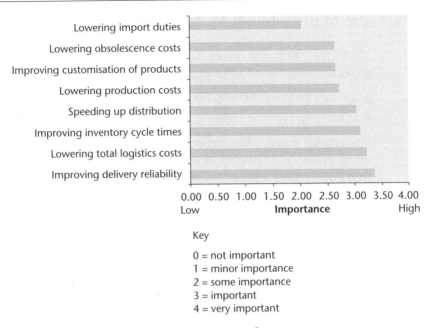

Figure 10.9 Why implement postponement?

production given the continuous nature of most of the processes. In comparison, the discrete nature of production in electronics and automotive is better suited to postponement applications. Automobiles are also sold at a higher level of customisation (through the specification of options etc.) than electronics products – particularly in consumer electronics, where the level of standardisation is higher.

Companies implement postponement for various reasons, several of which are ranked by priority in Figure 10.9, based upon the same study. Service considerations are the most important but in addition to responsive distribution and logistics systems and customisation, continued lowering of integral logistics costs remains important as well.

Postponement was found to be correlated to the dimensions of the agile supply chain as listed in the diagnostic in Appendix 2 and this, further substantiates its contribution to the creation of the agile supply chain.

10.3 The role of the Internet in supply chains

Key issues **How will the Internet become a key factor in reshaping supply chains?**

We have already discussed the role of the Internet in supply chain strategy, both earlier in this chapter and in Chapter 8. The Internet is going to be an ever more powerful force in reshaping supply chains. This section reviews four areas where the role of the Internet will have a major impact: use of the Internet by business, next generation enterprise-wide planning systems, product planning and development, and the e-supply chain.

10.3.1 Use of the Internet by business

Electronic business promises new ways of working for companies, allowing them to react in real time to changes in the market by:

● gaining more knowledge about their customers;

● increasing the visibility of demand across their supply chains.

It is forecast that the Internet will attract new entrants to many markets and even result in the restructuring of whole industries. Business-to-business (B2B) trade over the Internet is predicted to double every year over the next five years, surging from $34 billion to $3.2 trillion by 2003. This is forecast to outweigh business-to-consumer (B2C), growth by a ratio of nearly four to one.

The term *e-commerce* is usually used by the media to mean businesses trading with consumers via the Internet: that is, business to consumer. The hype surrounding e-commerce has resulted in organisations' stampeding to have web sites and then asking themselves 'What do we do next?' If they are managing to sell to consumers then there is the sudden realisation that the organisation's back-office processes and supply chains have to be aligned to meet a new set of consumer expectations.

E-business is a term used to cover trading with an organisation's suppliers and business customers – that is, business to business – by electronic means. A feature of B2B is the formation of online trading communities (see for example Ariba (www.ariba.net) and CommerceOne (www.commerceone.com)) and electronic marketplaces. Such structures have been made possible by the explosion of Internet technology, and seek to offer cost reductions in procurement of both direct and indirect goods and also in the processing of such transactions. The relationship of these terms in the context of the *e-supply chain* is shown in Figure 10.10.

Rather than define e-business by the technology, it is more useful to define it

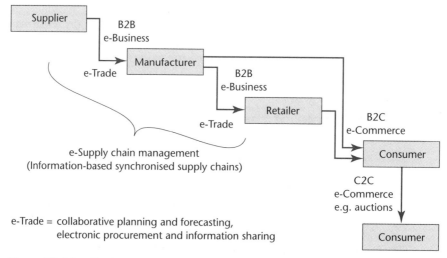

Figure 10.10 e-Business terminology

by its intent to allow the flow of accurate, timely and rich information. This flow of rich information starts with the consumer, and is shared with all organisations in the supply chain. It is therefore imperative that managers take every opportunity to understand the implications of electronic business for their own companies, and how they can develop an effective strategy to harness it together with an agile supply chain that will support this approach.

E-business allows businesses to do the things they currently do, but to do them better. The simplest example – and where many businesses start their exploration of e-commerce – is that of companies using web sites to provide information about products and services. This information has traditionally been transmitted via printed brochures or mass media advertising. A web site is not only likely to be cheaper to set up and update, it also allows customers to find the information on the particular product they require rather than be bombarded with information about products they are not interested in. A web site even allows the organisation to customise the information provided to each individual customer.

However, the excitement about e-business also stems from the fact that it allows businesses to do things that were not previously possible. This has led to the formation of certain types of business, or business model, unique to the Internet.

The ability to do new things via the Internet is not confined to Internet start-ups. It allows traditional, 'bricks and mortar' businesses to do new things, and in a way that benefits both the company and its customers. An example of the potential scale of savings can be taken from the financial services sector. A banking transaction made at an on-line bank is estimated to cost one-hundredth of a transaction carried out in a traditional branch. With banks undertaking many millions of transactions each day, such savings are highly significant.

CASE STUDY 10.3

Home shopping is reborn!

Home shopping is not new: some large, successful organisations have for many years been selling a vast range of products via mail order catalogues. However, the exponential growth in the number of users of the Internet, combined with changes in society, is expected to fuel a rapid growth in home shopping, particularly in sectors that have not traditionally used this shopping format. For example, sales of cars over the Internet in the US were worth $200 million in 1999.

The value of home shopping has been estimated to be worth £68 billion by year 2003, but will represent only 8% of total projected Internet revenue. Despite this, home shopping will generate the need for a variety of alternative distribution channels, which, when combined with the adoption of demand pull strategies, will lead to an increased need for warehousing, transshipment and consolidation facilities.

At present home shopping in the fast-moving consumer goods sector is dominated by retailers. Very few of these are profitable because of a lack of dedicated distribution systems and the high level of flexibility required to handle home shopping orders.

With the advent of Internet-enabled home shopping, both traditional and new organisations need to understand the implications for their organisation and supply

▶

chains of this new route to market. There are a variety of issues that need to be resolved in this type of electronic commerce:

- Where should the product be delivered?
- How should product returns be managed?
- How should conflicts with current supply chain relationships be dealt with?
- How can order fulfilment be assured?

10.3.2 Next-generation enterprise-wide resource planning systems

Legacy IT systems (typically, customised solutions that have been developed piecemeal for specific applications by previous generations of management) can lead to fragmentation of information, which in turn impedes supply chain performance and the integration of company-wide processes and information systems. The main problems with legacy systems are the cost of maintaining them, the risk of turnover amongst key staff who have evolved the system over the years, and the invisible costs of not being able to share information up and down the business. Accordingly, software suppliers such as SAP, BAAN and Manugistics have developed *enterprise-wide resource planning* (ERP) systems that bring several benefits compared with the legacy systems that preceded them.

ERP system benefits include improved control of the business and reduced costs arising from a faster flow of data and virtual integration across processes. To date, ERP systems have focused on connecting back-office operations such as manufacturing, financial accounting and human resource management into one system. Part of the future for ERP is to expand its capability to incorporate functionality in front-office applications such as sales force automation and customer care. An example of this is the trend to centralisation of customer care activities into service centres. Standardisation of processes, procedures and data on one site using ERP as a backbone allows the realisation of higher levels of service alongside cost savings through economies of scale.

The challenge for organisations over the next decade does not rest with implementing transactional-based ERP systems. Achieving true enterprise planning with more informed decision in the supply chain requires the implementation of additional *advanced planning and scheduling* (APS) systems. APS seeks to carry out material requirements planning (MRP – see Chapter 6) in ultra-short time frames, and to extend the planning process to scheduling of bottleneck operations.

In the search for competitive advantage, it is of paramount importance to achieve visibility throughout the supply chain. The exponential development of Internet technology, together with the increased power of the personal computer, offers organisations a relatively cheap means of integrating information systems across the supply chain.

The Internet provides a platform-independent communications highway that can be used as a cross-company interface to facilitate electronic commerce. It thereby fosters operationally efficient, connected and cooperative relationships among manufacturers, suppliers and distributors. The use of the Internet can provide an easy and cost-effective answer that is available to all organisations in the supply chain. The need for a dedicated electronic link between each partner is thereby made unnecessary.

Technology-driven improvements tend to favour larger companies, concentrating power in the hands of the bigger retail, distribution and manufacturing companies. Classically 80% of volume is channelled through only 20% of suppliers or customers, all handled by automated EDI links with much lower unit processing costs. The remaining 80% of suppliers and customers represents only 20% of volume and yet a massive 50–75% of sales order processing costs (see activity-based costing in Chapter 3). The vision for the Internet is that this technology could in fact encourage more equitable roles for smaller players, and ultimately improve choice, price and availability for consumers.

CASE STUDY 10.4 — Sharing information in the grocery supply chain

Lack of visibility in the supply chain is a significant barrier to the reduction of costs and the improvement of service levels, and a major inhibitor of supply chain agility. Major European grocery retailers have sought to overcome these barriers by sharing demand, promotional and stockholding information with their suppliers via extranets, which are limited-access Internet-based systems.

By making possible joint planning, product tracking and more efficient promotions management these systems allow suppliers to replenish more efficiently while improving in-store availability. This makes supply chains more responsive, and provides opportunities to reduce lost sales caused by stock-outs.

Tesco and Sainsbury are amongst the companies rolling out such systems to large and small suppliers alike. However, one problem arising from this is the lack of an industry standard, which results in manufacturers' having to deal with multiple systems. Although initial work in the area of standard communication protocols, interface standards and data definitions has begun, there is still a long way to go before the benefits of such a standardised approach are realised.

Question

Visit a supermarket web site such as www.tesco.com and find out about the policy for information exchange with suppliers in that organisation. Is the organisation sensitive to the needs of smaller suppliers?

10.3.3 Product planning and development

In B2B the ongoing supply of goods and services is only one of a number of transactions between organisations. Product planning and development is another area that is being empowered by new IT applications and by the widespread adoption of these technologies across the supply chain. In the early 1990s technologies such as computer-aided design (CAD) would have been rare amongst small companies. Today, few manufacturing companies are without it. The capability of suppliers throughout the supply chain to view and manipulate designs at the pre-prototype stage not only prevents costly mistakes, it also allows the supplier to contribute its expertise and significantly improves the speed of the overall product development process.

Collaborative and concurrent product development is being made possible by the simple ability to exchange designs digitally as file attachments to e-mails. Having demonstrated the cost, quality and responsiveness benefits of this way of working, large companies are likely to put more substantive systems in place to harness it. These systems have the potential to be very extensive.

> We believe that the product innovation management market (such as the product planning and development applications) will be significantly larger than the ERP and CRM (customer relationship management) markets.
>
> Sanjay Keswani, Oracle Industrial Vertical Solutions

10.3.4 The e-supply chain

Supply chain management is vital in the search for competitive advantage. Unless organisations can develop and implement supply chains that are capable of supporting this new route to market they are likely to lose out in market share. Consumers who buy through the Internet are likely to expect a different type of service in terms of cost, choice and value-added service levels. The Internet offers the consumer access to multiple countries, and gives rise to the need for price transparency. The use of electronic commerce also encourages organisations to rethink their marketing activity with the likelihood of short-term highly sophisticated Internet-based promotional activity aimed at individually targeted consumers.

The open and established standards of the Internet provide small and large companies with equal opportunities for exploiting e-commerce. The basis of the competition for consumers in the retail market centres on adding value for the customer since price becomes transparent. An important key to delivering customer value is the integration of information systems across the supply chain. Some of the examples reviewed in this chapter have illustrated the need to implement scalable e-commerce processes. Although an e-commerce presence may be easy to launch in the business-to-consumer market, it is the logistics and distribution issues that will determine success in the longer term.

10.3.5 Disintermediation or reintermediation?

Electronic commerce will not only shift power to better informed customers, it is expected to have a significant impact on the companies supplying a particular market. If manufacturers can quickly and relatively cheaply promote and sell their products and services over the Internet directly to the end users, then the role of intermediaries such as brokers, distributors and even retailers is unclear, and such companies may not survive. This removal of stages in the supply or value chain is known as *disintermediation*.

However, if the traditional type of intermediaries have an uncertain future, a new generation of intermediaries has already been born that companies wishing to undertake electronic commerce must consider. An example is *the Internet service provider* (ISP). If a customer wishes to access your on-line services via the Internet, then they will have to pass through such an intermediary. The service that customers perceive your site to be delivering may therefore be more dependent on the ISP's service levels than on your own. What is more, the future may well give rise to a whole new type of intermediary, one that acts on a customer's behalf to search for information about products of interest, and to filter incoming offers from companies. An important feature of such new intermediaries will be trust, since a customer would wish to be certain that the products found and recommended were indeed the most suitable and not those most heavily promoted by the suppliers.

10.3.6 Exchanges

B2B exchanges for *online reversed auctions* (ORAs) offer support to supply efforts that have been somewhat over-promised but which still have a role to play in the supply organisation. The theory is that through on-line exchanges companies can place orders on the Web and get interested suppliers from around the world to bid for those orders. This enables companies to find capacity in the supply market immediately – possibly from previously unknown suppliers. The bidding mechanism also lowers costs. Exchanges have a low participation threshold, as they are web based; member companies can just log on.

However, there has been a very fast growth of the number of exchanges. There are many exchanges for each industry, which reduces transparency for that industry. In fact many companies have involved themselves in multiple exchanges, thereby 'spreading their bets' but still leaving some coordination tasks to themselves.

Additionally, the buying behaviour leads to transactional relations, not partnerships, and the auctioning only really works if there are multiple suppliers bidding. This mechanism is typically best used for commodities. Such products are widely available from multiple suppliers as they are broadly specified, and supplier evaluation is concerned more with price than with technological capability – or any other complex metric that might require off-line interaction.

As a result there are two expected future avenues for exchanges: low cost and collaborative relations. The first is close to the current role of exchanges, but recognises that it plays only a limited role (perhaps 10–15%) as a part of the supply efforts, and does not replace others. The revenue model for these exchanges will have to be reconsidered because of the proliferation of exchanges (challenging scale and coverage of the market) and the focus on one-off orders (which may not generate a sustainable constant revenue stream). The second approach, that of supporting collaborative relationships, is a model that requires a migration of the exchange. To support collaboration, mechanisms other than ORAs with a large supply base are needed. Co-design, joint forecasting and sharing of confidential demand information are amongst functionalities to be developed. The establishment of private networks is currently thought to be more appropriate for that. Table 10.1 summarises the pros and cons of B2B exchanges.

Table: 10.1 Pros and cons of B2B exchanges

	Pros	Cons
Transparency	Ability to spot capacity in the market	Transparency lowered by growth of exchanges
Financial benefits	Cost-saving opportunity on transactions through auctioning and spot market nature	Transactional buying, particularly feasible of commodities; not all supplies
Supplier interaction	Real-time connection between supply and demand	Not supportive of relationship development
Systems support	Low threshold for application; web-based	Limited functionalities of supply chain integration offered

10.3.7 Further considerations

There are a few additional considerations relating to the Internet and IT that should be taken into account. First, technology is not the answer in itself to challenges that we face. The implementation of ERP systems, for example, today remains primarily within the walls of the organisation and does not yet widely stretch throughout the supply chain. Section 10.4 will focus on implementation, as the utilisation and integration of modern opportunities is ultimately more key than the technological possibilities.

Furthermore, the Internet has not yet led to a new world order. The bursting of the e-commerce 'bubble' and the failure of 'dot-coms' is very much based upon their lack of proven business experience and their reliance on technological possibilities rather than on operational expertise. Current understanding is that the Internet offers the opportunity to add new channels of commerce and distribution to complement existing channels. Following the first wave of e-commerce, led by dot-coms, we are now in the midst of a second wave, as the established companies such as GE move in and incorporate the Internet into their proven operating systems. B2B exchanges, for example, have been widely used in an effort to lower costs by applying the bargaining power of the buyers. The transactional approach is now being complemented by a stronger and more sustainable focus on the use of exchanges in collaborative supply efforts, including forecasting and collaborative design.

10.4 Implementation issues

Key issue: **How can the transition process be managed?**

The implementation of change in businesses is often frustrating, and frequently produces disappointing results. The process of change is particularly difficult in supply chains as it has to be undertaken in a coordinated manner across and between a number of organisations. It is therefore important to gain agreement from the top level of all companies involved before wide-scale changes can be made. As an example of the relevance of appropriate implementation approaches, it is well known that about three out of five third-party logistics out-sourcing implementations are discontinued after a year, based upon disappointing progress and accomplishment. Poor implementation skills leads to enormous wasted efforts and stalled progress.

'Where the rubber meets the road' is also the divide between idea or vision and reality. Operationalising for execution is a key task for logistics and supply chain managers. It is often seen as the most crucial organisational task. In the words of one logistics manager we talked to, 'We are not short of ideas, but we are also looking for proper execution.' Implementation requires more than a technical skill set. In fact communication, negotiation and convincing skills across functional domains are part of a broader skill set that logistics management needs to master.

The implementation of large-scale changes across supply chains benefits from the use of project management methods. At the outset, it is necessary to identify the *change objectives* (benefits, timescale) and to define the *scope* of the change project. Defining the scope clarifies the boundary of the project by identifying which areas and processes in the supply chain will be tackled.

In order to implement new ideas, a number of transitional forces need to be harnessed to give momentum to the change project. Figure 10.11 represents a structure that helps to illustrate these forces.

A viable route forward in uncertain circumstances is to initiate exploratory pilot projects, which should be viewed primarily as learning opportunities. Running these as joint ventures with other organisations will assist with the development of understanding.

Waiting for the 'mists of uncertainty' to clear may not be an option, given that brave and committed organisations are learning the lessons that trading in the digital era requires, ready to compete unshackled by the vestiges of the traditional business.

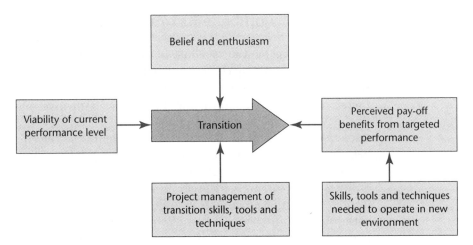

Figure 10.11 Transition forces

10.4.1 Viability of current performance level

The first priority for any organisation must be to transform the *supply* chain into a *demand* chain. This is more than mere semantics; it is a recognition that, in tomorrow's marketplace, customers and consumers will be looking for even greater value, and that the supply chain needs to be designed with the desired *value delivery* objectives in mind.

The viability of the current performance of the supply chain should be considered in the light of a number of market changes that are significant. These include:

- *Demographics.* For example, an ageing population with more single person households and fewer working people to support growing social costs. Value for money will increasingly be a customer choice determinant.
- *Time-stressed customers.* As a result of pressures of work and greater commuting, there is less time to shop. The implications for home shopping and delivery are significant.
- *One-to-one marketing and mass customisation.* The search for individual solutions to consumer buying needs requires a means to postpone the final product form and location.
- *The marketplace becomes the marketspace.* The development of the Internet and e-commerce will transform marketing and logistics.

The viability of current processes should be explored in the light of new developments that may render them obsolete, to establish whether not change is an option. For example, competitors may be developing the necessary understanding and putting into place the right electronic commerce strategy, supported by agile supply chains capable of meeting the significantly new forms of demand from business customers and consumers that will see the demise of many existing business.

10.4.2 Perceived pay-off benefits from targeted performance

An example of a change that could be implemented in order to take advantage of developments in supply chains is to embrace electronic business. In order to gain support for implementing new practices, the business must be convinced that there will be sufficient performance benefits from the investment required. While this may be calculated to a reasonable degree of accuracy, there will always be a discretionary element in the way the investment is perceived, including its likely benefits, and risks. Most often, it is the discretionary element that proves decisive.

The uncertainty inherent in any change project is particularly true of e-business projects. This is an environment of uncertainty, where there are no rules or boundaries that organisations can use as references. Instead they are faced with journeys into the unknown, while trying to maintain their existing businesses. It is clear that organisations face an enormous upheaval if they are to reap the potential benefits of electronic commerce.

Benchmarking projects provide a useful way both to quantify the potential benefits of making a change and also to give inspiration on how the new processes and systems should be designed.

Traditionally, arguments for change in logistics and supply chains have been based on anticipated cost savings. However, this is not always sufficient in the context of an agile supply chain; service is the more fundamental task. Even though service improvements may be more difficult to quantify, their revenue enhancing opportunities, and the ability to achieve pre-emptive competitive strikes, should not remain unconsidered.

10.4.3 Belief and enthusiasm

Belief in the ability to make the transition is essential for success. Tapping into enthusiasm and developing confidence is what motivates people to 'Just do it!', and maintains their self-belief that sees the project through adversity. Key here is the ability of the project manager to communicate belief in the change process with enthusiasm.

10.4.4 Ability to manage change

In order to make the change from the current system to the new one an organisation will need to be able to undertake a number of activities. First, they must be able to manage the change project. This involves planning the change, organising the resources needed to make the change and managing the application of those resources in order to achieve the necessary outcome.

Additional skills required to change a process include:

● the ability to analyse customer needs;
● the ability to quantify the current process;
● the ability to design the process that will achieve the customer requirements.

These skills may be present within a company already. If not, they can be acquired, either through training or through outsourcing them to consultants.

10.4.5 Ability to operate in the new environment

A further factor in making the transition to the new system is that people in the organisation must have the right skills, tools and techniques to operate it. Rather than wait until the change has been made, these should be provided in advance so that people are ready to operate the new process effectively from day one.

The management of the new process will require a new set of performance measures to be in place so that its efficiency and effectiveness can be assessed.

Summary

What does 'leading edge' logistics envisage in terms of the supply chain of the future?

- A combination of three factors will change the competitive landscape: the globalisation of supply chains; the convergence of low-cost computing and low-cost communications; and the increased capability to extend product variety and reduce product life cycles.

- Seven principles will guide the development of the new competitive landscape. The supply chain exists to serve the end customer, not the other way round. The output of supply chain management is a combination of time, place, form and function of a product or service proposition. Moving beyond the strategic vision established by the top team is a key challenge for logistics management. A linear view of the supply chain is too simple because it relies on an outdated, internal concept of 'our organisation' and its immediate neighbours. Immediate customers in the supply chain have an essential role to play in communicating, translating and coordinating end customer demand. Supply network priorities are constantly changing, and lead to an ongoing need for coordinated, time-based responses. There is no universal 'solution' to supply chain challenges and opportunities.

- Within retail supply chains, the challenges of replenishment ordering and 7-day 24-hour supply combined with efficient movement and tracking are being addressed by advances in information systems and distribution methods.

How will leading edge logistics be implemented?

- Three developments that will support the creation of the customer-focused, agile supply chain are the virtual organisation, the extended enterprise, and postponement.

- The Internet will be an ever more powerful force in reshaping supply chains of the future. E-supply chain management seeks to synchronise supply chains, while B2C links consumers to the supply chain.

- Enterprise-wide planning systems will be linked, using the Internet as a communications highway. This opens up possibilities of greater visibility and reduced transformation costs for smaller organisations.

- Four transitional forces help to achieve the vision of the future: the viability of current performance level; perceived pay-offs from targeted performance; belief and enthusiasm; and the ability to manage change.

Discussion questions

1 We started out in Chapter 1 by defining supply chain management as 'the alignment of upstream and downstream capabilities of supply chain partners to deliver superior value to the end customer at less cost to the supply chain as a whole'. How will leading-edge logistics contribute to this vision?

2 Suggest how the seven principles listed on pages 245 and 246 apply to our model of the supply network (Figure 1.3) and to the ideal of integrating demand and supply shown in Figure 1.6. How will virtual organisations, postponement and the Internet help to make such ideals a reality?

3 What is meant by the term *virtual organisation*? Select a virtual organisation (such as one of the dot-coms) and find out as much as possible about how the organisation develops economic value added (EVA – Chapter 3) by visiting the web site, searching for informed comment in a database search program such as Google or Northern Light. Is it basically a question of keeping minimum assets but still making a margin on buying and selling? Refer to the Batman case study in Chapter 2 in your reply.

4 Covisint.com is the web site for four of the major auto producers: Ford, GM, DaimlerChrysler and Renault. While suppliers are represented on the board of Covisint, there is much concern that this massive 'e-marketplace' will be used by the four major manufacturers as a further opportunity to squeeze prices for components. Visit the site, read articles about Covisint, and draw your own conclusions. Toyota has decided not to join, but to set up its own e-marketplace, which is aimed at sharing information across the supply chain. What does this tell you about supply chain relationships in these different chains (refer to Figure 9.1 in your reply)? What types of part (refer to the purchase portfolio index in Chapter 9) are most susceptible to auctions in e-market-places?

References

Aldridge, D. and Harrison, A. (2000) Implementing Agile Methods in Retail Supply Chains: a Scenario for the Future. *International Journal of Agile Manufacturing*, **3**, 2, 37–44.

Christopher, M. (1998) *Logistics and Supply Chain Management*, 2nd edn. London: Financial Times Pitman.

Franke, U. and Jockel, O. (2000) *Virtual logistics: an explanatory case study*. Cranfield University working paper.

McKinnon A. (1996) The empty running and return loading of roads goods vehicles, Transport Logistics, **1**, 1, 1–9.

Schuh, G., Millarg, K. and Göransson, A. (1998) *Marketchansen durch dynamische Netzwerke*, München: Carl Hansen Verlag.

Schonberger R.J. (1991) *Building a Chain of Customers: Linking Business Functions to Build the World Class Company*. New York: Free Press.

Van Hoek, R.I. (2000): *Postponement in European Supply Chains*, Cranfield University working paper.

Suggested further reading

Bowersox D.J., Closs, D.J. and Stank, T.P. (2000) Ten megatrends that will revolutionise supply chains logistics. *Journal of Business Logistics*, **21**(2) 1–16.

Van Hoek, R.I. and Harrison A.S. (2001) (eds) Creating the agile supply chain. Special issue of *International Journal of Physical Distribution and Logistics*, **31**(4).

Appendix 1: Company diagnostic questions

This chapter ends with a set of diagnostic questions that we suggest for reflection on logistics strategy and management. We propose these questions to help an organisation to diagnose its improvement opportunities in a practical environment, as well as to challenge future thinking in the logistics areas covered in this book.

There are two sections. Appendix 1 offers general reflective questions in four principal areas of logistics strategy and management. Appendix 2 offers an agile supply chain diagnostic. As is apparent from this book and its final chapter, the creation of agile capabilities will be central to logistics success in the coming years. In that respect we offer a set of questions that we have used in recent research to assess existing capabilities along four central dimensions of agility.

We propose these questions as a diagnostic for organisations, and as areas for further thinking about how to plan for change in the future.

1 Need for an agile supply chain mindset

● Does the organisation experience the shortening of product life cycles?

● Does the organisation experience the need to manage product or service proposition variety?

● Does the organisation experience the need to sense and respond rather than plan and execute?

● Does the organisation experience the need to respond to customer demands and request more accurately?

● Does the organisation experience the need to change the economics of organisation away from production- and technology-driven standardization, leading to volume and economies of scale?

● Does the organisation experience a status quo of everlasting change?

2 Methods of organising across functions, companies and borders

● Are functional 'silos' no longer the dominant structure for evaluation, compensating, organising and managing in your organisation?

● Is organising and supply chain unity based on a common goalsetting mindset, rather than on organisational trees?

● Are functional domains managed around interfaces rather than within those domains?

● Is achievement in functional domains largely recognised based upon supply chain evaluations: for example, earmarked by other functional domains?

● Are there opportunities to take advantage of competences outside your organisation to the benefit of the end consumer?

● Can communication and coordination systems be interfaced across companies?

● Is the capability available to manage relations along the transaction to market continuum, in which companies can migrate to different positions across time?

- Can product and service propositions be designed in discrete modules of added value that can be supplied by various players in an integrated manner?
- Are your supply chain's end consumers located in distinct market environments (e.g. culture, buying habits, application habits)?
- Does geography represent opportunities for positioning operations to benefit from differences in factor availability and costs?
- Can operations and coordination be organised in distinct facilities?
- Can intercultural organisation be supported by management systems?

3 Performance measurement and management

- Are broad-band measurement systems used (not just costs or financial metrics) to reflect multidimensional performance requirements?
- Are supply-chain-wide measures used to reflect the scope of agile organisations?
- Is the system shared in a horizontal setting or driven only by vertical, functional evaluation concerns?
- Is measurement information from the end consumer directly available throughout the supply chain?
- Are measures used to identify and mine market opportunities?
- Are measures guiding reconfigurability needs available as or shortly before they emerge?
- Are measures aligned to serving the end customer, or are they focused on the organisation's internal processes?

4 Management and people

- Is authority a function of position or of number of years in the hierarchy, or a function of knowledge and creativity?
- Are decisions justified on the grounds of economic joint decision-making or on politics?
- Is management focused on managing 'along the curve' (that is, within the existing status quo) or on 'establishing the curve' (that is, creating new grounds and reasons for being)?
- Is change approached from a technical point of view (and justified with highly technical systems such as OR models) or in an entrepreneurial spirit of goal realisation?
- Are frontline workers assigned near-total autonomy in their interactions with end consumers?
- Are frontline workers more committed to end consumers than to internal customers?
- Are managers capable of freeing up direct (line) authority, avoiding organisational slack to the benefit of frontline responsiveness?
- Are leaders evaluated in terms of their role of servant to management?

Appendix 2: Agile supply chain diagnostic

Dimension of agile supply chain	Measures used	Score (1–5)
Market responsive	● Ability to respond to demand with new product variants without overstocks and lost sales ● Products are customised rather than standardised ● Products are easy to adjust to demand rather than 'take-it-or-leave-it' packages ● Specific customer demands are included as part of the offering as a standard practice without additional costs ● Added value of base product proposition is expanded through additional services	
Network integration	The importance of shared investments in: ● purchasing ● logistics ● production	
Network cooperation	The importance of joint planning and strategic development in: ● purchasing ● logistics ● production	
Virtual integration I	Information integration in the supply chain: ● between factories ● with customers ● with logistics service providers	
Virtual integration II	● Information integration with suppliers ● Transactional internal systems ● Internal planning systems	
Process integration I	Linked to the ability to generate innovations based upon: ● the ability to generate and use market knowledge in processes ● the ability to generate and use customer knowledge in processes	
Process integration II	● Ability to develop process innovations ● Ability to develop product innovations ● Ability to develop management innovations	

Index